NOBLE IS MAN

Kate Mendels
and
Leopold Herzberg

Edited by Ursula Cher

makor
Jewish
Community
Library

The 'Write Your Story' Collection

© Ursula Cher 2010

Published by Makor Jewish Community Library
306 Hawthorn Road
Caulfield South
Victoria 3162
Australia

ISBN 978-0-9807027-1-2

Production: Inklink Advertising Pty Ltd
Tel: (03) 9528 2056

Cover design by Izi Marmur from Izigraphics Pty Ltd

Typesetting by Izigraphics Pty Ltd

WRITE YOUR STORY is a cultural activity of Makor Jewish Community Library.

DAS GÖTTLICHE

Edel sei der Mensch
Hilfreich und gut;
Denn das allein
Unterscheidet ihn
Von allen Wesen,
Die wir kennen.

THE DIVINE

Noble is Man to be
Helpful and good;
For that alone
Sets him apart
From all the living beings
We know.

First stanza of the poem
Das Göttliche
by Johann Wolfgang von Goethe, 1783
Weimar (near Buchenwald)

Contents

Editor's Preface

My mother, Ella Herzberg (née Mendels), died on 21 June 1989, in her ninety-third year. While sorting her papers I found the memoir *Lest We Forget*, which my father, Leopold Herzberg, had written in his native German in the early 1940s. The document relates the family's experiences during *Kristallnacht* and particularly his incarceration in Buchenwald concentration camp. Recalling his imprisonment upset him greatly and led my mother to discourage him from completing the report.

I could not remember having seen it previously and felt compelled to translate it for future generations – quite a challenge, as my use of German has been predominantly conversational. I have tried to keep as close as possible to the original in language, idiom, mood and style. It has not been an easy task.

I have since decided to combine my father's report with the absorbing family sagas of the nineteenth and twentieth centuries written by Kate Mendels, my father's sister. I am grateful to my cousins Erica Schwarz and her brother Paul Mendels, Kate's children, for agreeing to this.

For a wider understanding of the historical background, I have provided information which can be found in the appendices, footnotes and library sources that are listed in the bibliography. Non-English words, especially German *Jiddisch*, are in italics and are defined in the glossary.

Acknowledgements

My thanks go to my brother, Dr Walter Herzberg, for his thorough reading and advice; Professor Konrad Kwiet of the University of Sydney, for specific Holocaust information and final review; my friends Eva and Emeritus Professor Solly Faine, for their time spent reviewing the translation during a holiday we spent together; our friend Effie Ehrmann, for sharing his expertise in German-Jewish customs and linguistics; and to our children, Lawrence, Leonie and Nathan. It has been a pleasure working with Adele Hulse and Ruth Leonards of Makor Library and with Esther and Izi Marmur of Izigraphics; I am grateful for their careful processing and preparation of this work. My particular thanks go to my husband, Ivan, for pursuing the idiom of both languages, and for his many hours of thought and very punctilious support in editing. This publication would not have eventuated without his wise counsel.

Ursula Cher, Melbourne, 2010

Editor's Introduction
A Historical Background to Nazism and German Jewry

Nazi ideology divided German history into three periods. The First Reich was the Holy Roman Empire, 962–1806. The Second Reich was created by Bismarck, 1871–1918, and the Third Reich by Hitler, 1933–1945. Between 1918 and 1933 there was a short-lived democracy, the Weimar Republic.

In the lead-up to the Franco-Prussian War of 1870, Otto von Bismarck manipulated the expansionist designs of Emperor Napoleon III of France for two purposes. The first was to provoke France to declare war on Prussia, and the second to incite nationalist feelings among southern Germans, who were not yet members of the North German Federation. As a result, France was blamed for the war that Bismarck won and in defeat had to cede Alsace-Lorraine, accept an army of occupation and pay 5 million francs. This was a model for the Versailles Peace Treaty, in which the victorious Allies imposed similar draconian conditions on Germany after its defeat in the First World War (1914–1918).

Bismarck's success in 1870 led to the unification of Germany. The new Reich consisted of four kingdoms, five grand duchies, twelve duchies and principalities and three free cities: Hamburg, Lübeck and Bremen. Alsace-Lorraine was treated as a conquered province. Interestingly, Austria, the German-speaking part of the Austro-Hungarian Empire, later sought unsuccessfully to join the Weimar Republic. In the late 1930s, Austria was absorbed by Hitler's *Anschluss* into the Third Reich. The various princes of the states offered the crown to King Wilhelm I of Prussia, who was proclaimed Kaiser (Emperor) on 18 January 1871. Kaiser Wilhelm I died in 1888 and was succeeded on the throne by his son Wilhelm II throughout the First World War. A parliament (the Reichstag) elected from all of Germany accepted the existing Northern Imperial Constitution of 1867. Germany now achieved uniform legal procedure, currency and administration. Most restrictions on freedom of enterprise and movement were removed. Freedom of the press was secured in 1874.

Thus from 1871 the 'Jews of Germany' gained full civil rights constitutionally, becoming 'German Jews'. Despite these guarantees, however, they were not appointed to official positions as officers in the army, full professors at the universities, judges or civil servants. On the surface, until the outbreak of the First World War, Jewish life in Germany was more reasonable than it had been in any previous century.[1]

Of the 600,000 Jews in Germany in 1914, the number who served during the First World War in the German armed forces was 100,000, of whom 12,000 died in battle. At the end of the war when the monarchy fell and a democratic republic was established, the Jews finally achieved full emancipation. Any restrictions still in force were abolished by the Weimar Republic. Many of the leaders of the democratic and socialist parties were Jews, of whom the most renowned was Walter Rathenau. The Weimar constitution was drafted by Hugo Preuss, a Jew. In 1925 there were 564,379 Jews in Germany, 0.9% of the population.

After 1918 many Russian Jewish writers, intellectuals and publishers took refuge in Germany. The country became a centre for Jewish literature, publishing and Zionism. Some of the greatest Jewish poets and writers took up residence in Germany.

Reparation payments were imposed on defeated Germany. The general terms of the Versailles Treaty were so humiliating that they seriously weakened the infant republican regime. The legend that 'the German army had never really been defeated on the battlefield but had been stabbed in the back by the republicans, the socialists and the Jews back home' was repeated by the old establishment and the right-wing movements who were opposed to the republic. The mood of resentment created by the treaty meant that this legend came incrementally to be accepted by the populace. With hindsight, the seeds of Nazism, the Second World War and the destruction of European Jewry can be seen to have developed out of the severe provisions of the Versailles Treaty.

The years from 1920 to 1923 were times of crisis. Multiple parties were manoeuvring for power, including a newly founded Nazi Party (National Socialist Workers Party). Against this background the economy was dominated by inflation, due particularly to the government's decision to meet its reparation

---

[1] See Appendix 1

2

obligation by printing money. The inflation was such that from four Marks to the American dollar before the war, it required 4,200 trillion to buy one American dollar in 1923. The formidable leader Gustav Stresemann courageously declared an emergency in 1923. He introduced a new currency, the Rentenmark. One Rentenmark replaced one trillion of the old Marks. Security for this was provided by mortgages over the entire industrial and agricultural resources of the country. He also achieved Germany's acceptance into the League of Nations and negotiated the withdrawal of French occupation of the industrial Ruhr Valley. Germany's reputation was thus rehabilitated. Prosperity was real, but depended on foreign credits.

A drastic deflationary policy was necessary again after 1928. This succeeded in increasing exports and decreasing imports, but it led to bankruptcies and another collapse of credit, so that people could not borrow. The economic, social and political effects were disastrous, further encouraging popular support for extremist parties such as the Nazis.

With the crash of the New York Stock Exchange in October 1929, foreign credit was suddenly unavailable. Banks failed and there was not enough money to support the German economy. By 1932 there were 6 million unemployed. Depression and deflation, which were worse in Germany than anywhere else, had immediate political repercussions, increasing support for extremist parties, pitting Nazis and communists against each other and providing additional conditions for the Nazis' ultimate rise to power.

Elections in July 1932 gave the Nazis only 230 of the 647 seats, but after negotiations with various parties, Hitler secured the chancellorship for himself, attaining office in January 1933. He scheduled new elections for March that year, using the new medium, radio, for his propaganda. With the help of Hermann Göring he purged the Prussian police force, employing the Sturm Abteilung (SA), which was given 'freedom of the streets' to intimidate and control.

On 27 February 1933 the Reichstag burned down. There is enough evidence to establish beyond reasonable doubt that the Nazis planned and carried out the arson for their own political ends (see William L Shirer). On the pretext that this was a communist plot to seize power, the Reich government assumed emergency powers. Despite all this, the elections did not give the Nazis an overall majority. They still needed the support of the Nationalists.

Hitler now passed the Enabling Act, which allowed the government to issue decrees independently of the Reichstag or the President. This act remained the constitutional basis of Hitler's dictatorship throughout the period of the Third Reich.

In May 1933 trade unions were suppressed and merged with the German Labour Front. Soon all political parties except the Nazi Party were suppressed. Hitler needed the support of the army, the most powerful independent institution in the country. He needed its help to re-arm Germany and to acquire for himself the post of president. Using the conflict between the army generals and the radical Nazi leader Ernst Röhm, chief of staff of the Nazi SA, Hitler allowed the purge of his friend and ally Röhm and his lieutenants on 30 June 1934. They were seized and executed without trial. Having gained the support of the army, Hitler merged the offices of president and chancellor, assuming the titles of *Führer* and *Reichskanzler* (Leader and State Chancellor) after Hindenburg died on 2 August 1934.

The period of 1934 to 1939 saw the steady elaboration of a totalitarian police state. The principal instrument of control was the unification of police, security and Schutzstaffel (SS) organisations. All educational and artistic institutions and media were forced into the pattern of Nazi regimentation and the young were indoctrinated through the schools and the compulsory Hitler Youth movement. In April 1933, Jews were dismissed from government service and from universities and debarred from the professions. The Nürnberg Laws of September 1935 forbade marriages between Jews and persons of 'German blood'. By July 1938 Jewish children were no longer allowed to go to German schools. On the night of 9-10 November of that year the infamous *Kristallnacht* exploded throughout Germany.

In 1939 Hitler finally managed to bring under his control the two major institutions which had so far retained their independence: the army and the foreign service with its policymakers and diplomats. He achieved this by threatening to make public unsavoury aspects of the personal lives of senior generals and foreign-service officers. From this point on, Hitler's arbitrary power over Germany was total.

One of the German émigrés to England, Fritz Schumacher, described Germany as being like ' ... a glass of water with sediment at the bottom. The Nazis had stirred up the dirt so that the entire contents were now contaminated.' (Snowman, Daniel, *The Hitler Emigrés*, p 301.)

(Other sources: *Encyclopaedia Britannica*; *Encyclopaedia Judaica*; Shirer WL. *The Rise and Fall of the Third Reich*.)

BOOK ONE

Glimpses of Jewish Life in Westphalia 1886–1938

Kate Mendels (née Herzberg)

In the first years after our arrival in Australia I worked in our shop and later had a busy home to run. I had no time to tell the stories of our life in Germany and of our emigration. I don't consider myself an author, but believe my descendants would like to hear a faithful account of our family. As our younger generations grow up some may ask: 'How is it that you were able to escape Germany, yet so many of your relatives and friends were left behind?'

Kate Mendels, Sydney, 1971

1

The solemn atmosphere in the Herzberg family home in Gütersloh reflects the dim November afternoon. The year is 1886. Pauline Herzberg, mother of four small children, has just been laid to rest in the neat old Jewish cemetery. The house is filled with grieving relatives and friends paying last respects. For those who come from far away there is coffee and raisin bread on the table.

During the *Minjen* the widower Josef can barely utter the familiar words of the *Kaddisch*, his voice choked by sobs. He can't believe he has lost Pauline. He is emotionally drained, deeply concerned for the welfare of his motherless children: Salomon, aged seven; Rosa, five; Hermann, three; and Clare, just five months; and he pines for his baby son Arnold, just three weeks old when he died four years ago.

His brother, Salomon, living in the paternal home in Kleinen-Marpe (in the principality of Lippe-Detmold), comes to him to say goodbye, as do his five sisters and their husbands.

Betty Emanuel, the elderly spinster who has looked after the household during Pauline's illness, will continue on as housekeeper. She's not able to manage children longing for their mother. Josef is fortunate that Marie, the maid, looks after them so well.

Josef has now also inherited another responsibility: the care of Arnold, his late wife's retarded brother, who lives with them.

Although still in mourning, and with family responsibilities, Josef must not neglect his business, a successful butcher shop. To make sure that the meat he sells is of high quality he also has to visit farms to choose the best stock.

Ten years earlier, at the time of his marriage to Pauline (née Alexander), Josef had taken over the Alexander family house and two businesses. The second was a hardware shop selling pots, pans, cooking and heating stoves, coppers for washing and cauldrons for cooking cattle fodder. This business had been founded by Pauline's uncle, Marcus Alexander, who had migrated to Australia.[2] When buying cattle, Josef was often able to sell a stove or cauldron to the farmer. Busy as this kept him, he didn't neglect his children.

Eventually, friends begin to encourage Josef to remarry and even to suggest suitable prospects, but Josef isn't interested. Invited here and there, Josef won't accept, saying, 'I just don't feel I can be away from home and children.' His elderly, sick father suggests several times, 'You need a mother for your children.'

---

[2] Pauline Herzberg's uncle, Marcus Alexander, was the youngest of eleven children of Aaron Alexander, a Jewish master butcher who died in Gütersloh in 1843. Born 19 August 1820, Marcus also became a butcher by trade. As conditions in Europe, particularly for Jews, were difficult both economically and politically, Marcus, a bachelor, decided to try his luck in South Australia, where gold had been discovered. A facsimile of an 1853 letter to his Gütersloh family is preserved in the South Australian Archives and has been translated and published by the Australian Jewish Historical Society (Vol. VIII, July 1978). It describes his arrival, the limits of employment and the minimal Jewish life that he encountered. He went inland, and became a successful sheep farmer, till years later during a severe storm and flood, he lost his substantial livestock. This prompted him to travel back to see family in Germany. He returned to Australia via Baltimore, USA, where he visited one of his sisters. It is believed he died in New South Wales, place and date unknown, despite extensive research.

2

In the small hamlet of Barsinghausen, not far from Hannover, lived Jeanette Levisohn, widow of the late Levi Levisohn.

Levi had run a good business dealing in horses, very often travelling to foreign countries to import suitable livestock. Not long after the Franco-Prussian War of 1870–1871, on the way back from a journey to Denmark he took sick in Hamburg, infected with 'black pox'[3]. He reached home desperately ill, dying a few days later. Because of the great risk of contagion, nobody wanted to prepare his body for burial, so Jeanette intended to take care of this herself. A young man, Gustav Lehmann, came forward to assist. The Levisohns had often given a helping hand to the Lehmann family. This kindly reciprocal deed was exceptional and never forgotten.

At the time of Levi's death the couple had twelve children[4], the youngest only four years of age.

It was not possible for Jeanette to continue trading in horses. Realising that lace bonnets and hats were in fashion for married women, she engaged a milliner and opened a hat shop. Jeanette's resulting income made it possible for her to give the children a good education. She proved to be a capable businesswoman. Her late husband's spinster sister took care of the household.

Over the years as the business expanded, Jeanette's daughters worked there: Marianne, the first to train as a milliner, followed by dressmaker Elise, already married, and finally the youngest sister, Rosa.

---

[3] This was probably agricultural anthrax.
[4] Johanne born 1853, Marianne 1854, Helene 1855, Aron and Josef 1857 (twins), Magnus 1858, Benjamin (Ben) 1860, Elise 1861, Bertha 1862, Jenny 1864, Rosalie (Rosa) 1866, Meyer 1867.

Jeanette Levisohn (née Cohn).

Of the five Levisohn sons, the oldest, twins Aron and Josef, were successful grain merchants in Barsinghausen. Three others had migrated to New York. Two Cohn uncles, Jeanette's brothers, had been living in America for several years. The third youngest daughter, Bertha, lived with an aunt, Jeanette's sister, for four years to learn the finer points of cooking, then stayed on at a small wage. After the death of her elderly aunt, she returned home to take over the big household, with the help of a maid. A big fruit and vegetable garden had to be tended, a cow milked, butter and cheese made and bread baked. Gifted in needlework, Bertha would have preferred dressmaking or millinery to housework.

Before long the twin Levisohn brothers, Josef and Aron, would each marry. In fact, Aron had been secretly engaged for quite a time. Bertha, realising that with a bride coming into the house her services would no longer be needed, went into the workroom to help with the sewing whenever she could. If only she had learned a trade like her sisters! If only she could find an acceptable husband! There was little chance of that in the small town of Barsinghausen.

The Levisohns were very friendly with the family Lewin, whose married daughter from Bielefeld, on a visit asked, 'Bertha, would you be interested in an introduction?'

'I'd be delighted, if you know someone to recommend.'

'My sister-in-law, Rachel Langbein, in Gütersloh, near Bielefeld, knows of a man recently widowed. He has four children. If you like, I'll ask her to invite you.'

Bertha was excited when the invitation arrived. The Langbeins received her with great kindness. The following day Mrs Langbein took her visitor to Josef Herzberg's shop, ostensibly to buy meat. She introduced Bertha to Josef and invited him to visit on Friday night. Though he had previously resisted all such invitations, this time he accepted. During her stay Josef and Bertha spent what time they could together. She met the children, who liked her; and she them.

As Josef was overwhelmed with his many responsibilities, some weeks passed after Bertha's visit before he proposed marriage. He came to Barsinghausen and 25 December 1887 was chosen for their engagement. Advertisements were placed in the Gütersloh and Barsinghausen papers and printed notices mailed to friends and relatives in other towns.

Barsinghausen was deep in snow when Josef arrived for the engagement. Besides plain gold engagement rings[5], he brought a magnificent bridal present of garnet jewellery: a three-tier necklace, a bracelet and a brooch of finely cut stones set in gold and grouped into varied shapes. These lay as a set in a walnut jewel case lined with padded blue silk.

It was *Chanukah*. When the candles were to be lit, Josef was invited to say the *Broches*. Having a good knowledge of Hebrew and being fully familiar with the prayers, he didn't need a *Siddur*. This was unexpected of someone coming from liberal Westphalia. Josef had been born in Kleinen-Marpe, a tiny place in the county of Lippe-Detmold. His parents had sent him to Detmold for schooling and to study Hebrew and Judaica with Rabbi Dr Farmbach, who later supervised Josef's specialised training and qualification in *Schechite*, the kosher method of slaughtering animals for food.

During the winter Bertha was kept busy sewing her trousseau, for at the time one couldn't buy ready-made manchester. Having six daughters, Jeanette Levisohn had bought large quantities of hand-woven linen and damask. The materials for sheets, tablecloths and towels had to be hemmed, eiderdown covers made, chemises and nightgowns sewn. Some of the pillowslips had

---

[5] At the time, the custom was for the plain gold ring given at the engagement ultimately to be the wedding ring. It was first worn on the left hand and at the wedding changed to the right. Once married, a man would also wear a ring.

crocheted inserts and of course each item had the initials 'B.L.', finely hand-embroidered by Bertha herself.

After some weeks Josef came for a further visit. This time he brought Bertha an antique watch and a short, double, eighteen-carat watch chain with gold fringes, fashionable at the time. During the First World War, or soon thereafter, Bertha had the chain made into a necklace for me, her youngest daughter. Sadly the jeweller stole part of it. On our own at the time, we women weren't courageous enough to sue him. My sister Helene was given the attractive gold fringes. These were stolen from her many years later when her New York apartment was burgled after her migration.

Bertha had a brooch of chased matt gold, a diminishing coil set on a bar, with matching earrings, from which she later had brooches made for her daughters Rosa and Helene. Ilse Hynek (née Neugarten), Rosa's daughter, inherited this brooch, as it had originally belonged to Ilse's grandmother, Pauline.

Engagement of Bertha and Josef (1887).
Note the garnet jewellery.

Bertha Herzberg years later,
wearing the garnet jewellery and
the chased matt gold brooch.

16

The garnet jewellery from Bertha's engagement included a bracelet of linked rectangular units, each with several stones set in gold. Before leaving Germany in 1939, Bertha had rings made from these for her three daughters and two daughters-in-law. Later, in Sydney, she gave units to some of her grandchildren. Paul's and Walter's were fashioned into tiepins; for Erica a bangle, for Ursula a brooch.

The wedding was set for 11 April 1888. Josef and his family wouldn't have to spend *Jontef* on their own and Bertha could supervise the 'spring-cleaning' for *Pesach*. He had planned to be married by his friend *Chasen* Oberschützky of Gütersloh, but as the wedding was to take place in Barsinghausen, Rabbi Dr Gronemann, of nearby Hannover, insisted on officiating. The Rabbi's son, who later became a well-known writer, came with his father to the wedding.

* * *

A day after the Herzberg wedding, Josef's friend Josef Meinberg of Gütersloh married Sophie Rosenbaum of Hagen. This couple furnished their new home with modern furniture. Josef, on the other hand, preferred little change in his home, other than the purchase of a bedroom suite. Bertha readily agreed. She was happy with her new life and her caring spirit could be felt everywhere. For the wedding Josef had had new dresses made of fine fabric for his two daughters, Rosa and Clare. The dressmaker used a great deal of material but the dresses weren't a success. When Bertha later took the children to Barsinghausen for a visit, her sister Elise remade the dresses. Now the children looked charming. Out of two dresses she actually made three. Josef was pleased that, in Bertha, his four children had found a capable and loving mother. During the summer Bertha realised to everyone's delight that she was pregnant.

Autumn brought the High Holidays. As always, Josef *daven*ed *Schacharis* on *Rausch Haschono*. On *Kol Nidre* night he *daven*ed till the sermon, and at the end of the service he sang *Jigdal*, alternating verses with the community. Mrs Meinberg played the harmonium. She was a professionally trained soprano and claimed: 'Nobody can sing *Jigdal* like Mr Herzberg.' On *Jaum Kippur* he again *daven*ed *Schacharis*, singing his melodic *Nigunim* in a fine baritone voice.

Some years earlier the congregation had wanted to enhance the synagogue service with a harmonium to accompany the choral singing. My father and Hermann Ruthenburg advanced money for the purchase and the community repaid it progressively. Piano teacher Lina Stern was the first to play the

Josef Herzberg davening in the Gütersloh Synagogue, sketched by Paul Meinberg.
Writing on Sketch: (left) Grandfather Herzberg is davening;
(right) One has to acknowledge he is a wonderful Chasen.

instrument. The Lewandowski melodies with harmonium accompaniment rang out, enriching the service. The community learnt many tunes from the *Chasen* and teacher Louis Löwenstein.

This same Hermann Ruthenburg, one of thirteen children, was quite a character. He told the following amusing story of his father.

> My father had been on a trip looking for a husband for one of my sisters. I picked him up from the railway station and asked, 'How did you get on, Father?'
>
> 'Let's get home first.'
>
> After a while Father said, 'Hey! You haven't asked me anything about my trip. Aren't you interested?'
>
> 'Oh yes! Tell me, how was it?'
>
> 'What can I say? Well, they did have plush carpets on the floor and silverware on the table. But how can one tell if those things belong to them or to the bank?'

* * *

In December Gütersloh held its annual fair with merry-go-rounds, cake stalls and toy stalls. Our two maids took the children, having been given ample spending money. On their return home, when the children were called to dinner, little Clare didn't want to eat. Mother looked at her throat. It was very red. The maid suggested the child had eaten red sweets. During the night Clare became very restless. The doctor diagnosed diphtheria and prescribed several medicines, to no avail. The poor child suffered terribly. A surgeon was called. He opened the child's windpipe to ease breathing. Nevertheless, little Clare died on 21 December 1888. The parents were heartbroken, Bertha distraught, and there was concern she might miscarry.

Five weeks later, on 27 January 1889, Bertha bore a little girl by difficult forceps delivery. She was named Helene. 'She's a little princess,' said the attending doctor, as her birth coincided with Kaiser Wilhelm II's birthday, his first as Emperor. The streets were decorated with flags; schools and offices were closed. Helene grew up to be a real beauty, and because her birthday was on such a special day people always remembered to send her greetings.

A year later, on 29 January 1890, a son, Paul David, was born, and on 22 September 1891, another son, Leopold.

Yes, Bertha had her hands full with three small children, as well as looking after the schoolwork of the older ones. She also helped in the business and did the bookkeeping. The many responsibilities made Bertha very tired, so during the children's summer vacation, she travelled with them to Barsinghausen to relax in the clear Deister air. (Deister is a forested mountain area near Barsinghausen.) The children were well cared for and enjoyed their holiday. Bertha returned home invigorated.

During the summer of 1894 Bertha felt exceptionally tired. Josef said, 'You look pale, perhaps you're anaemic. You should go to Bad Pyrmont to take the baths and drink the waters.' They consulted the doctor who smiled and said, 'A health resort will make no difference – Bertha is pregnant.'

She wasn't thrilled. 'We already have six children. If they are all to have a good education, however will we manage?' 'Don't be discouraged,' Josef answered. 'If we can care for six, we can care for seven. We just need to stay healthy.'

For some months the eldest son, Salomon, had been serving his apprenticeship in a hardware/homeware shop in Minden. Josef had in mind that Salomon could eventually build up their sideline business selling stoves, and ultimately have that for himself. Consequently Father built a two-storey house in the garden, the new building fronting Moltkestrasse. On the ground floor was a stall for the carriage horse, a slaughter pen and support space for the butchery. The first floor was a storeroom for cooking and heating stoves, oven pipes and replacement parts. The big loft was to be used for drying laundry. In the other house on Königstrasse, the old loft was now to be the drying area for hides of calves, lambs and goats, bought from Bertha's brother, Josef Levisohn.

The eldest daughter, Rosa, now thirteen and at a girls' high school, was already a great help in the house and very caring towards her smaller brothers and sisters.

On 25 February 1895, a baby girl was born into the Herzberg household. (This was Käthe, recorder of this family saga). 'Thank G-d, mother and baby are well,' Josef said. 'Bring the youngsters to see their little sister.' (They were fascinated to see how small I was.)

'Yes, she's tiny.'

Her head's about the size of an apple.'

'Look how lively she is.'

'See how she moves her fingers.'

'Mummy,' Rosa said, 'may I take the little one out for a ride in my doll's pram?'

'Not today. First the baby has to grow.'

As soon as the warm spring weather arrived, Rosa proudly took me for an outing in her doll's pram, into which I fitted comfortably.

At work in Minden, Salomon had the job of picking up the firm's mail from the post office. A postcard from his father was addressed to him. Having read it, he put it back with the incoming letters. His boss noticed the card and handed it to him. 'Congratulations on your new sister.' Salomon blushed and didn't reply. It seems he didn't welcome an addition to the family.

'Little Käthe' continued to do well. I was tiny compared with the Meinbergs' daughter, born two days earlier. The Meinbergs and Herzbergs had much in common. They married at the same time and each couple ultimately had four children of similar ages. Naturally, they became close friends.

In addition to the children, Bertha took care of Albert Alexander (brother of the late Pauline), who had always been part of the household. He was not capable of looking after his late father's business, but helped wherever he could. Bertha got on well with him and he was very attached to her. One Friday night Bertha and Josef were invited to the home of friends. When they returned,

Josef said, 'I'll just check on Albert. He told me this afternoon he wasn't feeling well.' Moments later he was back very distressed, having found Albert had died, apparently peacefully.

Later that year Rosa became *Basmizwo*. Soon after, she left school to help Mother run the big household.

Hermann's *Barmizwo* was celebrated in November 1896. In the following year he went to Barsinghausen apprenticed to Levisohn Brothers, a produce firm, and boarded with his uncle, Josef Levisohn, and wife. His washing was sent home to be laundered.

Washing then was done every three to four weeks. It was hard work and done by hand as there were no washing machines. The clothes were boiled in a big copper filled with water, bucket by bucket. Rinsing and wringing were also done manually. Even the wringer we later bought had to be turned by hand.

The Herzberg children.
Back row (l-r): Salomon, Rosa, Hermann. Mid row (l-r): Leopold, Käthe, Helene.
Front: Paul.

3

In a community as small as Gütersloh, it was accepted that everyone who could would attend synagogue on *Schabbes* and *Jontef*, including children of the Jewish primary school. Students who went to high school from the age of ten learned at the Jewish school every Wednesday afternoon, when government schools were closed. Only two or three Jewish high schools existed in the whole of Germany.

The Herzbergs worked hard all week. For some years the shop opened on Saturdays because of growing competition. Josef and Bertha took turns in going to synagogue. But *Erev Schabbes* was honoured by all. The table was set with a white, starched tablecloth, highly polished silver cutlery and fresh *Barches*. Mother *bencht* the *Schabbes* candles, Father made *Kiddusch* and *Mauze*. After a beautiful dinner we always sang *Semiraus* before *Schir Ha-maalaus* and then Father would *bensch* Grace after Meals. Sometimes the boys would be given that honour. Then we children would ask Father to tell us stories. He had a great repertoire, most with a moral message and enlivened with local context.

I recall his telling of the fable 'The Fox and The Wolf':

> Wolf comes to Fox and says, 'Go get me something to eat or I'll gobble you up.'
>
> Fox answers, 'Look, I'm only a small animal; you need more meat than you'll find on me! Here is half a chicken for you meantime. Now run to Barkey's bakery where Herzberg's maid is picking up the fresh *Barches*. Grab the loaves from her.'

Wolf hurries to seize the *Barches* but the girl is not alone; her boyfriend is with her. With his stick he gives Wolf a big hiding. Howling, Wolf runs away as fast as he can. In great pain he comes back to Fox and tells him what has happened.

'I know something even better for you,' says Fox. 'Do you know Meier Merklinghaus's big paddock near the Dalke River? There you'll find a fine, red horse grazing. Jump onto his back from behind and bite a big piece out of his rump.'

At daybreak the following morning Wolf runs into the paddock and Horse turns to face him and says, 'Dear Wolf, what brings you here so early this morning?'

'I'm hungry and I want a piece of your hind leg.'

Horse says, 'I can't stop you biting me, but first I would like to ask you a favour. There's a nail in my right hind foot. You know humans put iron shoes on my feet. Well, one of their nails is stuck in my flesh. It hurts. Please pull it out.' As Wolf goes to pull out the nail with his sharp teeth, Horse steps with all his might on Wolf's nose, making it bleed. Wolf runs off howling. The peasants and workers of the nearby big Meierhof farm hear the noise and chase Wolf, but he escapes and comes back to Fox, quite out of breath and lamenting.

'You're a big *Schlemihl*,' says Fox, 'but I'll tell you of another delicacy. When the big circus left town, a mother monkey stayed on. She now lives with her two babies in the big tree behind the three oaks. Go there. Remember to tell her how beautiful her babies are and she'll show them off to you. You can then snatch them and run.' Wolf wastes no time and goes to the monkey.

From far away Monkey cries, 'Look dear Wolf, how beautiful my babies are.'

'They are really ugly *Menubbel*s,' says Wolf.

'You're a nasty liar,' says Monkey, and scratches Wolf's head with her long nails till he bleeds. Again Wolf comes back plaintively to Fox.

'What happened, didn't you eat the baby monkeys?'

'No! The mother monkey was furious when I said her babies were ugly *Menubbel*s. Please dear Fox, tell me once more how I can get something decent to eat.'

'If you want to make any kind of a deal,' says Fox 'sometimes you must praise things even if they aren't worthy of praise. I realise now, I'll have to send you to a timid animal. Go up Berliner Strasse to the area known as the Busch. The people there have a goat in their stable. You can kill the goat quick and easy and you'll have food for a long time.'

'Thank you,' says Wolf and hurries to the Busch and finds the stable.

Being very friendly, Goat says, 'How are you dear Wolf?'

'I am so hungry. I'm going to gobble you up.'

'Oh!' says Goat. 'I'm not strong enough to resist. I guess I'll have to resign myself to my fate. Do you know that tomorrow is *Jaum Kippur* and tonight is *Kol Nidre*? I am already wearing my white *Sargenes*. I beg you let me first sing the *Ja-aleh*.' So Goat starts to sing, 'Maeh Maeh, Maeh Maeh.' Wolf with his deep bass voice joins him and they sing their *Jaum Kippur* duet.

The farmer in the house jumps up and says, 'The way our goat is bleating there must be a wolf in the stable.' They run to the stable with spades and sticks and beat Wolf to death.

I, Käthe Mendels, youngest of the nine Herzberg children, have been privileged to tell this story in English to my own grandchildren, changing the places of action to Sydney. I would sing the *Ja-aleh* imitating animal voices, to the great amusement of the children. My father's stories were always so colourful that I remember many of them. I was four years old when I first heard 'The Fox and the Wolf', yet, here I am at seventy-six, recounting it from memory. Perhaps I've left out some detail.

Before the First World War, *Schnorrer*s from Eastern Europe came through Westphalia, about whom many *Moischelchen* were told. Every *Schnorrer* who came to our home was given a hot meal as well as money. My father told numerous tales about them. Here is a sample:

> Every Friday night, a certain pious man would invite a *Schnorrer* home for dinner. His wife was miserly, begrudging these guests the delicious meal. So she would give them vegetables and potatoes and a bone with almost no meat on it. But no gravy!
>
> The gravy always smelled just so good and one Friday night the *Schnorrer* really wanted some. He was cunning. He said to the lady, 'Madam, may I tell you about something that happened to me?'

'Alright, if you must.'

The *Schnorrer* then told a far-fetched story. The wife interrupted him, 'That couldn't possibly be true.'

'If it's not true, then may my blood be spilt just as I spill this gravy.' Saying this, the *Schnorrer* took the gravy boat and poured gravy freely onto his plate.

'Stop! Stop!' said the lady. 'I believe you. I believe it all.'

Thus, when we as children were given strawberry sauce for our vanilla custard we always said, 'Then may my blood be spilt ...'

Here is another of his stories:

Two Jewish tradesmen move into a little hamlet to open a shop. They've been warned that the local parson insists that his parishioners buy only from their Christian brethren. Therefore the two men decided to seek out the parson and tell him they wanted to convert to the one and only Church of Salvation. The parson asks them to come back the next Saturday afternoon for instruction in their new religion.

It's a hot summer day, the sun shines brightly into the room and the parson drones on. One of the Jewish men dozes off, wakes with a start and, half asleep, blurts to his friend, 'Listening to all these *Stussen*, I've forgotten to *daven Minche*!'

I could tell many more! Are fables still of interest? Here is a story that is true. It actually happened:

In Aerzen, in the county of Lippe, near Hameln, the city of the Pied Piper, lived a poor Jewish man known as Jekevche Aerzen. In his youth, Father lived near Aerzen. Incidentally, my mother-in-law, Riekchen Mendels née Gronsfeld, was born there and also knew Jekev. My father told us that one day he came across Jekev lying nude in a paddock. He had washed his only shirt and was waiting till it dried.

During his wanderings Jekev came to Barsinghausen to my grandmother Levisohn, played a little melody on his two-string violin and said, '*Auch nit schön?*' (Nice, eh?) He was given a good meal and some money and then walked on. He went on to Kleinen-Marpe, also in County Lippe, to my other grandmother, Karoline Herzberg. As he greeted her she said, 'Jekev, don't come into the house; you could do with a wash.'

'*Nu*,' he said, '*Ein paar hat a Jeder.*' (Everyone's got a few.) He was referring to *Kinnim* (lice). Quite likely, given the lack of bathroom and washing facilities in those days. In our family this comment became a household word.

During the First World War my brother Hermann was fighting in Russian Poland and complained bitterly about plagues of lice. We then wrote to Paul, my brother in the trenches in France, to ask whether he was similarly plagued. Back came the reply: 'I say, as did that Great Philosopher of County Lippe, '*Ein paar hat a Jeder.*'

Both brothers were to die for an ungrateful Fatherland.

* * *

Our family was always on good terms with our non-Jewish neighbours. Children played together; parents helped each other. It was not unusual for a neighbour to come and say, 'I've a promissory note to pay. Could you lend me 50 Marks?' Sometimes it was 100 Marks or more. The money was always paid back, without a *Pfennig* interest charged.

I went to kindergarten with a neighbour's two daughters. Often, when I called for them in the mornings, the family, who were religious Protestants, would still be saying prayers. I would also put my hands together and join in singing hymns. When they lit their Christmas tree I was always asked to join the singing. 'Käthe, it's wonderful. You know all the carols.' When *Pesach* came we always gave them *Matzo*.

Protestant Pastor Meinshausen lived in our street. Before every Christmas I had to go to his home taking a basket of meat cut into portions and say, 'Best regards from my father. He asks Herr Pastor to be kind enough to give this meat to the poor in your parish.' Herr Pastor would then respond with thanks and good wishes, and Frau Pastor would give me a bag of home-made biscuits. After many years Pastor Meinshausen was transferred to another town. His successor bought meat only from co-religionists.

The Herzberg butcher shop was known for its good quality meat. There were, of course, no refrigerators or cool rooms at the time, so butchers couldn't keep much meat in stock. All they had was a big icebox[6] and an external meat safe with walls of fine wire mesh accessible from inside the shop. Butchers from the surrounding areas or towns often asked Father for his special cuts. One such wholesale customer, Moses Mendels of Rheda, a town near Gütersloh, supplied the household of the Prince of Rheda-Bentheim-Tecklenburg. I was still a child at the time and couldn't know that Moses Mendels was the grandfather of my husband-to-be.

In early February 1903, Paul's *Barmizwo* and Helene's *Basmizwo* took place. Helene was fourteen. We had a beautiful double celebration in the synagogue on a mild winter's day. For the occasion a fine dinner was prepared by Rosa and the two maids under Mother's supervision. Opening the doors between our two living rooms, we were able to seat thirty people at one long table.

Leopold's *Barmizwo* took place in September 1904 – Louis Löwenstein's last official function in Gütersloh.

In time for the High Holidays, Markus Gottlieb of Berlin came to the community as *Chasen* and teacher. He was very musical, highly intelligent and an excellent teacher. The congregation was very fortunate in appointing such a capable man. He had been employed in an orphanage in Berlin, but a difference with the director brought him to us. His sister Sofie was a well-known opera singer in Charlottenburg, who often performed Wagner.

The women of our community had already formed a choir trained by *Lehrer*[7] Spier of Rheda. They rehearsed psalms and hymns in harmony, as well as the *Kedusche* (sometimes in German), *Ma Tauwu, Adaun Aulom, Ja-aleh, We-je esoju*[8] and *Tal* for *Pesach*, mostly with Lewandowski melodies. During singing lessons at school Mr Gottlieb taught us those same melodies, so we could be part of the choir. For years the 'German *Kol Nidre*' prayer[9] had been sung by the congregation, with Mrs Sofie Meinberg singing the solo parts. During the

---

[6] Iceboxes were insulated cabinets, forerunners of refrigerators, kept cold by a large block of ice, which was replaced as needed and sold by the 'ice man' who delivered them to the business or the home. In those days there was also the 'milk man' who came around daily with horse and cart.

[7] The term '*Lehrer*' is equivalent to Reverend.

[8] 'All the world will come to serve Thee, and bless Thy glorious Name,' from the *Kedusche* of *Rausch Hashono*.

[9] The 'German *Kol Nidre*', '*Oh Tag des Herren*' was sung in many communities in Germany from the latter part of the 19th century onwards as a substitute for the *Kol Nidre* declamation. This was initiated because anti-Semites falsely chose to take Kol Nidre as evidence that the oath of a Jew was worthless.

service Mr Gottlieb, as *Chasen*, also had harmonium accompaniment. Passers-by would sometimes stop to listen to the music.

I had lessons with Mr Gottlieb for six months at our small Jewish elementary school. His excellent teaching, combined with what I learned at home, gave me a good basis for the future. The general education was also of high standard. About this time Else Meinberg and I were ready to go to the girls' high school. In the entrance examination we were the only ones of approximately thirty-five students who could correctly parse a sentence using the appropriate Latin terminology. I can still see the bearded, white-haired Headmaster Hark shaking his head and hear him saying to the teachers, 'It's interesting that these two girls are well ahead of students from other schools.'

Mr Gottlieb was quite the artist; he could draw and paint well. He made a wonderful portrait of the blind Mr Max Daltrop.

With parents' permission, Mr Gottlieb took twelve of us, including one of the Ruthenburg twins (Karl and Fritz), to the City Theatre in Bielefeld. The other twin couldn't come as he had an abscess at the base of his spine. Leaving the train station, we visited the old castle Sparenburg before going to the theatre. We were impressed enough by the outside of the building, but wide-eyed at the gilded stucco and the tall mirrors in the foyer. We couldn't get enough of viewing our images from all directions. Suddenly Karl Ruthenburg called out, 'There's our Fritz!' We burst out laughing. The twins were so alike that Karl, seeing himself in the mirror, thought the image was Fritz. We could tell them apart only because Fritz had a small brown spot on his nose. The show we had come to see, a fairytale with wonderful costumes and many coloured lights, made a big impact on us. We had never seen anything like it.

Sadly, Mr Gottlieb stayed only one and a half years in Gütersloh.

* * *

We were very friendly with Amalie Meinberg, who ran something like a finishing school, boarding a young girl for a year to learn the finer arts of cooking, needlework and etiquette. This brought her extra income. Sometimes Amalie even took two girls at one time; her friends frequently referred to her home as Amalienstift (Amalie Institute). Her husband, Salomon, was often away on business as he was a commercial traveller. Occasionally one of her 'old girls' would come to see her. While there they would also visit us, to be with the young people in our home. Sophie Meinberg, Josef's wife, also took in girls while her children were young. One of these, Jenny Buchdahl, married Julius Daltrop. Another, Clara Levy, would later become my sister-in-law, on marrying my brother Salomon.

My older brothers and sisters were friendly with the Rosendahls and the Daltrops, who had sons and daughters of the same age. Occasionally they arranged a ball, put on a comedy, or wrote and performed their own amusing play in rhyme, about members of the congregation. Sometimes we went to the nearby town of Rheda, about ten minutes by train, to attend a *Purim* or *Chanukah* ball.

Some summer Sundays our business carriage was converted into a landau[10] with seats. Paul and Leopold would clean the carriage and groom our horse thoroughly. Once the horse was harnessed, Father would drive his family into the countryside, to the garden of a coffee house. On Whitsunday[11] afternoon, *Pfingsten*, we liked to drive to Castle Tatenhausen, enjoying the view of the castle surrounded by water. In the nearby café, where tables were set out in the lovely garden, we would order coffee, fresh country bread and butter. Cake we brought from home. Music of the band added to the pleasure of the afternoon. Usually Amalie and her boarder came with us. We often met friends and acquaintances there: I recall the Maass family from Borgholzhausen, relatives of Marcus Alexander, the Isenbergs from nearby Halle and families from Bielefeld. These outings were unfortunately rare, as Father preferred not to work the horse on weekends. Instead, we would simply go for a Sunday stroll.

After Mr Gottlieb's departure the community employed two Rosenthal brothers in succession as the *Chasen* and teacher. Karl Rosenthal stayed for two years, then went to the town of Hörde, where he completed his studies. He later became a progressive rabbi in Berlin and migrated to London, where he lived till the end of his days. His brother, Hugo Rosenthal, also stayed about two years. He eventually became director of a Jewish boarding school in southern Germany. During the Rosenthal period a literary club was founded for the Jewish families of Gütersloh, Versmold, Rheda, Wiedenbrück, Neuenkirchen, Herzebrock and Oelde. Lectures were usually given at the Hotel Allerbeck in Rheda on Sunday afternoons, followed by interesting discussions over coffee and cake. Occasionally the subject was Zionism, though few people at the time were Zionists.

---

10   A four wheeled, horse-drawn vehicle usually open, but capable of being closed by an adjustable hood.

11   Whitsunday is the seventh Sunday after Easter and, being a public holiday, was often used for family occasions.

It cost very little to go to Rheda on Sundays, the tickets being discounted for the day. A Mrs Steinberg from Wiedenbrück had moved to Gütersloh and opened a horse-hair spinning mill. She had two grown-up sons. One Sunday we were all once again at the railway station buying our cheap Sunday tickets to Rheda, when one of the Steinberg sons asked rather pretentiously for a first-class ticket to Paris. The Station Master at the counter said, 'It'll take a while sir. I'll have to write that ticket out for you by hand, sir.'

'If I can't have the ticket to Paris straight away, then I'll take a Sunday ticket to Rheda.' We all burst out laughing. He was just showing off.

* * *

As a matter of course every household had a maid or two, mostly from the country. They had much to learn but often became real gems. We once employed a girl, Alwine, who was willing but simple. Our family liked to sing, especially my sister Helene, who sang popular songs and Hebrew songs while doing housework. When I came home from school we often sang *Ma Tauvu* as a duet. The maid would then say, 'Fräulein Lenchen (Helene), sing *Man Tau* again.' It seems she confused it with '*Man zu*' which, in the Low-German spoken by the peasants, means 'Hurry up'.

Mother frequently suffered bouts of gallstone attacks. On one such occasion she was ill in bed and we were expecting visitors for midday dinner which was being prepared by Rosa. She told Alwine, 'Please pour the water off the potatoes, then let the steam out.' The girl took one of the pots and poured out the liquid. 'Miss Rosa, water all gone. But there's soup balls in there. No potatoes!' The *Schlemilte* had taken the wrong pot and poured the soup down the sink.

My brother Paul was in *Unter-Sekunda* (Year 10) at the boys' high school. He was tall for his age and the maid expressed surprise that he was still at school:

'Paul, you still at school? What you going to be?'

'Oh! I think I'll be a millionaire.'

'What's that? You go to 'nother *gymmi-nasium* to be one of them? (The term *Gymnasium* signifies boys' high school.)

One day Alwine was ironing handkerchiefs and Paul took one to blow his nose. This upset the girl. 'Oh Paul! How can ye do that in clean hankie.' She was friendly, always grinning. My father would say, '*Sege schmechelt schon wieder*' (The bumpkin is grinning again.) *Schmecheln* is *Jiddisch* for smiling or grinning. On one occasion, having heard this, the girl took it that she was to bring *Schmirgelpapier* (emery paper) and actually brought some into the dining room.

In 1905 we received an invitation to the wedding of our cousin Emma Hesse of Meschede, a daughter of Father's sister Minna. Our parents decided that Rosa and Salomon should attend. For the occasion Rosa got a beautiful white satin-silk dress and wore Mother's garnets. She looked lovely. At the reception Rosa and Salomon met Louis Neugarten and his sister Bertha, from Rüdinghausen. They were friends of the Hesses, with whom they had gone to school in Meschede. Having lost both parents, Bertha was keeping house for her three brothers, of whom Louis was the eldest. During the dinner he was seated next to Rosa. They thoroughly enjoyed each other's company.

Louis felt he shouldn't marry before his sister. When, a year later, Louis's sister, Bertha, announced her engagement to Albert Bähr, Louis began to correspond with Rosa. Before long they too were engaged. Bertha and Albert set their wedding date for 4 December 1906, Louis's thirtieth birthday. He suggested both couples marry on the same day. Louis's brothers, Paul and Salli, would stay on to be part of their new household.

We younger siblings would miss our big sister who had looked after us so lovingly. She had always helped Paul, Helene and Leopold with their schoolwork, especially when there were essays to write.

The separate *Chuppes* and combined wedding reception took place in a Dortmund hotel. I wore a beautiful white dress and even white silk shoes. I was so proud of those shoes, even though they were hand-me-downs from Rosa. I was nearly twelve years old. Helene and I carried Rosa's train; Cousin Gretchen Königheim from Blomberg carried Bertha's. Before the ceremonies began, our cousin Lina Königheim, also from Blomberg, sang, '*Gott der Liebe, schau hernieder auf diese jungen Paare ...*' (G-d of love, look down upon these young couples ...). Bertha was very tearful. Rosa was all smiles.

As was customary, there was a wedding 'newspaper' put together by family members specifically for the occasion, with photos of both couples on the front page. The paper contained a variety of original *Tischlieder* (table songs), poems, stories and amusing 'advertisements' written by a number of people for the occasion. During the dinner, between courses, the songs were sung by all.

I recited my poem to Rosa:

Du liebe Braut wo alles daran denkt
zum Hochzeitstag Dir Liebe zu erweisen,
da sei von denen Dir auch was geschenkt
die stolz Dich ihre grosse Schwester heissen.
Oft bei der Schularbeit, die schwer uns fiel,
hast Du mit viel Geduld uns beigestanden
kurz überall, sei's Arbeit oder Spiel,
bei Dir wir immer sich're Zuflucht fanden.

The poem said that we, the younger sisters and brothers, were proud of our big sister, who always had patience to help us with schoolwork and found time to play with us. I then presented Rosa with a framed photo of us, her four younger siblings. Rosa burst into tears and threw her arms around me. I don't remember the other verses. After all, the wedding took place sixty-five years ago.

The weddings were just beautiful.

Wonderful that our grandmother, Jeanette Levisohn, almost eighty years of age, was able to be at the weddings. She had come to Gütersloh weeks before, to help sew Rosa's trousseau. After a few days, she and the other guests left to return home to Barsinghausen.

Our lives returned to normal.

Bertha's four children: Paul, Helene, Leopold, Käthe.

* * *

Paul had started his apprenticeship at an office in Bielefeld. Hermann had finished military duties and was working for a corn merchant in Steinheim, Westphalia. After finishing conscription, Salomon didn't want to go back into the hardware business and started work in Father's butcher shop.

Leopold attended the Protestant *Gymnasium* and was an exceedingly good student. There was a great deal of *Risches* from both teachers and pupils. Religion was a main subject, but Jewish pupils were denied credit for this in their results, as were our girls at their high school. Despite this, Leopold was always one of the first in his class. The classic languages Latin and Greek were compulsory. French was taught in *Quarta* (upper form of junior high school); English only after the Intermediate. The Professors (teachers) came to my father pressing him to send Leopold to university. Father's response: 'I can't give preference to one child over the others!'

Leopold's last school holidays were not far off. In April he would start his apprenticeship with Gebrüder Bing Söhne (Bing Söhne Brothers) in Cologne. His Christmas holiday visit to the newly wed Rosa in Rüdinghausen was the first by any family member.

Mother was worried that Leopold, only fifteen and a half years of age, was to live so far away during his apprenticeship, and might face challenging situations. She travelled with him to Cologne, where she found board and lodgings for him with a nice Jewish family. She warned him, 'Be careful of Albert M. He may earn well, but he goes to the races and gambles. He's "not married" you know.' (This was her code word. Albert M was homosexual, something not talked about or explained to youngsters in those days.)

'Don't worry Mother, I know about that'[12] was the confident response.

She bade him a worried goodbye.

* * *

Helene had grown into a real beauty. Heads turned when she was out and about in Gütersloh. It was no surprise that Paul Neugarten, Louis's younger brother, fell in love with her.

Though Salomon was working full time in the butcher shop, it still didn't leave Father enough time for the hardware store on busy Königstrasse.

---

[12] Leopold had been in Cologne for only a very short time when he was encouraged to go to the races. He bet on various horses and lost his entire first wages, an experience that cured him of gambling for life.

Consequently it wasn't doing well. He now planned to sell off the stock and lease out the shop.

A worrying letter arrived from a doctor in Steinheim telling us that Hermann was in hospital, seriously ill with pneumonia. Both parents immediately went to visit. By the time they arrived Hermann was out of danger but had to rest for several weeks. The doctor recommended he should not work in the corn business again. Dust settling on his lungs put him at particular risk.

The sell-off of the hardware shop was in full swing when Hermann came home. To occupy himself he sometimes served customers. When Hermann felt stronger he challenged Father: 'I don't understand. Closing a shop is easy, but opening one is not so simple. Let me have the shop. I'll run the business under my own name.'

At first Father refused, but then relented: 'You can have the shop for a year and we'll see what you make of it.' Hermann, a good businessman, friendly and amiable, soon had regular customers. He concentrated on quality and service, seeking limited profit. He delivered and set up all coal stoves, whether for cooking or heating, and even suggested to customers how best to arrange their furniture. Gradually he enlarged his stock, increasing the range of household products. Later, once electricity became available, he was among the first to replace his gas lamps with modern electric lighting. Hermann was popular.

4

After the annual *Purim* ball, we began our thorough *Pesach* house cleaning. Helene was cleaning wardrobes and drawers when she found in Salomon's room a writing compendium whose blotting paper had the same scrawl repeated in reverse, many times. Being curious, she held the blotter up to the mirror and clearly saw the words 'Fräulein Clara Levy, Lünen'. She ran downstairs, calling, 'Mother, Salomon is corresponding with Clara Levy!'

'I know. Father isn't happy about it. He thinks she might be physically fragile. He knows from personal experience how hard it is to have a sick wife.'

Clara had come on a visit to Gütersloh a few months earlier, invited for a much-needed rest by Sophie Meinberg, with whom she had trained some years before. Her mother had died after a long illness, during which Clara had nursed her throughout the previous summer. Besides the responsibility of the household, she had also been looking after her father, three brothers and three younger school-age sisters. As she was in mourning and wearing black, her pale face and fine features, framed by full jet-black hair, looked even paler. Salomon had 'fallen for her'.

The stay in Gütersloh improved Clara's health only marginally. She had a stomach complaint and couldn't put on weight. A doctor in Düsseldorf prescribed medicine and a special diet. Salomon travelled to Lünen whenever he had free time. Through his brother Paul in Bielefeld, he ordered flowers to be sent weekly to Clara. While both our parents really liked Clara, their concern for her health led to excited exchanges between them – something that was a rare occurrence.

For years Father had worked very hard without a real holiday. In September 1908, the doctor suggested he go to Bad Neuenahr to drink the waters and take the baths. Father liked the recommendation. Mother suggested visits to Rosa in Rüdinghausen and Leopold in Cologne on his return trip. Hermann added, 'Father, I know Salomon intends to marry Clara, and you like her. Why not go to the doctor in Düsseldorf to ask if Clara has a serious illness?'

'Now that's an idea!'

Father sent enthusiastic reports from Bad Neuenahr. He went on long strenuous walks in nice company, felt well and was really refreshed. En route home, he first travelled to Cologne to ask Leopold's employer whether he was satisfied with his son's work. The boss was very pleased with Leopold and the firm intended to send him to Italian classes. He would then handle that correspondence as well as the French.

Card from the Firm Marcello Mainetto to Gebrüder Bing Söhne (Bing Söhne Brothers), regarding payment for goods received.

Leopold in Cologne aged 18 years, 1909.

Düsseldorf was Father's next port of call to visit Clara's doctor. He introduced himself saying he had not come as a patient, but to inquire about Miss Clara Levy. The doctor replied that he could not give out private information.

'Look doctor, my son loves Clara. We like her too, but are concerned she may be seriously ill. What would you do in our position? Perhaps you can answer that?'

'I'd welcome the marriage. No hesitation.'

'That's all I need to know and I'm very grateful.'

Father took the next train to Lünen and went to Levy's butcher shop. Clara's eldest brother, Emil, was working there. Father asked him,

'Do I look like anyone you know?'

'No. Not really.'

'Do you know Salomon Herzberg? I'm his father. May I have a word with Clara?'

Father greeted her, 'Regards from Salomon. He doesn't know I'm here. Do you think we two could set a date for your engagement?'

Over a cup of good coffee and cake it was agreed that the engagement would take place in May, on Whitsunday. By Easter, Clara's sister Else would have just returned from finishing school in the Rhineland. The wedding was set for the following year, to make it easier for Else to take over the household and look after the family. From Lünen Father travelled to Rüdinghausen to spend a day with Rosa and Louis. He came home refreshed and triumphant.

That evening, Salomon walked in to a real surprise: 'Special greetings from Clara. She wants to know whether you'd like to celebrate your engagement on Whitsunday holiday!' Salomon was speechless. He didn't even ask why Father was no longer reluctant about the marriage.

In May 1909, we celebrated Clara and Salomon's engagement in Lünen. My parents, Salomon, Hermann, Helene and I travelled together from Gütersloh; Paul from Essen and Leopold from Cologne. Paul Neugarten had also been invited as it was thought he and Helene were secretly engaged. But after meeting Clara's brother, Emil Levy, Helene changed her mind. Paul Neugarten was very disappointed.

The celebration was memorable: a dinner with many delicacies, even imported fresh apples, which at that time were a great rarity. Clara kindly sent some of these to my frail elderly grandmother, Jeanette Levisohn, in Barsinghausen. Sadly, my grandmother died in December of that year.

On the following Saturday I celebrated my *Basmizwo* in our synagogue – solo. Though Else Meinberg was my age, her parents thought a *Basmizwo* unnecessary. I was taught by Mr Hugo Rosenthal, our *Chasen* and teacher. I studied the Ten Commandments, verses from the Prophets Amos, Micah and Isaiah, general Jewish knowledge and memorised a special prayer for the occasion. The subject of Mr Rosenthal's sermon was: 'The world rests on three things: righteousness, truth and peace'.

We came home for a festive dinner at which I thanked my parents for the love and care they had given me, my teacher for the lessons, and the guests for their participation and presents. I was thrilled to receive many books, for I loved reading. The family in Barsinghausen gave me a watch of dark Tula silver with two flowers etched on the back, one gold and one silver, with a long, matching chain necklace. The watch could be worn linked with a brooch, the latest fashion, or at the waist on a belt. Clara was in our house for the first time since her marriage. She gave me a brush, comb and mirror set.

Friends came over in the evening: Amalie with her boarder, Josef and Sophie Meinberg with daughters Irma and Else, and nieces Erna and Julie Rosenberg from Hagen, who happened to be visiting. The girls were conservatorium students, Julie playing piano and Erna violin. The Meinbergs were all very musical and great entertainers. Mr Rosenthal sang some *Lieder*, as did my aunt, Henny Levisohn, who had a fine soprano voice. Between musical items, coffee, homemade cakes, *Platenkuchen*[13] and *Torten* were served. I so enjoyed the occasion.

Twelve months later, we celebrated Helene's engagement to Clara's brother, Emil Levy. The day had been very hot, so we walked up and down Moltkestrasse to catch a breath of air and enjoy the scent of lilac from the neighbour's garden. To transform our adjoining building into a home for Salomon and Clara in time for their wedding planned for June 1910, an enclosed staircase leading to the former hardware storeroom was being added. During our evening stroll we heard a strange noise in the renovations. My brother-in-law Louis Neugarten quickly climbed up a ladder and found a tramp, set to spend the night squatting there. He was disappointed!

* * *

I had always achieved good school reports. Nevertheless, Mother wanted me to leave school, learn needlework and sewing and then take an apprenticeship as a milliner in order to be self-sufficient, able to stand on my own two feet. Unlike Mother, I was not suited for this craft. Only years later, when I first saw an eye specialist at age forty, was I told I had limited vision in one eye. There had been no medical examinations in schools in my day. Once I had glasses my needlework improved.

I started my apprenticeship as a milliner, already doing small tasks. Sometimes I had to deliver hats. My boss's sister was a dressmaker and lived in the building. One day one of her girls and I had to deliver dresses and hats to a big farmstead, about half an hour's walk away. On our way back a sudden electrical storm and subsequent downpour drenched us. We returned to work without changing our clothes, which dried on our backs in the warm workroom. This was to have consequences for me.

A day or two later, I felt severe pain in my right leg and knee. My right hand, especially the middle finger, was very sore. I had hardly any strength in the hand. When I complained to Mother, she said, 'They're growing pains. Many young people have them.'

I was sent to buy milk and butter from neighbour Ükmann's grocery shop. Mrs Ükmann commented, 'Käthe, you don't look well. What's the matter?'

---

[13] *Platenkuchen*, a flat yeast cake, brushed with beaten egg, dotted with small pieces of butter, sprinkled with sugar and slivered almonds, was baked on a metre-long tray and carried to the local bakery oven. *Torten* are tarts or flans.

'My right knee and hand are very painful. Mother thinks I've growing pains.'

No one in the family had noticed I looked ill. The pain was worse at night, sometimes making me sob. One night it was so bad that I cried out, waking Mother in the next room. She calmed me down, promising to call the family doctor, Dr Kranefuss, first thing in the morning.

The doctor couldn't come till midday, it being his busy Saturday. I was on the couch in our big living room. He saw me through the wide-open door and immediately said, 'She's very ill.' He diagnosed rheumatic fever and prescribed a medicine containing salicyl (aspirin), as well as ichthyol ointment to be applied to the sore joints, which were then wrapped in cotton wool. Because I was feverish I was kept in bed. The weather was hot and I remember being very uncomfortable. Good friends gave a variety of advice: some thought that salicyl was bad for the heart. My parents were very worried. Helene would come upstairs with a dish full of hot water and towels and apply hot packs around my aching joints. This soothed the pain only temporarily as the packs cooled in no time. The heavy tin or copper hot-water bottles then in use were of no help. Rubber hot-water bottles and electrically heated pads did not exist. Electricity supply came to us three years later. Gütersloh had only gas at the time.

After a few weeks, my right side started to jerk. I couldn't keep my arm or leg still. Dr Kranefuss prescribed bromide – this I liked! Suddenly I got red lumps on my face and on top of my head. Combing my hair was painful. Friends advised my parents to consult a neurologist from Bielefeld. Although it was expensive, my parents asked the specialist to make a home visit. He prescribed a foul-tasting medicine and allowed me to get up, as the rheumatic pain had gone. He advised that I shouldn't be left on my own. I asked, 'Can I travel to Lünen next week for my brother's wedding?' 'Of course! What sort of dress are you going to wear?'

Shortly after the specialist left, it was evident that one side of my mouth had dropped and my whole face appeared swollen. Eating was difficult. Intending to bring Dr Kranefuss up to date themselves, my parents had asked the specialist not to contact him directly. The specialist had disregarded their request and had actually informed Kranefuss that he'd taken over my care. On this account, when father phoned our family doctor, he refused to come, but did say the swelling could mean the kidneys might be affected.

My parents were so worried that they rang a second neurologist, Dr Kramer, also in Bielefeld, who said I was probably overdosed with bromide. To be on the safe side my urine should be examined at a pharmacy. Thank goodness this test showed the kidneys were unaffected.

As it turned out I was not the only convalescent guest at Salomon's wedding! A few days before the occasion, Helene was called to Rüdinghausen to help Rosa, whose husband, Louis Neugarten, had to have an urgent operation for haemorrhoids, having delayed surgery too long. He couldn't be taken to hospital, as motor transport was basically unknown. Two doctors performed the operation at Louis's home. He recovered well, being generally in good health, so was able to come to the wedding, but not by rail. The journey would have been additionally awkward because of the need to change trains. His brother Salli drove him from Rüdinghausen by horse and carriage directly to the hotel in Lünen.

Salomon and Clara married on 26 June 1910, a cool and rainy Sunday. On the train to Lünen I wore a navy blue woollen dress. Mother had packed my thin white dress, but I was still not well enough to wear it. Paul came from Essen, and Leopold from Cologne. Although they knew I'd been ill both were shocked by my disfigured face. Paul went outside and shed a few tears. Leopold immediately sat and chatted with me.

The *Chuppe* took place in the hotel and was a lovely ceremony. I remember Paul giving me a glass of champagne soon after. I liked it so much I asked for another, after which I felt much better! At the dinner Helene had to feed me as I had no strength in my right hand. I could hold neither cutlery nor glass.

Once again, plays, sketches and table songs had been prepared for the occasion. While I'd been sick Hermann and I had made up some amusing rhymes about the bridal couple, set to the music of current popular songs. Copies were printed and handed out to the guests. Everyone joined in the singing, setting the mood for the evening.

It was usual that a collection take place at a wedding in honour of the bridal couple. In those years it was normally for an orphanage or an old-age home. Inspired by his boss, my brother Paul had become a passionate Zionist and asked for donations to plant trees in Palestine. Everybody donated and Paul happily sent the sum off. In 1910 people in Germany were scarcely aware of tree planting and land redemption in Palestine.

Paul had heated discussions with my father and brothers about his views on Zionism. At the time, most Jews subscribed to *Der Zentralverein Deutscher Staatsbürger Jüdischen Glaubens*, which implied they were 'German Citizens of the Jewish Faith'. Paul believed we must have a land of our own for Jews of Russia and Poland because of pogroms in those countries. Father just couldn't accept that Jews needed a homeland. He argued, 'I don't want to go to Palestine. We have a good life here.' On *Seder* night he would not say, '*Leshono habo be-Jeruscholajim*' (Next year in Jerusalem), but '*Leshono haboh in Gütersloh*'!

Not being used to alcohol, I became drowsy at the wedding and had to go to bed early. During the night I perspired heavily. Next morning I felt better and my face was back to normal.

The newly completed apartment for the couple had still to be cleaned. It was a Sunday job and the maids didn't want to do it. Salomon paid our apprentice butchers some extra cash and together with him, they cleaned and scrubbed floors. Normally he wouldn't even touch a broom. Hermann said, 'I'd love a photograph of him doing that', but wasn't able to organise it. Being a jokester, he had a photo taken of himself, trousers rolled up, bucket, brush and floor cloth in hand. From another photo he exchanged Salomon's face with his and had it re-photographed. Under the doctored photo, Hermann wrote a parody from an operetta of the time, *The Merry Peasant*: 'I'm a good spouse; that's all I want to be.'

After a fortnight's honeymoon the newlyweds came home to their comfortable modern dwelling. We loved Clara and welcomed her into the family. On Friday nights and *Jontef* we usually ate together. When this wasn't possible we would gather after dinner for coffee and home-made biscuits. Salomon was a fussy eater and would sometimes say, 'I always liked Mother's recipe, which was different.' Clara, a good cook, was clever enough to take the hint and later ask Mother for that recipe. Theirs was a happy home.

Helene now worked on her trousseau. I had given up millinery and took the opportunity to learn to cook. I also worked in Hermann's shop. He was always on the lookout for new items to stock. Incoming goods had to be unpacked and priced. I made sure everything was *blitzblank und staubfrei* (spic and span) and helped with window-dressing. Hermann taught me how to give good service to customers so that I could look after the shop when he was out delivering goods.

* * *

For the High Holidays the community again appointed a new *Chasen* and teacher from Bavaria. He came to our home to introduce himself to Father, the long-term president of the congregation: 'I'm Arnold Stein.' (Stein means 'stone' in English.)

Father's response was instant: '*Even moassu habaunim hoissoh lerausch pino.*' (The stone which the builders rejected has become the chief cornerstone.)

Touched by this quote, Mr Stein said, 'Thank you, Mr Herzberg. I'll do my best to live up to your greeting.'

He achieved what he promised in his care of our spiritual welfare. He was popular with the whole congregation and also with many non-Jewish citizens. He had a friendly manner and helped wherever he could. He involved himself in politics, founding the local branch of the Free Democratic Party, unfortunately with little success because the Deutsche Nationale Partei was predominant. The Catholics voted for the Centrum Party and the workers for the Social Democratic Labour Party. There was as yet neither Communist nor Nazi Party.

During Mr Stein's time in Gütersloh, the community organised a ball and put on a play, *The Camp of the Gypsies*, with singing and dancing. The actors, including Arnold Stein, Helene, Hermann and myself, wore elaborate costumes.

Mr Stein also encouraged us, the younger members of the community, to meet once or twice each week to improve our French, a language we all loved.

Porta Westfalica, one of the local amateur musicals, (1913).
Actors in regional costumes still worn by farming families at the time.
Left back: Käthe Herzberg, Hermann Herzberg; Seated right front: Amalie Meinberg.

* * *

Capable and hard working as he was, my brother Paul had difficulty finding satisfactory employment, as he had not yet done his military service. Employers therefore wouldn't give him a responsible, higher paid position. It was compulsory for every twenty-year-old to serve two years in the army unless, like Paul, they had reached *Ober-Sekunda* (Year 11) at *Gymnasium*. They then served only one year. This service could be delayed till age twenty-five. Paul wanted his army service behind him, so decided to join the Cologne Infantry Regiment in early April, allowing him to spend his free time with Leopold, who was still working in that city. Paul had to buy his uniform and after four weeks in barracks had to pay board and lodging. He'd not been able to save enough and needed subsidy from home.

A few months earlier, Clara had told us she was expecting in the spring. We were thrilled. I admired the baby clothes she had bought and then embroidered. On Friday 7 April 1911, my parent's first grandchild, my first nephew, was born at home as there were no maternity hospitals in Gütersloh. Everyone was so excited about the new baby that the parents were all but ignored. One after the other, we went to greet the baby. I had never seen a newborn and was thrilled when allowed to hold him.

We arranged for the *Mohel* to come on the following Friday. In Gütersloh the men of the congregation were always invited to a *Brissmille*. There was usually a celebratory cold lunch and plenty of alcohol. On this occasion, as it was *Chaul hamaueid Pesach*, we served a hot dinner, soup with *Matzo* balls, ragout of ox tongue with meatballs, several compotes and for dessert, *Matzo Lockschen* (matzah pudding) with wine sauce. The youngest member of the family, being honoured, slept through the celebration, sucking on a corner of a kerchief that had been dipped in wine. The baby was given the name of Kurt and the Hebrew name David ben Schlaumo after his great-grandfather, David Herzberg, of Kleinen-Marpe.

It was a happy and busy time for us. With great interest we watched little Kurt develop.

The wedding of Helene and Emil, Clara's brother, was set for 18 June 1911. Helene received a substantial dowry of furniture for four rooms, ample linen, *milchig* and *fleischig* crockery and cutlery. She needed additional crockery and cutlery for the six men employed by the Levys, workers who lived next door and were entitled to hot midday and evening meals.

As always happened on Helene's special occasions, the weather on her wedding day was beautiful. Adding colour, the houses in Gütersloh were decorated with flags marking a military festival. The ceremony and reception took place at Hotel Barkey. Flowers decorated the *Chuppe*, enhanced by tall potted shrubs. Our cousin, Hete Levisohn, sang '*Wo Du hingehst, da will ich auch hingehen*' ('Whither thou goest, I will go'), before *Chasen* Arnold Stein's admirable ceremony. Helene was a radiant bride and Emil a good-looking groom. They made a handsome couple.

It was one of the merriest wedding receptions ever. Most of the guests were young. There were recently married couples and more young men than girls. Paul and Leopold composed the wedding newspaper with much *Chein*. One of Helene's early admirers had been Louis Mond (meaning 'moon' in English). The 'journalists' turned it into a newspaper story headed '*Der Mond schon erobert*' ('The Moon Now Conquered'). It told of a Miss Helene Herzberg, who in her first amorous encounter had almost been hooked by 'the moon'. There were more such items and many table songs. When the song with the refrain *Ta ra da boom di rah* was sung, at the exclamation – boom – the young men leapt into the air!

With the help of our neighbour Ludwig Walger, a good artist, Hermann had put together a book of coloured cartoons with accompanying rhymes telling something about the bridal couple, our parents and Helene's father-in-law. With much singing and dancing, time raced by. The bridal couple slipped away. We young people partied on till the early hours of the morning. After their honeymoon we received happy letters from the newlyweds in Lünen.

Life at home came back to normal. Mother's sister, Marianne, had come to the wedding and stayed on for a while. She and her sister Rosa were now running the millinery shop in Barsinghausen, supplying us every season with the most fashionable hats.

We learned that German and French aeroplanes were giving displays at Brackwede racecourse. So my parents went there with Aunt Marianne and Salomon, reporting that the planes had flown high, circling gracefully then 'looping the loop'. Father was very enthusiastic: 'It looks safe. I wouldn't mind flying in one.' While we had once seen a Zeppelin, we had never seen a plane. After all, even motorcars were rare at the time.

The following March the Levy's first child, a girl, was born and named Ingeborg (Inge). Mother travelled to Lünen to help Helene. I was just seventeen but I looked after our house and did the cooking. As Mother stayed with the Levys through *Pesach*, I even cooked our *Pesach* meals.

5

Some of my girlfriends had done a secretarial course and now worked in offices. They boasted about the money earned and the easy work. I made up my mind to go to such a course in Bielefeld, twenty minutes by fast train from Gütersloh. The hours were from eight to noon and two to four, allowing me a hot midday meal at home. I bought a monthly rail ticket and started the course on 1 April 1912. Great importance was attached to fine handwriting skills, which took time for me to master, but other subjects were no problem. The students, boys and girls, came from the surrounding district and I got to meet some very nice people. A group travelling on the train from Oelde would always look out for me so I could join them in their compartment. On the morning of 15 April we heard the tragic news that the English luxury liner, the *Titanic*, had sunk after colliding with an iceberg and only a small number of people had been rescued.

At the completion of the six months' course we went for a celebratory outing to a coffee house set in a large garden – teachers and pupils together. Later we went dancing for some hours at a garden tavern with its own band. We had a marvellous time.

Now that he was receiving rent from the shops run by Salomon and Hermann, Father decided to retire in autumn 1912. He could take it easier now. We encouraged our parents to exchange dwellings with Clara and Salomon, whose new home was smaller and would be easier to care for. I moved with them of course. We took most of our furniture with us, but replaced the old black cooking range with a modern white one, which not only burned wood

Käthe Herzberg.

Graduating class of The Franz Kohlhase Private Technichal Business College,
Summer Semester, 1912.
Käthe and Irma Meinberg third row from the top, 5th and 7th from the left.

and coal, but also had an added feature – two gas burners. During the move Father was upset and shed a tear or two: 'I always thought I'd live in that house till I was carried out feet first.' We calmed him, persuading him that our new apartment was nicer and would be more comfortable.

The following morning Mother suffered another of her abdominal colics. Dr Köhne recommended she eat no solids and drink only black tea or thin black coffee. 'How can I drink without eating?' Mother pleaded with the doctor for some dry toast. Answer: 'No!'

To ease her pains I made hot compresses, using towels dipped in hot water, wrung out and put between two blankets. As I had to replace them frequently, I was unable to set up the household fully or hang the curtains in our new home. Some of the old furniture looked out of place in the bright new rooms, so was stored in the attic. A few days later Rosa came from Rüdinghausen and together we soon had everything looking just right. The first-floor apartment had one single and two double bedrooms, a living room and a kitchen. The bathroom was down several stairs.

Father soon became rather proud of his new surroundings and showed them off to his friends. He still went into the business most mornings. Several afternoons a week he took horse and cart to the farms to buy livestock for Salomon's shop. He also bought calves for resale through an agent at the cattle market in Dortmund, bringing him extra income. As Clara was expecting her second baby, Mother helped in the butcher shop.

On 4 December 1912 Clara's second boy was born. They named him Werner. All the men of the congregation once again came for the *Brissmille*. After the ceremony a cold lunch was served of salads, many different meats and plenty to drink. We cooked a hot meal for Clara's father and brothers from Lünen and for Louis from Rüdinghausen, who had all travelled a long way. I made beef soup with *Eierstich*[14], various vegetables and, for the first time, a roast goose. The meal was a great success. When Mother tasted the lemon crème desert she asked, 'How many eggs did you use?' She was shocked by the reply. 'It doesn't matter. Nothing's too good to honour our Werner,' laughed Clara.

In February 1913 Mother went to Lünen to be with Helene, whose son Hans was born 27 February. I enjoyed looking after the household and in the

---

[14] A savoury egg custard cut into little squares and added to chicken or beef soup, instead of noodles or *Matzo* balls. It was a delicacy.

afternoons went to a sewing course to improve my skills in making a variety of linen towels, pillowcases and nightgowns. I was kept busy.

* * *

It wasn't easy for me to find employment. Few offices wanted female employees. Mr Stein, always helpful, came one day with a message: 'I met Mr Verleger, a partner in Miele GmbH (Pty Ltd). His firm is looking for a capable girl to work in their office. You should apply immediately.' I went right away, walking the half-hour to the factory. During the interview, Mr C H Walkenhorst, the office manager, gave me a lengthy dictation test in shorthand. As Miele was then making automobiles, the test included such words as 'chassis' and 'cabriolet'. I had no problem reading it back. Next day I was invited to start work on 1 April.

Working hours were from 7.30 in the morning till 6.30 in the evening with a two-hour mid-day break, allowing staff to go home for the main meal of the day.

I liked the 'set-time' working hours. I walked to and from work in every kind of weather, come snow, rain or shine. These were easy working hours. Shops stayed open every evening till eight. Thirty men and three girls, including me, made up the office staff. We all got on well together. My desk was in the same room as that of a Mr Shöning, who did the French correspondence. I would frequently be called to the adjoining office to take dictation from Mr Bischoff, the director responsible for purchasing materials for the enormous factory.

With the outbreak of the First World War, Miele gave up producing cars and concentrated on milk centrifuges, butter churns, manual washing machines and also electric washing machines[15] with wringers attached, kitchen tables with drop-down mangles[16] and timber handcarts. These days they are making hi-tech washing machines, dishwashers, vacuum cleaners and clothes dryers.

* * *

---

[15] Washing machines were made of timber staves, similar to beer barrels, but not bowed out-wards. The timber could not be allowed to dry out, otherwise it would shrink and the tubs would leak. My sister-in-law Ella Herzberg brought such a washing machine to Australia.

[16] These mangles were made of a pair of timber rollers worked by a large rotating handle. They were used to pre-press bed linen, linen or cotton towels, tablecloths, etc. Some of these were built into kitchen tables between two leaves which could slide apart to allow the mangle itself to drop down below the table-top for storage. When we migrated to Australia in 1939 we brought such a table with us.

The twenty-fifth anniversary of my parents' wedding fell on Friday 11 April, a week and a half after I'd started at Miele. As Father had done so much for the congregation, my parents were to be honoured during the Saturday morning service in the synagogue. I didn't dare ask for time off. Apparently Mr Bischoff had heard of the occasion from Mr Daltrop of Daltrop Brothers, a Jewish firm which supplied Miele with office furniture and equipment. He came to me on the Friday to tell me I could have the Saturday off to join the celebrations.

What a surprise, when on Friday afternoon a delegation from the congregation delivered a comfortable sofa which fitted perfectly into our large bright living room, as well as a superb silver ornament inscribed 'To Mr Josef Herzberg in grateful acknowledgement of his services to the Jewish congregation of Gütersloh'. Regrettably, this fine memento was left behind when we migrated to Australia.

Decorating one of the walls of our living room were two *Misrachs*: one a print, the other an original work done by a scribe, Dr Auerbach, in 1857. In this *Misrach* the complete *Hallel* is artistically written with minute Hebrew lettering in a series of interconnected scrolls and whorls. This *Misrach* is still in the possession of my sister-in-law, Ella Herzberg,[17] of Dover Heights, Sydney.

On *Schabbes* the synagogue service was festive. It was also the silver wedding day of Sofie and Josef Meinberg. Cantor Stein gave the sermon, again praising the years of devoted service by Father, whom he always held in high esteem, as did many others, including Rabbi Dr Coblenz of Bielefeld. He and Father were friends who enjoyed discussing a wide range of Jewish topics, valuing each other's opinions.

The following day we had a memorable family celebration. My sisters, Rosa and Helene, came with their husbands, as well as Paul from Mainz, where he now had a good position. Leopold came from Frankfurt, my aunt Betty Herzberg from Kleinen-Marpe, and several Levisohn aunts and uncles from Barsinghausen. Aunt Betty, always the lively one, played the piano. With table songs and humorous speeches the time passed only too quickly.

Next evening we gave a party to thank the congregation. We were able to seat all our guests comfortably. Opening double sliding doors and clearing bedroom furniture combined the living room and our parents' bedroom into a large entertainment area. Wonderful cakes and plenty to drink helped to make the evening a success.

---

[17] In 2003 the Misrach was taken to Melbourne by Ella's daughter, Ursula, editor of this work, when she and her husband, Ivan, moved there.

The orderliness of work at Miele was very satisfying. At the end of the month, gold coins in my first pay packet tinkled onto my desk – music to my ears. On my way home I bought the first fresh fruit of the season for my parents. They were thrilled. From day one Father always banked part of my wages into a savings account for me and would not relinquish that task to anyone.

Besides my main job, I helped Hermann whenever I had time, as his business was steadily growing. On the last four Sundays before Christmas, when all shops were open, I worked all day. Totally unexpected was a full month's Christmas bonus from Miele, a wonderful surprise. I was so excited I ran home quickly over icy streets to share my good news.

During the cold winter months I didn't want Mother to get up early, so I ate a sandwich and had a drink of milk warmed on the gas stove. My *Butterbrot* (sandwich) for morning tea was made the night before. When Paul visited in December he brought me a thermos flask, something very new and the first we had seen. Given that there was no canteen or cafeteria at work, my parents were pleased I could take hot milk in the new thermos. The aunts from Barsinghausen had sent me a stylish fur cap and matching muff. The muff not only kept my hands warm but was big enough for the thermos flask as well!

Paul and Leopold were happy to be living near one another again, Frankfurt being only a short distance from Mainz.

Leopold now had a better-paid position and Paul had at last found a satisfying office job in a factory making men's suits. His wages had also improved. The boss liked him and often invited him home. On those occasions Paul would help the boss's children with homework. He had every prospect of progressing in his job.

My brothers had nice friends. They spent the weekends together and enjoyed the surrounding countryside. They sent our parents a crate of fine table wine and occasionally parcels of tinned delicacies. Wine in the area was less expensive than in Gütersloh. Our parents were pleased at their thoughtfulness.

One of Amalie Meinberg's young trainee girls, Paula Horwitz, had fallen in love with Paul. When he was an apprentice in Bielefeld, he would come home to Gütersloh every few weeks. Hermann really would have liked this girl for himself, but realised she was interested only in Paul. One day he decided to advise: 'Marry her, Paul. She loves you. What's more, her father has a business, a drapery shop in which you could work.'

Misrach, by Dr Auerbach, 1857.

Detail of the Misrach, by Dr Auerbach, 1857.
Note the minute Hebrew lettering which spells out the complete *Hallel* prayer.

'When I marry, I want to be ready to support a wife and family on my own. I don't want to be a prince consort.'

Paul and Paula corresponded for a long time. Paula's parents were eager to see her married. Being an obedient daughter, she accepted their advice. Through mutual friends she met our cousin, Gustav Königheim, to whom she became engaged. We didn't believe the two were well suited. After a few months we heard the engagement was broken.

The Herzberg shop on Königstrasse, early 1919.
Note sign on shop window: Hermann Herzberg Eisenwaren (home/hardware).
Standing in front (l-r): Emil Levy, Bertha, Käthe, Leopold, and (the child) Werner.

6

I had always been intrigued by the closeness of my mother's friendship with Amalie Meinberg. One day I asked her, 'How come you two are such intimate friends? You even *duz*[18] one another. You don't do this with any of your other friends. Sometimes I think you could even be related.'

'You're actually right. It's time I told you her story':

It centres on Moses Cohn, one of your grandmother Levisohn's brothers. This Uncle Moses Cohn and his brother Simon, both of Hannover, inherited a pig-iron business moulding iron products, founded by their father Meier Cohn (of Rodenberg). They expanded it considerably. With their own sons, they eventually established Hannover Railway Industry, a large and well-respected firm.

Uncle Moses married Marianne Michelsohn from Hausberge. I guess he must have received a large dowry, for the Michelsohns were wealthy, owning several quarries. When Marianne was due to have another child her younger sister came to nurse her and help look after the house and the older children. The young girl fell for the handsome Moses. This had its consequences. In those days, most young girls didn't know about contraception or abortion. Eventually, she couldn't hide what had happened. Her parents were distraught and didn't want anyone to know of their daughter's disgrace. Before

---

[18] '*Duzen*' in German is to use the pronoun *du* (you) instead of the formal version *sie*. *Du* is the intimate form of address used only when speaking to family members, very close friends, children or subordinates.

the baby was born the Michelsohns bribed the midwife with a considerable sum of money for the baby to be registered as their child. The newborn girl was called Amalie. A few weeks later she was fostered to a kind and caring peasant family, who treated her as their own. They were, of course, well paid. As a toddler she was sometimes dressed in the customary local folk costume of red woollen skirt, white blouse, black velvet bodice and a little black cap with a large silk bow.

She stayed with this family until she was ready to start school, then went to live with a Miss Esther Cohn of Wadersloh, near Oelde in Westphalia. Miss Cohn was told that Amalie was to learn everything appropriate for a young lady, but not to know her origins. Beautiful clothes were always sent for Amalie and people thought she might even be a daughter of nobility. When Amalie was growing up she asked Aunt Esther, 'Why don't I have a mother, father, brothers, sisters or grandparents?' Esther's answers avoided the issue.

One Saturday afternoon an elderly gentleman, a friend of the Cohn family, came for a visit. He greeted Amalie, now a beauty, almost an adult, 'Let's go for a walk. I have a story to tell you.' Halfway through his tale, Amalie broke into tears. 'This is about me, isn't it? Please don't go on.'

When my mother placed the announcement of my engagement to your father in the paper, she signed it Jeanette Levisohn, née Meier Cohn. Salomon Meinberg, Amalie's husband, saw the announcement, came to your father and asked, 'Did you realise that your fiancée, Bertha, is my Amalie's first cousin?'

'That I didn't know! When next in Barsinghausen, I'll tell Bertha.'

That is how I, Bertha, learned that Amalie is my first cousin, a fact hidden from me until then.

Amalie eventually found out that her birth mother was now married and living in Beckedorf. She ultimately got up enough courage and, accompanied by her friend Ricka Cohn from Rheda, went to Beckedorf. As they entered the mother's home she seemed immediately to recognise Amalie as her daughter. She implored Amalie to leave at once, 'Please go. Nobody here knows of you. Don't make problems for me.'

Tearfully, Amalie pleaded, 'Mother, give me a hug and a kiss. Just this once.'

'No! You must go! Leave now! Instantly! I could never explain you to my husband and children.'

A cruel disappointment.

Amalie was not the only one noting the absence of family connections. In later years her only son, Siegfried, would often ask his mother why she had no immediate family. A remarkable story isn't it Käthe?

Amalie has had a heart condition for a long time. I decided to write to her wealthy uncle Michelsohn in Hausberge suggesting he send money for her to go to the health resort at Bad Nauheim. He sent it last week and she's thrilled. By the way, she wants to take you and her trainee girl to a performance at the City Theatre in Bielefeld to celebrate.

The *duzen* mystery was now fully explained and I was flattered that my mother had shared the story with me.

7

I enjoyed the work in the office at Miele. I know my efforts were appreciated. When Mr Reinhard Zinnkann, a partner in the firm, came from Darmstadt, I was always called to do his correspondence, usually typing direct from his dictation. Sometimes he gave me notes written in his very individual, hard-to-read handwriting and it was left to me to finesse the letters. I had already been working for the accounts department, where I had to remind customers when payment was overdue, sue when necessary and correspond with solicitors. I would talk things over with our main bookkeeper and style those letters also.

I was frequently introduced to visiting members of the firm by Mr Hartmann, our chief bookkeeper. One day Mr Hermann Walkenhorst, a senior representative, came from Wetzlar. I knew his status from references to him in the office. Mr Hartmann introduced us. During our conversation I mentioned that one of my brothers lived and worked in Frankfurt and another in Mainz. 'Oh! Really! I'm often in Frankfurt. Give me your brother's address and I'll look him up.' Some days later his postcard arrived from Frankfurt, to which Leopold had added his greetings. Mr Walkenhorst continued to keep in touch.

During my fortnight's vacation in 1914, I travelled to Barsinghausen to celebrate the *Barmizwo* of my cousin Adolf, son of Mother's sister, Elise Traube. After her husband, Ernst, died, Elise had given up her dressmaking business to keep house for her two sons, Adolf and Werner, and her spinster sisters, Marianne and Rosa Levisohn, who had the millinery shop.

I stayed at Uncle Aron Levisohn's place. His wife, Henny, was a very lovable and well-educated woman. Their eldest daughter, Hete, was three years older than me, and their twins, Käthe and Walter, were four years younger. Uncle Aron was a cheerful fellow and there was always a lively atmosphere in their house. I felt very much at home.

The *Barmizwo* was a lovely occasion. During the rest of my holidays we went on excursions and walks in the beautiful Deister Wald as far as Bad Nenndorf. The coffee house of this health resort was set in a beautiful park, where we enjoyed the music of the band while having coffee and cake.

The relatives kindly gave me presents when it came time for my return home. I was delighted to receive a lovely hat from the aunts. Hats had become an essential part of one's wardrobe.

Levisohn Siblings.
Back row (l-r): Josef, Elise, Bertha, Rosalie (Rosa), Meyer, Aron.
Seated (l-r) Johanne, Helene, Marianne.
(Magnus and Benjamin [Ben] were already in the USA. Jenny had died in childhood.)

Letters arrived from Paul and Leopold saying they would spend their fortnight's holiday with us in Gütersloh. My cousin, Hete Levisohn, and Clara's younger sister, Emmy Levy, from Lünen, came at the same time, making a happy group of young people. The weather was particularly pleasant and together we enjoyed the long warm European summer evenings. When work finished the group would come to meet me on my long walk home. We spent a magnificent time together, one that I will always remember.

After our boys returned to Frankfurt and to Mainz, we three girls were invited one evening to the Ruthenburgs, whose daughter, Liese, was a friend, a few months younger than me. Her parents were relatively young and full of life. Among the guests were Mr Wesel, the new *Chasen* and teacher for the community (Mr Stein having left for a position in Mülheim a short time before), Sophie and Rudolf Wolf and their half-sister, Lucie Hope, and Else and Paul Meinberg's niece, Lilli Schreiber, from Oelde. There were others whose names I can't remember. Presumably in an oversight, my brother Hermann had not been invited, so missed a wonderful party which lasted till late into the night. Hete, Sofie Wolf, Lucie Hope, Emmy and I went home together. We were in a merry mood, laughing and giggling all the way. Hete and Sofie were close friends, reluctant to part, so we stood on our street corner laughing loudly. Suddenly a window opened at our neighbour Osthus's house. Old grandfather Roggenkamp complained that he was wakened by our noise, couldn't get back to sleep and would report us to the police. We hurried away. Silently we crept into our beds and slept the untroubled sleep of youth.

The following day when I came home for lunch as usual, Hermann was waiting for me: 'What on earth did you do last night? Old man Roggenkamp complained to the police and you all have to report at the station.'

'If I didn't know what a prankster you are, I might believe you!'

He waited for Else Meinberg and repeated the tale. She knew immediately he was stirring, for she'd taken a different route home the previous night. He then told us, 'I've rung Mrs Hope about the girls' behaviour. She was very upset. She told Lucie she couldn't visit her aunt Mathilde in Applerbeck and then boxed her ears. I heard Lucie crying.'

When Hermann made the phone call to Mrs Hope he had pretended to be the police inspector. He told Mrs Hope her daughters were required at the police station. Mrs Hope responded meekly, 'My daughter Sophie can't be there before six o'clock.'

'Both girls! No later than six.'

Else told Hermann, 'Mama Hope will take this seriously. You'd better tell her the truth.'

Hermann conceded and rang Mrs Hope, 'This is Hermann Herzberg. I heard that Sofie and Lucie, as well as our Käthe, were told to report to the police. While I do think they behaved badly, I've spoken to our neighbour Roggenkamp. He's withdrawn his complaint. I also spoke to the police. The matter is settled.'

Mrs Hope burst into tears. 'Hermann. Thank you so much. The girls will come over tonight to thank you personally.'

That evening a very emotional Mrs Hope came, bringing Sofie and Lucie. Lucie gave Hermann a hug. 'I don't know how to thank you.'

'Oh Lucie, don't be taken in. The whole thing was a joke. I think Hermann was just miffed that he hadn't been invited to the Ruthenburgs' party,' burst out Sofie.

Mrs Hope and Lucie wouldn't believe it was a joke and repeatedly thanked him. Eventually Hermann said, 'I invite you all to the patisserie for ice cream!' Ice cream was still a novelty and therefore special.

8

On a fine Sunday afternoon, 28 June 1914, the family took its usual stroll down the Kökerstrasse, past the Post Office, over the railway line, along the Lindenallee, an avenue of lime trees, to the coffee house Meier's Bäume. We were passing the Post Office when a postal clerk Salomon knew called him over to share astounding news: 'It's just come through on the telegraph that in Sarajevo, Franz Ferdinand von Habsburg, the heir to the Austro-Hungarian throne, and his wife, Sophie, Duchess of Hohenberg, have been shot by a Bosnian Serb. This is threatening news.'

A very serious Salomon returned and told us what he had learned. 'I hope this won't lead to war.'

In no time, special newspaper editions appeared announcing the assassination. Even though Germany was allied to Austria-Hungary, I found it impossible to believe that these assassinations could involve us in war. Was there now the possibility that gruesome war would supplant the good times?

I had been so enjoying life.

The following days were tense and stressful, but the mood improved as the threat seemed to recede. My parents took their three-year-old grandson, Kurt, with them on a visit to their daughters in Lünen and Rüdinghausen. Rosa and Louis as yet had no children and thoroughly enjoyed little Kurt's amusing manner of speech.

During that lull there were reports that war was still possible. The situation turned and became more acute day by day. A concert by the Marine Band was to take place in the garden of the Hotel Kaiserhof in Gütersloh. Friends and family, as well as staff from our Miele office, had bought tickets. It promised to be a wonderful night.

On 28 July 1914 Austria declared war on Serbia. Special editions of the newspapers appeared with the headline: 'The Kaiser has ordered general mobilisation.'

The concert never took place.

Russia mobilised to support Serbia, leading Germany to declare war on Russia on 1 August 1914. Two days later, Germany entered Belgium and France, expecting little risk, given the strong alliance with Austria-Hungary[19]. The average German citizen believed: 'The English, our cousins across the channel, will never declare war on us.'[20]

In the Miele office everything was topsy-turvy. Many of the young men called up for the army or navy said their goodbyes. Our director, Mr Bishop, told me to stay home for the month of August. 'Sorry, but it'll be without pay.' Nobody knew whether the factory could be kept open. Nobody knew what would happen. Everyone was on edge.

When I came home from work, Father had just come back from Rüdinghausen with little Kurt. Mother had gone on to Lünen to be with Helene, as Emil had also been called up. His father was still fit enough to look after the large butcher shop. Helene was more than busy with her two young children – Inge just two and a half and little Hans eighteen months – and expecting her third child in February.

On the third day of mobilisation Hermann had to be in Bielefeld at six in the morning. Not knowing what would be required of Paul and Leopold was a concern for us. Everyone was worried and rightly so. Every family would have at least one young man called away to war. Paul was already a corporal in the reserves. Leopold had not done military service because his level of education exempted him till the age of twenty-five; besides, he was short by military standards. Rosa's husband, Louis, was not called up at that time; he too was not tall enough for active service. Salomon had done military training but now

---

[19] Actually, following the assassination of Franz Ferdinand on 28 June 1914 by a Bosnian nationalist, it was Austria-Hungary that declared war on Serbia, with whom it had had some years of political conflict over minority nationalist aspirations, particularly those of the southern Slavs. Austria-Hungary sought and gained the support of Germany. Germany had its own agenda and took control, placing its own strategic and national plans above Austro-Hungarian interests. This changed the Balkan conflict into a world war.

[20] The royal families of Germany, England and Russia were headed by cousins, all grandchildren of Queen Victoria of England.

had a heart condition and was disqualified for war service. Once war really got under way the rules changed.

There was a patriotic demonstration in front of the Town Hall across the street from our home. I went over with Hermann. Next to us stood a young man named Jacke. His father had been coming to our house for years every Tuesday and Friday, to give Father a shave. This Jacke was an only child. He said, 'Yes, these men can make fine speeches, but we're the ones who'll be sacrificed!' Like so many others, he later gave his life in a foreign land.

It was dark by the time Hermann and I headed home. We could see the shop, illuminated by electricity, which he had just installed to replace the gaslights. He had improved many other things to make the shop look attractive.

He said to me, 'You know the song "*Was nützet mein schöner Garten, wenn andere drin spazieren gehen*"?[21] Well, by the same token I say, "*Was nützet mein schöner Laden ...*"!' ('What's the use of my beautiful shop ...' – implying that others would end up with the benefits.)

'Oh Hermann, everyone says that with all the big cannons and machine guns we have, the war will be over by Christmas. Our parents and I will do our best to manage your shop for you.'

Early next morning we took Hermann to the railway station to catch his train to Bielefeld. The railway was closed to civilians, open only for the military. The trains came through constantly, crowded with soldiers. Apparently they'd been given lots of alcohol and they sang in full voice: '*Die Vöglein im Walde sie singen so wunderschön. In der Heimat in der Heimat da gibt's ein Wiedersehen.*' ('The birds in the woods, they sing so beautifully. In our Homeland, in our Homeland we'll meet again.') We shuddered as we questioned how many would ever return home.

That was the day England declared war on Germany.

The Kaiser ordered a day of prayer for all religions. Our *Chasen*, Mr Wesel, had to report for army service the next day. Before leaving he held a short and moving service. Nobody ever heard of him again.

I walked home from the synagogue with Father on my arm. We had to stop several times, as he didn't feel well. With difficulty I managed to take him to Clara and Salomon's home, into their ground floor living room, and sat him on the sofa. He vomited several times and we called the doctor. The tension of the past hours had been too much for him.

---

[21] A German song: 'Of what use is my beautiful garden when only others walk in it'. Note Hermann's rhyme between *Laden* (shop) and *Garten* (garden).

When Father had recovered a little, we took him home to our own flat next door. The doctor diagnosed a slight stroke. Father continually asked for Mother so we phoned Lünen. Mother was deeply shocked to learn of the illness and was concerned about how she would get home, the railways now being closed to civilians. Jacob Levy, Emil's father, calmed her: 'Our neighbour Bennemann is a hackney coachman. We'll order a horse-drawn carriage and driver and I'll come with you to Gütersloh.'

Father was glad to hear she was on her way. He urged me to have a hot dinner ready for her. It was getting later and later and Mother didn't arrive. On that hot August evening the windows were wide open, so all the while we could hear the never-ending trains and the singing of the soldiers: *In der Heimat, in der Heimat, da gibt's ein Wiedersehen,* then *Gloria, Victoria, mit Herz und Hand fürs Vaterland* ('Glory, Victory, with heart and hand for the Fatherland'). Our thoughts went from Hermann to Paul to Emil and back to Hermann.

It was about midnight when the carriage finally arrived. Father seemed better once Mother was with him. She told us that the drive had taken so long because police stopped them in every town and village, concerned about spies. Fortunately Jacob Levy and the coachman had their papers with them. When they came to the outskirts of Gütersloh, a local policeman recognised her and said, 'Good evening, Mrs Herzberg. You can head on home.' Mother asked him whether he knew where our boys had been sent.

The following days were full of anxiety. Despite the best intentions we could deal only with essentials. Hermann's civilian clothes arrived. He wrote to us on his way to the East and gave his address: Infantry Regiment 158. Presuming that Paul had also been called up, we wrote to Leopold wanting to know if he had heard from Paul.

He answered immediately:

I was very worried about Paul because I hadn't heard from him for days – unusual as he always keeps in touch. I went to Mainz. His landlady told me Paul had gone out and not come back; that a policeman had come and asked for him; that his room was just as he always left it. I then went to Scheuer & Plaut, the firm where Paul worked, and was told that a policeman had come for him on 26 July, five days before the declaration of war on Russia, and taken him to the military barracks. He was not even given time to go to his lodgings to pack. I went immediately to the military barracks, where I found Paul already in uniform. He was to have gone with the first troops to cross the border, but his group had been given a further medical examination and, as he had an inflamed foot, Paul was kept back. He had inadvertently knocked and injured his foot on his bedstead a few days earlier.[22] He will probably stay in Mainz for the time being to train recruits, but he wasn't sure about this. He will write when he knows what is to happen. As he is not allowed to go back to his lodgings, I will pack his civilian clothes and send them to you. Of course, I've also had to report to the military but I don't know what my orders are going to be.

Father recovered quickly, but his face was very drawn. Concern for his sons gnawed at him. On occasion we found him reciting prayers for their welfare, using the book of prayers by Rabbi Moses Philippsohn, *Bei drohender Kriegesgefahr* (At the Threat of War).

We learned of successes in the East. Hermann wrote via the army postal service: 'If you hear about victories, they were not only due to Hindenburg's strategy. Believe me, it was our legs that won the victories. I can tolerate the hardships, knowing our efforts keep you safe. So many farms and homes have been razed. It breaks my heart to see crowds of refugees fleeing.'

There was very little, or no, motor transport. The soldiers were ordered on long forced marches along muddy roads in what was then the Russian part of Poland. Supplies were not able to keep up with them and our parcels took time to reach the advancing regiment; as a result the soldiers suffered severe hunger.

We were allowed to send 500-gram parcels by army post. Many of my cousins on both sides of the family were at the front. Sometimes we packed as many as twenty parcels of smoked sausage, small-goods, cigars, cigarettes and cake. We had a small cake tin, just right for a 500-gram cake.

There were victories in the West also. Despite the non-aggression pact, our German army had swept through Belgium, to attack northern France. A second army was on its way to Paris, but was held back by the French in heavy battles.

* * *

The High Holidays came. Our *Chasen*, Mr Wesel, had gone into the army. The congregation engaged a man studying to be a rabbi. His sermons were excellent

---

[22] Leopold later said, 'If it hadn't been for this injury, I would never have seen Paul again.'

but he didn't have a good singing voice, a disappointment for our musically inclined community. Father led a big part of the prayers. Some time earlier, an orthodox family, the Eisensteins, had moved to Gütersloh. Mr Eisenstein was at home with Hebrew. Father approached him to *daven* a short *Tefille*. He was reluctant at first, but later was happy to do more.

From 1 September, I was back at work in the Miele office. When I went home at lunchtime, I would first call into Clara's house to see if there was any army mail, which was always delivered there. Many of my former colleagues wrote to me and I answered each with a parcel. I answered Hermann Walkenhurst's weekly letters from the Eastern Front and sent him cigars and cakes.

Letters arrived regularly from Paul and Leopold. The latter was not yet in the army. In early November, Paul told us he was leaving for the front and gave his new army address. While he would certainly have had the option of farewell leave, our serious-minded Paul wanted to avoid the inevitable tension for both him and for us. Leopold later told us Paul had said, 'I've had such a lot of bad luck in life. Frankly, I don't expect to come back!'

Helene's husband, Emil, was another on the Eastern Front, a trained butcher working in the mess kitchen. Most of my cousins were fighting on the Western Front. Paul was in the north of France, where opposing armies had settled into trench and dugout warfare, after extremely bitter fighting. Paul's letters were uncomplaining, while Hermann wrote of hunger and lice: 'The beasts just won't let us sleep. Is there nothing that will get rid of them?' We bought something at the chemist and sent it off. 'Sorry but it didn't help' came the reply. 'It's as if the lice had drunk champagne. They just went wild after tasting it!'

I must mention one touching episode experienced by Hermann:

Marching through a Polish village on my empty stomach, I saw Jewish *Ponem*s and asked my lieutenant whether I could talk to them, hoping I might get some bread. Permission granted, I approached one of the men: 'It's between *Rausch Haschono* and *Jaum Kippur*. Would you do a *Mizwo* and give me some *Lechem*?' The man returned with a large loaf. The amazed lieutenant asked me what I'd said. In the evening I was on guard duty with this same lieutenant: 'Herzberg, do me a *Mizwo*! Lend me your mittens.

For Christmas, ten-pound parcels could be sent to the front. Mother knitted mittens. We bought warm headgear and underwear and included smoked meat and *Wurst*, cakes and sweets in the package. Hermann wrote that it took quite some time before the first big parcel arrived. He always acknowledged immediately the many parcels from friends and relations for, as he would say, 'Many letters bring many gifts'.

At the end of 1914, after four months of war, thousands had given their lives for the Fatherland, yet the terrible fighting continued.

Leopold now received his call-up, first being allowed home for a few days leave. We were glad to pamper him and hoped to see him again before he was sent into action.

He told us, 'I think I'll be going into the Army Service Corps.'[23]

'That means you won't be going to the front, but will you be able to handle the heavy horses?' asked Salomon, who knew from his time in the army what his brother would have to cope with.

Leopold trained with the Army Service Corps and did find it hard to manage the big horses. After a time, he was transferred to the infantry and soon sent to France. The losses in France had been great and more troops were needed.

We now had three brothers and a brother-in-law at the front.

The four Herzberg sons in the army.
Paul wearing a *Pickelhaube*, Hermann, and (below l-r) Leopold and Salomon.

---

[23] Its main role was transport of all supplies required by the army.

Our parents were looking after Hermann's shop. Clara would stand in while they had lunch. If a problem arose she would contact them by the house telephone. I took over the bookkeeping and correspondence, despite being very busy at my own job. At Miele I had seen to it that all outstanding debts owed to the company by customers in German-occupied areas of Belgium and France were collected. This earned me a raise in salary.

On 9 February 1915 we received news that Helene had given birth to a third child, a girl to be named Paula. Mother again went to Lünen. Even though a maternity nurse was employed, there was still plenty for her to do looking after the children and the big household. Emil managed to write to Helene regularly, despite big battles being fought in Galicia.

On that same 9 February the big Battle of Masuria took place. The Russians were driven back into the swamp[24] by the strategy of Field Marshal Hindenburg. It was a famous victory. The church bells rang out. Their clang seemed to me like a death knell. Once again, how much young innocent blood was being spilled? We worried about Hermann, who would almost certainly have been in that battle.

During Mother's absence I would hurry home in my lunch hour so Father and I would have our main meal at Clara's. Usually the day's mail would already be there. Thank goodness that during this period mail from Hermann didn't take long to arrive: 'I survived the big Battle of Masuria. Again we had to go on exhausting forced marches. Your small parcels reached me in the last mail, fifteen of them; some from Barsinghausen as well as Meinbergs and Daltrops. I will write to all.'

Father's seventieth birthday was on 19 February 1915. We had always planned a big celebration for this day. Congratulations came from relatives and friends and of course a lot of army mail from all our soldiers. Hermann, yearning for home, wrote, 'All the family had been looking forward to spending this day together and I hope that we can make up for it and celebrate this occasion next year. But if we are still on the battlefield, then our thoughts will be with you; and if we are under the field, then your thoughts will be with us.' ('*und ich hoffe, wir können die Feier nächstes Jahr nachholen. Sind wir noch im Felde, dann sind unsere Gedanken bei Euch, und sind wir unterm Felde, dann sind Eure Gedanken bei uns*'.)

---

[24] The Battle of Tannenberg had been fought in this region in September 1914.

There was much to be worried about. Salomon was now called up, but thank G-d was sent home again.

Hermann's next letter came from a military hospital in Gleiwitz, Silesia. At the time this town was still part of Germany. He wrote that he was suffering from malnutrition: 'I have lost so much weight that even Leopold's suits would be too big for me. The Catholic sisters nurse us with much compassion.' We were glad that Hermann was out of danger. Louis and Salomon visited him in Gleiwitz, taking goodies such as roast chicken, small-goods and cake. On their return they confirmed Hermann's loss of weight and subsequent weakness. We hoped that he would not be sent to the front again, but after some weeks he was discharged from the military hospital and sent to Reserve Infantry Regiment Number 5 in Marienburg, West Prussia. Mother wrote to Hermann that he should contact her married cousin living there. They were very hospitable to him.

* * *

Ration cards had been introduced for the civilian population. Each person was allowed weekly: one pound of bread or flour, some semolina and macaroni, two eggs, a small portion of meat, some margarine, sometimes a little butter, but no oil. There was milk only for children, for persons over seventy or for those with medically certified illness. Even potatoes were rationed. To buy *Matzo* for *Pesach* we had to give up equivalent ration cards for bread.

Shortly after *Pesach*, Mother had just exchanged the old ration card butts for new ones when the telephone rang. She picked up the receiver and heard a man's voice, asking, 'Would you like a visitor?'

'Yes, I always like visitors.'

'Do you have ration cards for bread?'

'Yes. I've just got new ones, but who's calling?'

'Look out the window!'

'Oh, Hermann, you clown! Do you have to tease me like that? How wonderful to have you home.'

Hermann had phoned from our neighbour Osthus's stationery shop. He came into the house and was embraced by young and old. I was phoned at the office and excitedly shared the good news with my colleagues. As soon as the workday ended, I hurried home. In no time news got around that Hermann was home for two weeks. The doorbell didn't stop ringing with people dropping in.

He told us, 'One day I was caring for eight seriously wounded Russians.

Under heavy fire I brought them food. There was no water to quench their thirst. In a damaged house I found a barrel of pickled cabbage, skimmed off the brine and at the risk of life brought it to them. Salty though it was, they gulped it down.'

Hermann's leave passed too quickly. Parting was easier because we hoped there was now no danger he would be ordered into battle yet again.

We were mistaken! At the end of April, a few days after Hermann's return to Marienburg, he was sent to the front. He wrote he had been awarded the Iron Cross for having taken care of wounded comrades. He was proud of this honour, for apart from officers none of the other soldiers in his company received the award. He sent the Iron Cross home: 'Take good care of this. I am very proud of it.' Leopold's bravery was later recognised by the same award.

Mail from France did not take as long to get to us as that from Russia. Paul was in the trenches in northern France and wrote regularly, as did Leopold, who would later survive the terrible battles of Verdun in early 1916.

Provisional Certificate

Pte (1st Class) Leopold Herzberg

12th Comp. Res.Inf.Reg't 87

on 5 April 1917

was awarded the

Iron Cross 2.Class

Regimental Colonel

Leopold Herzberg's Iron Cross.

9

I had made up my mind to take my summer vacation at the beginning of June so that I could go with my parents to visit my married sisters in Rüdinghausen and Lünen. I was so proud of my outfits: a navy suit, white batiste blouses, nice summer dresses and black patent-leather shoes in the latest fashion. Until then only laced-up high boots were worn. The aunts from Barsinghausen had sent me a charming hat, dark red lilac in colour, with a flat, straight brim. The hat was covered in tulle of the same colour. On one side were clusters of tiny ears of corn and a lilac flower front and back. That hat must really have suited me. It turned heads!

We had an enjoyable time in Rüdinghausen, with regular good news from all at the Front. Nonetheless, the safety of our boys was constantly on our minds. We were lucky with the weather and went on outings into the surrounding areas and to Dortmund to see a show. After a week we travelled to Lünen, arriving there on a Friday. It was soon evident that Helene's readiness to help in the two Levy butcher shops during staff shortages was much appreciated by her new family.

Next morning there was a phone call from Clara: 'The maid's had an accident and burnt her foot, and we've heard that Paul's been wounded. I think the three of you should come home.' After our first shock we rang back for details and Salomon told us he knew only that Paul's wounds were serious.

We decided to return home immediately. Jacob Levy said, 'I'll go with you as far as Hamm,' where we would change trains. Helene said, 'I'll come too.'

As we were saying goodbye to them both on the platform in Hamm, we bumped into Sofie Meinberg from Gütersloh. Mother asked, 'Where've you been?'

'In Hagen.'

'It's so hot and humid today.'

'In Gütersloh as well.'

'I thought you'd just come from Hagen?'

'I meant on Friday. I was away only yesterday and today.'

The closer we came to Gütersloh, the greater our concern. The train rolled into the station. Salomon and Clara were waiting for us on the platform. Salomon's usually rosy cheeks were chalk white and showing fine veins. Clara wore a green blouse and her face seemed the same colour. There was no need to ask anything. Their faces told us all. Sofie Meinberg had travelled from Gütersloh to Hamm to make sure that no one would approach us to express sympathy before we heard the sad news at home.

We dragged ourselves home. Mother burst out crying, sobbing aloud. Father sat quietly, tears running down his cheeks. I couldn't and wouldn't accept that we would never see Paul again – this strong young man, so full of life and vigour. When I think back about this now, after so many years, I still hear my mother's cries of despair.

When we had composed ourselves a little, Salomon said, 'Would you like to go to your apartment now? I've prepared everything so we can sit *Schiwe*.' We went upstairs, but I could not sit *Schiwe*. I kept thinking, 'This is a bad dream, it can't be true!'

When Salomon and Clara joined us later she told us:

Saturday morning we were very busy in the butcher shop. We'd not even had time for breakfast. At about nine the postman came. There was some army mail, which we intended to read while eating. I told Salomon, 'There's a letter from Paul. He writes there've been some days without fighting.'

Salomon meanwhile took another army letter and started to read. He suddenly screamed! His face turned ashen.

'What's the matter?' I asked. 'What's wrong?' Without a word Salomon passed me the letter in which the Sergeant Major of the Company informed us: 'Reserve Corporal Paul Herzberg was killed by the blast of an exploding grenade. He had been asleep with other soldiers in the dugout. He died immediately, bleeding from nose and mouth. He was buried at the Louvière Farm, between Pusieux-au-Mont and Hébuterne.'

The letter from Paul was dated 13 June 1915, that from the Sergeant Major, 15 June. Both letters had reached us on the same day, a terrible coincidence!

Some time later we received a Memorial Testament honouring Paul's memory, signed by Wild von Hohenborn, Minister for War. [25]

Many friends came to express sympathy. Their condolences brought our loss painfully home. Sofie Meinberg said, 'Nobody had such a good influence on our Alfred as Paul. The boys being about the same age were always good friends. Alfred always listened to Paul, till his job took him to Düsseldorf and Paul's to Mainz. Surely he would have encouraged Alfred not to marry the non-Jewish girlfriend from such an ordinary family. You see, we too are going to miss Paul.'

Of course Amalie Meinberg came immediately and stayed to comfort our parents.

In the evening, during the first *Minjen* of the *Schiwe* week, it was heartbreaking when Father joined in saying *Kaddisch*, to hear the words which he usually said so effortlessly, interrupted by sobbing.

Monday morning Rosa and Helene came. Both had eyes red from crying, but they tried to be outwardly calm when with our parents.

It was customary to wear black during the period of mourning. We sent our maid to a shop to bring home a selection of blouses. Mother didn't need, as she always wore only black. Clara chose a black-and-white check, Rosa and Helene each fully black. They selected the same for me, but I could not make myself wear it. It took a few days and great emotional effort before I could convince myself to do so.

My sisters stayed on with us during the week of the *Schiwe*.

In the synagogue on the *Schabbes* of that week, our minister spoke well. He

---

[25]   Hypocrisy! This same man was responsible for the census of Jewish soldiers early in the war with the expectation that it would show that the German Jewish community was underrepresented. When the survey proved the opposite, the results were not published. (See Appendix 2) The memorial document from the Ministry of War mentioned above was followed by a memorial scroll signed by the Kaiser. On the top of the scroll is a quotation from the Gospel of John.

Memorial Testament honouring Paul Herzberg and his family.
(Translation below)

In fighting to defend the German Fatherland, a beloved member of your family has suffered a hero's death. In remembrance of the honoured dead, fallen on the field of battle, His Majesty the Kaiser and King in sincere commiseration of the severe loss and in eternal recognition of his supreme sacrifice has awarded this

Memorial Testament

May this commemorative symbol of the historic era and the unending gratitude of the Fatherland bring perpetual honour to your family.

Supreme Headquarters, the 10 Dec. 15

Minister of War

Wild von Hohenborn

Memorial Scroll signed by Kaiser Wilhelm II honouring Paul Herzberg.
(Translation below)

It is for us to lay down our lives for our brothers 1 John.3.16.	To the memory of Paul Herzberg N.C.O. in the Res. Royal Prussian Infantry Regiment 186.12. R He died for the Fatherland On 15 June 1915 *Wilhelm Rex*

chose the text *Ma tauwu oholecho Jaakauw* ... (How goodly are thy tents, O Jacob ...), connecting this quote to our family life. His words were very comforting.

Salomon, who rarely wrote family letters, had taken over the task of writing the sad news to out-of-town family. Their replies all began much the same way: 'When we saw Salomon's handwriting we knew to expect bad news.'

Much mail came, including many letters from Paul's army comrades. Hermann's letter showed how deeply affected he was. We had held back from notifying Leopold of Paul's death, since they had both always been very close. We knew Leopold's formation was currently involved in heavy battles. Within days, we had mail from Leopold: 'My last letter to Paul was returned stamped "Killed in action". A terrible shock. Paul was a wonderful person. His death is such a loss for all who knew him.'

The many condolence letters and sympathy visits served to emphasise the sad reality, as did my nice hat, now dyed black by the aunts.

Life had to go on as usual, for we each had our responsibilities. I went back to work at Miele. My sisters and Salomon had their businesses to manage. Our parents helped where they could. The cute speech of their little grandsons, Kurt and Werner, was a diversion for them.

Rosa wrote that Louis was called up and would go to Detmold for military training with the infantry. After a very short period he was sent to the Russian Front. Leopold's regiment was in the Champagne. The newspapers told of heavy battles there and of many losses. He wrote in one letter: 'If I live to see my birthday in September I believe I will survive.' Hermann also took part in big battles. We had many reasons for constant worry. Whenever a letter arrived from any of the boys we always thought: what might have happened since that letter was sent?

* * *

For the High Holidays of 1915, Father could no longer lead the prayers as he had always done, nor stand for such long periods. We had to take him to the synagogue in a wheelchair. On the short route, he was warmly greeted by many with respect and affection. It was fortunate that Mr Eisenstein was there to take over Father's responsibilities. A reduced congregation assembled. Everyone prayed with great *Kavoneh*. In the still of the synagogue, thoughts drifted to our soldiers in harm's way. Every family had someone in the forces.

Our good friend Amalie Meinberg became seriously ill with heart failure.

Her favourite trainee from her finishing school, Paula Horwitz, came for a visit and stayed over *Jaum Kippur*.

The *Jontef* days brought much stress for all, especially *Yizkor*, the *Seelenfeier*, on *Jaum Kippur*, which in our synagogue was always said in the twilight between *Minche* and *Ne-ile*. It was an emotional time for the family as we were all so conscious of our loss during the year. What might we have to face in the coming year?

During the *Seelenfeier* Irma Meinberg, from the women's side of the synagogue, sang *Ruhen in Frieden alle Seelen, alle Seelen ruhen in Frieden …* (Rest in peace all souls, all souls rest in peace …). Mother, Clara, and I, clad in black, were sobbing softly. In late afternoon the last sunbeams suddenly shone through the open window adorned with a red and blue *Mogen Dovid*. A large black-bodied butterfly with wings of many colours flew in on that sunbeam and settled on Mother's shoulder, then onto Paula Horwitz's shoulder, again to Mother, to Paula, then out the window. Did that butterfly bring a greeting from 'The Other World'? Paula was thinking of her beloved Paul. From crying, her eyes were as red as her red blouse.

The conclusion of *Suckes* brought September to an end. We had had a hot summer but now it was suddenly cool. Life went back to its busy routine, including dropping into Clara and Salomon's to look at the mail on my way home for lunch. And so it was on 4 October 1915. I entered the house finding it unexpectedly quiet. Usually the children greeted me full of joy. I went into the large living room and found Clara lying on the sofa, eyes closed. Salomon was sitting on a chair with his back to me.

'Clara, aren't you feeling well? What's the matter?'

'Everything's the matter.'

'Where's the mail?'

'Upstairs with our parents,' Salomon said.

I went home next door. The same strange quiet was present there also. My parents were lying down. No lunch table set.

'What's happened, where's the mail?'

'Hermann … he too, is gone!' said Mother, weeping.

I couldn't speak.

I picked up the letter and read that our good, unselfish Hermann was killed while bandaging a wounded comrade. Hermann had been shot in the back. His last words were, 'Give my love to my parents.' This happened on *Jaum*

Kippur, 18 September 1915, in the trenches at Schaulen, close to Makarowka, in Poland. Once again tears would not come. I felt I was choking and had a stabbing feeling in my chest. We three sat together for some time. Then Mother said, 'You have to eat, you're young. You need nourishment and you can't change anything.' It was impossible to eat a morsel.

The front doorbell rang. It was my colleague Mieze Gött, who often called by for our walk back to the office. I told her our tragic news and asked her to explain my absence from work.

Visitors had already arrived. In the evening Rosa and Helene came. Helene could not stay long, as she had responsibility for the business and her three small children. Rosa stayed for the *Schiwe*. As her husband was away at the Russian Front and she had no children, she had closed her shop. Finding stock was often difficult, so what she had on her shelf would certainly not lose value.

We had a daily *Minjen* in the house for the week. It was physically distressing for me that I couldn't shed tears, until one evening when relief came in a burst of sobbing – then I couldn't stop crying for hours.

It was hard to accept what had happened. I kept thinking, 'Hermann will come back, even if it takes a while. He'll be glad that we've looked after his shop so well.'

I went back to the office and everybody expressed sympathy. Mr C H Walkenhorst called me to his office and gave me his condolences: 'I'm so sorry to hear you've lost another brother to the war. Surely now your youngest brother should be transferred to a support role. I'll tell you what we'll do. Let's compose a letter requesting his withdrawal from the front.'

I typed the letter, had it certified by the town's mayor and sent it to Leopold's regiment, hopeful that in the future we would not have to worry about his safety. Sadly, our effort was in vain. After a few weeks we were informed that our petition was not granted as there was yet another son, namely Salomon! Unfortunately having already mentioned our petition to Leopold we now had to disappoint him.

10

large contingent of soldiers was stationed in Gütersloh for army training, men between thirty and forty years of age, most married. They had not been taken for military service in peacetime and had originally been rejected for active service, due to age or health defects. Young people of the town were asked to organise dances to entertain the soldiers, among them a very good opera singer. My friends Irma and Else Meinberg sang with him in a number of concerts. A few theatrical plays were also staged. I was asked to participate, but declined out of respect for the memory of my brothers and for my parents. We were still in mourning.

Salomon was now also called up and stationed in the large prisoner-of-war camp in Sennelager, a town not far from Gütersloh. A butcher by trade, he too was assigned to the mess kitchen. While there, he met Willi Gronsfeld, a prison guard who was so skinny that at mealtimes Salomon would dish out an extra serving for him. (When I later married Karl Mendels, Willi became my cousin-in-law.) As the camp was close by, Salomon could sometimes come home and help in his own shop, but even so, it was difficult for Clara to keep the shop going. The few men available for employment were either unfit for military service or elderly.

Just before the war, a big regional asylum had been built on the outskirts of Gütersloh. It was now a prisoner-of-war camp, housing captured Russian and French officers, with batmen, guarded by the military, who also censored prisoners' mail. Two German Jewish soldiers were working in the camp as interpreters for the prisoners and as mail censors. They asked Clara if they could come daily for a hot mid-day meal. She was happy to do this for them and it also gave her a little extra income. Mother sometimes invited them for dinner on Friday night and they accepted readily. They acknowledged the hospitality by inviting me, together with two other girls and another soldier, for an outing to the Teutoburger Wald once the weather was warmer.

During the summer of 1916 Leopold came home on a fortnight's leave, which passed all too quickly. At the time we had photos taken, one of Leopold with Salomon and one of Leopold with me[26]. We all look very solemn. Our farewell was very distressing.

I had severe flu in August. I was very down and the doctor suggested a fortnight's rest. I went to Barsinghausen and, despite food rationing, the relatives did their best to nourish me back to health. While there I received the sad news that Hermann Walkenhorst had also 'died for the Fatherland'. We had been corresponding regularly. I was shattered.

With autumn came the High Holidays and their added demands. Jacob Levy visited and counselled: 'Käthe, you should give up your job. Your father is weaker and needs more care; wood and coal have to be brought up from the cellar; the hardware shop is getting busier. There's just too much for your mother to do even though she now has a maid for the mornings.'

I didn't want to hear this. I liked my job and valued the monthly wages.

* * *

In mid-December 1916, I was home for lunch when Mother whispered, 'Father's in bed. He isn't at all well. Dr Kranefuss was here and prescribed camphor. I remember when my mother was failing they gave her camphor. Father's heart must be very weak.'

I went into the bedroom. His eyes lit up. He always waited impatiently for me to come home, often with pocket watch in hand. 'You're late. What happened?'

As I was young and unaware, I thought the illness would soon pass. Unfortunately that was not to be. His severe breathing difficulty forced him to sleep sitting up in bed. We took turns to stay with him, even at night. Such care was very demanding.

I rang the Miele office and asked for leave of absence for a few weeks, not only because of Father's illness, but also because our shop was busy, with Christmas in the offing. Our wares were in great demand.

---

[26] This picture is the cover photograph of this book.

Rosa and Helene came for a visit. Mother's sister, Elise Traube, came to help look after Father. Salomon suggested sending a notarised telegram to Leopold's regiment, seeking compassionate leave. I was concerned that Father would be alarmed if Leopold returned so soon after his summer furlough, so asked Private Jordan, one of the interpreters who went for meals to Clara's, to write an army postcard in Leopold's name foreshadowing another visit.

Leopold arrived the day after Christmas. His presence seemed to improve Father's health. The swelling of his legs almost disappeared. Attacks of shortness of breath were less frequent. He began again to eat a little of the light meals Mother cooked with such love and care. We had a few quiet days and began to feel confident. Even Dr Kranefuss believed: 'He may soon go for a walk to Unter Meiers Bäumen.' But it was a last surge of life. At about seven in the morning of 31 December, I heard Father calling, 'Mother, Mother'.

I went to him. 'Let Mother sleep a little longer. I'll stay with you.' Within minutes I regretted my suggestion, for Father lost consciousness and began thrashing his limbs about. I wakened everyone and ran next door to Salomon and Clara. From there I telephoned the doctor. He came immediately, diagnosed kidney colic and gave an injection to relieve the intense pain. Father was on the sofa when this happened. We contacted the Jewish nurse who was looking after our sick friend Amalie Meinberg. With her help, Salomon and Leopold were able to carry Father, a heavy man, to bed. There was nothing more we could do for him. Mother's meals, prepared days earlier, stayed untouched.

Rosa and Helene both returned and some men of the congregation also visited. Mr Eisenstein sat at Father's bedside reading Psalms.

It was noon on New Year's Day 1917. Mother said, 'Children, you must eat. Go! Eat! Everything's on the table. There's nothing we can do to help.' We were just going to the table when we heard Mr Eisenstein proclaim: '*Shema Jisroel Adauschem Elaukenu Adauschem Echod*!' 'It's over,' Mother said and fell against me sobbing. This was now the third death in our family within fifteen months. We had lost our much-loved Father, but at least in his case we had been able to care for him to the end.

We were all overwrought.

German law required a delay of three days between death and funeral. The body rested in the coffin during that period. Many relatives gathered for the funeral – some we had not seen for years – as well as many friends and acquaintances from nearby towns and villages. Our cousin Moritz Herzberg, being medically unfit for active service, had been assigned to the outfitters section of his regiment in Detmold, so was able to bring *Pickelhaube* (spiked) helmets for our uniformed soldiers to wear at the funeral. These were more stately and dignified than the rimless caps usually worn.

That Father was well known and well liked was confirmed by the long funeral procession. Salomon arranged for the coffin to be brought into his home, where Father had lived and worked for so many years. As our own *Chasen* had been called up only recently, the minister from the nearby town of Neuenkirchen, Max Vorsänger, officiated. It was the first time that the tall, imposing man had assisted us in Gütersloh. The service and eulogy took place in the house. I was too upset to recall any part of the speech. Surely, Mr Vorsänger would have praised my father for all his good deeds in both the general and the Jewish community.[27] As was customary, Mother and we three daughters did not go to the cemetery.

At the time of Father's death, our former *Chasen* and teacher, Arnold Stein, was recuperating from war wounds in a military hospital in Berlin. He had always idolised Father. As soon as he learned of our loss he came to Gütersloh and spoke at the graveside, praising his fatherly friend.

Amalie Meinberg sent words of consolation written for her by the nursing sister, then signed by Amalie in a tremulous hand. She was daily more frail.

Even with Salomon and Leopold home on leave it was sometimes hard to get ten men together for the *Minjen* during the full week of the *Schiwe*, as men under the age of forty-five were away in the army. The two interpreters, Jordan and van Geldern, came to every *Minjen,* as did two Jewish prisoners of war, (batmen of imprisoned Russian officers) who had been granted permission to attend. One was a shoemaker and the other, Sam Skolnikov, a watchmaker. Arrangements were already in place for them all to attend synagogue services.

---

27 Josef Herzberg's death left the community without a *Schauchet.*

Kommandantur
des Offizier-Gefangenen-Lagers
Gütersloh.

J.-No. 3217 I

23. August 1915.

An

den Magistrat der Stadt

G ü t e r s l o h .

Stadt Gütersloh
Eing. 24 AUG. 1915.
Tgb. No. L 849

Im Gefangenenlager befinden sich 19 jüdische,
russische Soldaten, welche die Bitte ausgesprochen
haben, am jüdischen Neujahrstage, den 9. und 10.
September, und am Versöhnungstage, den 18.September,
zum Gottesdienst in die Synagoge geführt zu werden.

Das General-Kommando hat in ähnlichen Fällen der
Teilnahme von Gefangenen am allgemeinen Gottesdien-
ste zugestimmt, falls die Kriegsgefangenen auf be-
sonderen, von dem übrigen Publikum getrennten Bänken
sitzen, und der Eintritt in die Kirche und der Aus-
gang aus derselben vom Publikum getrennt stattfin-
det.

Ich bitte ergebenst um recht baldige Aeusserrung,
ob dort der Gewährung der Bitte Bedenken entgegen-
stehen.

Oberstleutnant z. D.

Enquiry from Prisoner of War Camp on behalf of POWs seeking permission to attend
Synagogue services and Minyanim. (Translation below)

In the prisoner of war camp are 19 Jewish Russian soldiers who have made a request to
be taken to the Synagogue services for the Jewish New Year on 9 and 10 September and on
the Day of Atonement on 18 September.

The General Command has in similar circumstances agreed to allow the participation
of prisoners in inter-faith religious services, on condition that the prisoners sit on benches
separated from the general public and that on entering and leaving the church they are again
kept apart.

I request most humbly a speedy reply if the situation there meets these requirements.

Lieutenant-Colonel

Reply by Josef Herzberg to Commandant of POW Camp and the latter's
conditional permission. (Translation below)

There is nothing to prevent the Jewish prisoners who are in the local prison camp from participating in our religious service and the prisoners can be seated on specially allocated benches, separated from the rest of the public.

The Board of the Jewish Community

J. Herzberg
President

* * *

Sam Skolnikov [28] didn't want to return to Russia. When war ended he was able to settle in Gütersloh. He first worked for a local watchmaker and was able to save enough to start his own business, going to surrounding villages repairing watches. Communicating in *Jiddisch* and broken German, he managed to make a name for himself and built up a clientele. The Stern family in Gütersloh introduced him to a fine young Jewish girl, Minna Hamberg, of Wolfhagen, whom he subsequently married. Minna's only brother had been killed in the war. She had kept her late brother's suits, so Sam became instantly a well-dressed man. The young wife was industrious and the couple soon opened a shop repairing and selling watches and gifts. Minna contracted multiple sclerosis and some years later became lame and confined to a wheelchair. Being a positive person, she was determined to get about and continue to manage the various responsibilities. She was perceptive, decisive and selfless. When Hitler came to power she sent her elder son, Josef, to her sister in New York and later ensured that her husband and her younger son, Ralf, also emigrated. They went to Shanghai, no other country being open to them. They left as late as 1 July 1939. Minna bravely stayed behind to avoid jeopardising their migration.[29] She went to the Jewish Hospital in Cologne, where she died two months later, just after the start of the Second World War.

Immediately after the war Sam wrote to Leopold from Shanghai, seeking a permit for himself and his son, Ralf, to migrate to Australia. Leopold obtained the two permits.[30] Meanwhile, Ralf married and so Leopold had to organise an additional permit for Alla, Ralf's wife. The three Skolnikovs arrived in 1949 and stayed for some weeks with the Herzbergs. We (my husband Karl and I) then found them a furnished flat in Bondi and later they lived near us in Eastlakes. The two men found work straight away. Alla, a Russian from Harbin, had difficulty with the language at first, but was soon able to work in our Nut Shop (in the Strand Arcade, Sydney) till the birth of their only child, Michelle. Ralf built up his own jewellery business and now has a fine home. Sam Skolnikov remarried in Sydney. He died in 1961.

---

[28] Because of shortage of manpower the government allowed employment outside the camp. Sam Skolnikov worked as a jeweller in Gütersloh, even while a prisoner of war. Sam had a good Jewish education so sometimes took the service, as there was no permanent *Chasen* or teacher.

[29] There was no country in 1938-39 that would take in migrants who were not in good health, certainly not invalids.

[30] These permits required personal guarantees given by an Australian resident.

After Father's funeral came many days of heavy snowfall, which took weeks to thaw. Mother wanted to go to the cemetery but snowdrifts made this impossible.

In the last days of January 1917 we lost Amalie Meinberg. Though this was anticipated, Mother was going to miss her cousin and good friend. After that funeral Mother realised, 'There've been so many people at the cemetery treading a path through the snow, we will now be able to go.' We found Father's grave decked with many wreaths from non-Jewish friends.

* * *

Now I really had no choice but to give up my position at Miele. Mother couldn't look after the shop by herself and, furthermore, she was exhausted. Housework had been neglected; laundry not done. Automatic washing machines and electric irons were still unknown and there was no commercial laundry in Gütersloh.

The winter of early 1917 was bitterly cold. Coal was hard to get so people used whatever alternative fuels they could for heating. As a result, many iron grates in heating and cooking stoves had been damaged. Hermann had always kept a large supply of grates in a range of sizes stored in the loft. It was very draughty up there and the wind blew snowflakes through the dormer windows. These metal articles were so chilled that even with thick gloves I could still feel the penetrating cold. I would choose the sizes of grate needed and, despite their weight, lug them down to the shop. Interestingly, they were sold by weight. Straight and elbowed stove pipes were also kept in the loft. They varied in size and had to be cut to measure. Learning this took me some time.

America now entered the war. Consequently Germany was totally blockaded, no goods entering the country. Rationing, while helpful, could not solve the scarcity of food. In the previous autumn a friendly farmer had given us a generous supply of potatoes. One day an inspector arrived at our house, assessed the quantity of potatoes and ordered us to give up a large proportion.

We were not entitled to buy milk but could sometimes find skim milk, often not fresh and sometimes smelling sour. The two of us were allowed very little bread, as Mother chose to keep some of our ration stamps for flour to bake cakes and biscuits for our many visitors to have with their 'coffee'. Coffee of course was *Ersatz*. From a friendly farmer one could get rye kernels, to boil and then roast in a coffee roaster. This produced a pleasant aroma. Coffee made this way tasted far better than coffee bought at the grocery. Coffee roasters were in

Reference from Miele & Co for Käthe Herzberg. (Translation below)

We hereby certify that Miss Käthe Herzberg was employed as a secretary in our bookkeeping department from 1 April 1913 to the end of December 1916.

Miss Herzberg was ambitious, industrious and conscientious and after brief instruction, carried out the work assigned to her completely independently to our satisfaction.

Her resignation was at her own request and we wish her all the very best for the future.

Gütersloh, 28 March 1917.

Miele & Co

big demand in our shop. Flour was brown, and artificial honey was substituted for sugar. There was very little fat or butter available; no oil at all. Consequently we sold many cast-iron fry pans, which needed little fat to fry a range of foods.

Meat had been rationed for a long time, but Clara made sure we had sufficient. As bread was our scarcest food, Mother would bring cooked vegetables from the day before with a few tiny pieces of meat for my ten o'clock morning break at the shop. I would warm this on Clara's stove and eat in her kitchen. One day Salomon, on leave, noted this:

'What are you eating?'

'Turnips.'

'Don't you have bread?'

'No. Bread's very scarce.'

'That's unbelievable. My mates throw bread away once it's not fresh. I'll send you a parcel of army bread.'

A few days later his parcel arrived. That bread was magnificent!

Coal for heating and cooking was hard to get. If you were lucky you might get a hundredweight or two, but you would have to fetch it using a handcart. There were neither enough miners nor people to transport the coal. Due to the very cold weather people were also hungrier. Meals were scant, with little or no fat. No wonder people went to farmers to forage for potatoes, bacon, eggs – anything they could get. Labourers came from the Ruhr to our district seeking food at almost any price. The black market flourished.

The German people were hungry. Their hunger would continue. Bartering also blossomed, people exchanging soft goods, manchester and sewing cotton for food. There were also many *ersatz* goods: towels and sheets woven with paper fibre in them, bread with turnips in the mixture. With so much *Ersatz* many people became ill. Clara developed bronchitis with a severe cough. We were very worried about her. Fortunately, we had been able to get enough extra coal to heat her bedroom. The doctor's recommendations didn't seem to help. We asked Güthenke, the tailor, who had studied 'nature healing' to look at her. He had helped many people by applying water treatments of various kinds. In this instance he advised hot compresses on the chest. These gave Clara relief.

Our Christmas sales had considerably reduced our stock levels. Most suppliers needed long delivery times for poor quality, wartime goods. Many had nothing to sell. A circular arrived from a firm in southern Westphalia, advertising a large stock of household goods. Salomon encouraged Mother and me to act on it and said Clara would look after the shop for us. On the Saturday night we travelled to Rüdinghausen and stayed the Sunday with Rosa. Very early on Monday morning we went on foot through the snow to the railway station in Annen, there being no trains or buses from Rüdinghausen. All the windowpanes in the train to Schalksmühle were broken and the seats covered with snow. It was difficult to find a corner where the chilling wind could not blow in. The scenery outside was like a fairytale. The houses and trees were covered with masses of snow. Icicles hung from the roofs, some two metres long and thick at the base. We had never seen anything like this. At last we reached our goal, pleased to be in an overheated office. But heat was all we got! In their circular, they had promised immediate delivery of goods but even though we were offering payment in advance, they now told us delivery would take several months. None of the goods ordered ever arrived.

We came home Monday afternoon. Clara had prepared food and a hot cup of coffee to warm us up. We went upstairs to our flat, which was so cold that the tiles in the kitchen had cracked.

I regularly travelled to the factories of our long-term suppliers. As 'sweeteners' I took meat, sausages, even fat, which helped to obtain goods we needed. The factories were usually on the outskirts of town. I would also go into the town centre, for I could often find and buy pre-war goods at reasonable prices in small shops. It soon became known that despite shortages, we carried a range of stock unavailable elsewhere.

* * *

The relatives in Barsinghausen urged Mother to come for a visit. She accepted gladly but wanted to take her oldest grandson, Kurt, who would soon be starting school. On the Sunday morning, Kurt came dressed in a neat sailor suit, the fashion of the day, to accompany his grandmother. The child had an odd look about him. Mother said, 'You'd better go home. You've got black rings round your eyes. Perhaps Mummy didn't wash your face properly.' Minutes later, Clara sent the maid to tell us that the boy had vomited and was not able to travel. We went next door straight away. As Kurt also had a high temperature, Clara had called Dr Kranefuss, who diagnosed pneumonia. Of course Mother postponed her trip.

When Salomon came home on leave, Kurt still had a high temperature. He questioned, 'Why didn't you seek Güthenke's advice?'

As soon as he arrived, Güthenke filled our galvanised tub with about five centimetres of lukewarm water, put the feverish lad into the tub and sprinkled him with cold water. Next, he wrapped the boy in a cold wet sheet, covered him with two thick, woollen blankets and put him to bed. Kurt started to perspire and within a few hours his temperature was normal. The pneumonic crisis was over. Now we could relax.

In the evening when the doctor returned, he was surprised that the boy was relatively well. Else Levy, Clara's younger sister, who had done a nursing course at the beginning of the war, volunteered, 'I gave the boy a cold bath.' We could hardly tell the doctor of Güthenke's visit.

'You've been very lucky. If he didn't have a strong constitution he might not have survived.' We were just happy that young Kurt was recovering.

Else Levy had already been in Gütersloh for some time, helping Clara in the shop while Salomon was away. She was engaged to our cousin Gustav Königheim from Blomberg, also a butcher in an army kitchen on the Russian Front. Else had always worked in a butcher shop and was better suited to be Gustav's wife than was Paula Horwitz.

During February we made another attempt to have Leopold recalled from the frontline. Salomon had argued, 'Mother, you've always cared for us equally, as though we, all of us, are your natural children.[31] But Leopold is your actual son, your only surviving son. We must try again to get him recalled from the Front.'

Salomon and I put together a letter, which Mother signed. It was certified at the mayor's office before being sent to Leopold's regiment. This time we didn't tell Leopold, so he couldn't be disappointed if we didn't succeed.

We heard from Leopold in no time! As it turned out he would have preferred to know we were applying. Unaware of the reason, he had been summoned and questioned by the Sergeant Major. Consequently he was moved to a depot behind the frontline and as an experienced non-commissioned officer was training new recruits. He gave us his new address. We were relieved. At last he was out of danger.

* * *

In the spring Mother and I used the first fine Sunday to visit Father's grave. Throughout summer, after the close of business we went there regularly.

---

[31] Helene, Paul, Leopold and Käthe were the children of Bertha and Josef. The other five children – Salomon, Rosa, Arnold, Hermann and Clare – were from Josef's first marriage.

There were now new worries. Mail sent to Rosa's husband, Louis Neugarten, had been returned, stamped 'Missing'. We wrote to his commander, who replied that Louis had been in a fierce battle and, together with a few of his mates, had become separated from his platoon. It was not known whether he was dead or alive, wounded or a prisoner of the Russians.

After some days Rosa came to stay with us. She was very composed and said over and over: 'I know Louis is alive; we'll get mail from him soon.' But we heard nothing. Rosa went home for a short while before returning, her neighbour agreeing to send on her mail. There was nothing to keep her in the big house in Rüdinghausen. She had no children. Unsold stock in her shop would gain value every day.

I was always busy in our shop. One day we had to deliver a stove to a place close to the town park in exchange for fruit and vegetables. We lifted the stove onto a two-wheeler handcart and our maid set out, with Rosa and me walking behind. We had not gone far when we heard someone calling. It was cousin Henny Levisohn from Barsinghausen, who was staying with us for a few days. She was waving something in her hand. 'That must be for me,' said Rosa. It really was! A postcard from Louis, addressed to us. He wrote that he was well and in good spirits. We were overjoyed. Several members of the family got mail from him but none came addressed to Rosa. Louis later told us he had received none of the cards and letters we had sent, some even addressed in Russian.

During summer Leopold had a fortnight's leave. For his nephews, Kurt and Werner, he brought a live rabbit from France. The children were delighted with the pet and fed it constantly. Sadly after a few days the little creature went to rabbit heaven!

Kurt, already at school, heard about the undernourished *Belgerkinder* (children of Belgian refugees). He asked his mother for soup bones for the children and of course Clara gave him a parcel.

Battles on both fronts continued. There was talk of peace negotiations but they came to nothing. Our troops were trapped in trench warfare in both France and Russia. The struggle was bitter. Lists of soldiers injured or killed were published daily. In this way we learned of the death of Willi Wolf in the last months of the war. Orphaned, he had been brought up by his uncle, old Mr Garty of Gütersloh.

In March 1918, the Russian government, now Bolshevik, concluded the Treaty of Brest-Litovsk with Germany, Austria-Hungary and the Ottoman

Empire. (The latter two combatants would pull out of the war altogether in late October.) Months after Brest, a postcard from Russia arrived for Rosa from Louis, but to our address, as he didn't know she had gone home. 'Have been exchanged for Russian prisoner of war; am being sent back to my regiment in Detmold.'

How wonderful!

He gave the date and time of his arrival at the railway station in Gütersloh. We passed on the good news to Rosa, who said she would like Louis to go straight through to Dortmund, where she would meet him. As Leopold was also just home on leave, we all went to the railway station to meet the train. When we saw Louis on the platform looking around for Rosa, we called out to him, 'She's waiting for you in Dortmund.' After giving him a packet of sandwiches, we attempted to get him back on the train. It was so overcrowded with returning soldiers that some of his mates had to lift him in through the window.

Next day we received a phone call from Rosa. She was just so happy. 'I want you all to come to Rüdinghausen next Sunday. We'll have a celebration. Louis's homecoming will be like another wedding.' Leopold was still home and Salomon managed to get leave, so we were all able to go. Louis's two brothers, their wives and Helene were already there. Everyone was in a jolly mood and somebody chuckled, 'Babies often follow wartime weddings.' The couple had been childless for twelve years.

Our two soldiers returned to their regiments and we to our various occupations. A few weeks later we received a letter from Rosa telling us she was pregnant. Mother was unconvinced: 'I won't believe it till I see Rosa.' But true it was.

* * *

As a result of the extreme scarcity of food, riots began to occur in the big cities, particularly in Hamburg and Berlin. Kaiser Wilhelm abdicated, escaping to Holland. Negotiations for an armistice with the Western Allies began.

At last. The Peace!

The soldiers' homecoming was now anticipated with great excitement. The first to return to Germany were those few who could find transport. Most had to walk to the border before being picked up. Trucks carrying troops started coming through Gütersloh. We had to billet two soldiers for several days and were later asked to take another. That young man wanted to take me to several end-of-war balls and festivities but I didn't accept his invitations. He felt so at home that we had difficulty encouraging him to leave. We needed the room for Leopold, whom we expected any day.

Naval and military mutinies were breaking out.[32] Soldiers no longer respected officers, to the extent of tearing off their insignias. Workers' councils and soldiers' councils were formed. Unbeknown to us, Leopold had been elected to a soldiers' council involved in preventing riots in their area, causing delay in his return home. We went to the railway station a number of times, but Leopold was not on any of the troop trains passing through. We realised we would have to be patient till we heard from him.

On an afternoon in late November, Liese Ruthenburg burst into our house. 'Here's your soldier. You didn't even go to pick him up!' With great joy we threw our arms around Leopold, hugging and hugging him. He was home.

Leopold wrote to his firm in Frankfurt asking to be re-employed. The firm offered him a job but for a reduced salary. As there weren't many goods available, certainly none for foreign trading, his old position as correspondent in French and Italian no longer existed. He intended to stay in the clothing business and became an agent for various menswear firms, but that was not what he really wanted.

Our household and hardware shop was expanding rapidly. We welcomed Leopold's decision to join the business, which then became known as L & K Herzberg. We sold off the wartime goods. As war receded, better quality stock became available. We expanded our range, adding china, glass, crystal and silverware. Additional shelves were installed in the loft of the business house to store stock. Each year we went to the Leipziger Messe, the Leipzig Trade Fair. We worked hard and were successful. Mother took over the household, and was needed only occasionally in the shop.

On weekends we would socialise with other Jewish families, sometimes

---

32 Unrest began with a sailors' mutiny at Kiel 29 October 1918. By 3 November this had developed into armed insurrection. Disturbances broke out in Hamburg and Bremen; councils of soldiers and workers like the Russian soviets were formed in inland industrial centres. This led to the abdication of Kaiser Wilhelm II. In the four years of war nearly 80 million men were mobilised in total, of whom nearly 9 million were killed and 21 million wounded. 12,000 German Jewish soldiers died fighting for their nation, and tens of thousands of Jews were wounded. Germany, together with Austria-Hungary lost 3 million dead. Their associated countries (Turkey and Bulgaria) lost 400,000. Of the Western Allies more than 5 million lives were lost – 1.7 million from Russia and 1.3 million from France.

going to the theatre in Bielefeld. Leopold joined the Gütersloh Turnergesang Verein (Gymnastics and Choral Society) and was active in the synagogue. The evenings were spent reading, we women doing needlework at times. We were a happy family.

I had several proposals of marriage, but the suitors didn't appeal to me.

Advertisement in the book celebrating the centenary of Gütersloh as a city.

Hermann's shop became L. & K. Herzberg after World War I.

11

In the early spring of 1924 I spent a pleasant weekend with relatives in Blomberg, a little town in the principality of Lippe-Detmold, near the Teutoburger Wald. On one of its mountains, Grotenburg, is the massive monument of Hermann the Cherusker,[33] who defeated the Romans in the year 9 CE. For this he has always been idolised by the Germans. I didn't know at the time that the Nazis were using this area to hold secret meetings.

On my way home I had barely sat down in the Gütersloh train when several young men came into my compartment, dressed in hunter-green suits and hats, but none among them had hunter's knapsack or rifle. With them was a young woman.

As the train pulled into the next station, the man sitting next to me took a stack of leaflets out of a case and threw most out the window. I was curious to know his purpose. There were no elections due in the near future. Did the leaflets have some commercial purpose? Advertising for a store perhaps? I took a side-glance and was shocked.

---

[33] Armin (Arminius, Latin), ca 18 BCE–19 CE, a Roman-trained chief of the Germanic Cherusci tribe, defeated the Romans at the Battle of the Teutoburger Wald in 9 CE. The Romans had difficulties bringing the German tribes under control and the Rhine remained the north-eastern border of the Roman Empire for 300 years. Arminius was slain by his own tribesmen in 19 CE. Although the Roman historian Tacitus labelled him 'the liberator of Germany', the concept of a united Germany was not even imagined in Arminius' time. But that did not prevent the German nationalists in the 19th century adopting Arminius as a German hero. Martin Luther gave him the warrior name 'Hermann der Cherusker'. In 1875 a colossal statue in his honour was completed in the area of the battle.

> Jews hold too many top positions in Arts, Commerce and Industry.
>
> Germans work hard, while Jews pile up lots of money, sucking blood out of German veins.
>
> During the war Jews were nowhere to be found at the Front or in the trenches.
>
> Jews manoeuvered themselves into safe positions and made tons of money, while Germans were bleeding to death.

There were more lies and accusations on the leaflets. I can't remember them all. I was furious, but calmed myself and thought, 'I must get hold of some of those papers.'

It took all my courage to address the man next to me: 'Excuse me, could I have a look at what you're handing out? I'm interested. I'm from Gütersloh, where there's a Deutscher Schutz-und-Trutz-Bund.'[34] At this, he handed me some without any comment. When I read the appalling, false accusations I couldn't restrain myself: 'Your pamphlets say Jews avoided dangerous frontline positions during the war. Factual records show there were higher proportions of losses and casualties among Jewish soldiers than among soldiers of any other faith.'

'Obviously such statistics are wrong; falsified by the Jews.'

I thought of my two wonderful brothers Paul and Hermann, killed in action fighting for Germany. I was livid.

My eyes filled with tears: 'My forebears have lived in Westphalia for over 200 years. We have a close connection with the land and the people. We are Germans of the Jewish faith. I'm a Jewess from Gütersloh, which has only a small Jewish community. Every one of the men between the age of eighteen and forty-five was in the war. In my family alone, four of my brothers and two of my brothers-in-law served at the front from the beginning of the war. Two of those brothers were killed in 1915, one in France, the other in Russian Poland. One brother-in-law just escaped being captured by the Russians; the other was a prisoner of war in Siberia for over two years. My oldest brother was in the army before being invalided back. My youngest brother served four years, including Verdun, and returned only at war's end. I'm talking of my immediate family only.

I can give you many such examples about friends and wider family. If you

---

[34] A very well known anti-Semitic organisation that existed before the Nazis came to power.

check you'll find that recruitment of Jewish soldiers and the percentage of Jewish casualties were both very high.'

The man replied, 'Of course there were exceptions, as in your case. Most Jews think only of making money. They were cowards during the war. They cheat and deceive us Germans.'

'That's simply not true. If they cheat and deceive, why are there so few Jews in jail? Are you implying Jewish judges are acquitting Jewish criminals? As there are so few Jewish judges, surely you're not saying non-Jewish judges are accepting bribes to keep Jews out of jail!'

More people, mainly women, had come into our compartment. The train stopped several times, but the men didn't throw out any more leaflets. One woman asserted, 'Most of the big stores are owned by Jews. One shouldn't buy there. I wouldn't.'

Noticing she had a cardboard box from Alsberg Bros of Bielefeld, I asked, 'Aren't you aware the owners of the big Alsberg store are Jewish?'

'Yes, I know. They use cheap prices to tempt us. I just can't resist.'

'Do you mean that charging lower prices and thus reducing their profit is somehow the wrong thing to do?'

The man who had been talking to me interrupted, 'I think we should stop the argument. *Ich sehe ein, ich habe es hier mit einer Dame zu tun.*' (I realise I'm dealing with a 'real lady' here.)

At every stop other people came in. The compartment was full and almost everyone joined in, but nobody spoke in my favour. The young woman who had come in with the men in the hunter-green suits kept silent. Some time later, I came across a photograph of the quiet woman on the arm of the man who had argued with me on the train. The picture identified the couple as Hermann Göring and his first wife Carin.[35] Being Swedish, she had kept out of the debate.

I had involved myself in this argument, which was difficult for an inexperienced person, and was still very agitated when I arrived home. I showed the leaflets to Salomon and Leopold, who were shocked by the slanderous libels and lies. None of us had ever seen or heard the like.

Against this anti-Semitic background one postwar scandal drew attention

---

[35] After a period as a commercial pilot in Denmark and Sweden, Göring met the Swedish Baroness Carin von Rosen, who divorced her husband in December 1922 and married Göring within a month. She died in 1931. Göring later remarried in 1935 and established a great baronial home, which he called Carinhall. There he enriched his art collection with art confiscated from Jewish victims in occupied countries.

to two Balkan Jews, Barmat and Kutisker. They had acquired from the German army and navy a number of railway vans packed with goods. Having paid a low price, they profited from a population which had already been suffering food shortages throughout the wartime blockade. When the story hit the headlines neither Barmat nor Kutisker could be found. They had probably left Europe for South America. As the saying goes: 'In a flock of sheep you'll find one that is black.' None of our non-Jewish friends and neighbours ever raised the subject of these men with us.

Without participation of non-Jewish Germans, Barmat and Kutisker could not have profiteered like that. Senior German military officials probably had their hands in it as well, but that aspect was not proven. Some newspapers, especially anti-Semitic ones, carried the story, emphasising the Jew Barmat and the Jew Kutisker. The Nazis took such situations as opportunities to spread their hateful anti-Semitic propaganda.

* * *

German citizens slowly recovered from the war. During the subsequent inflation, when the value of the German Mark fell progressively against the American dollar, one could make a fortune buying goods and storing them to sell at a later date. Many seeking even bigger profits bought on promissory notes payable after three months. But all this proved risky, for in November 1923 a new currency, the Rentenmark, was introduced: one Rentenmark replacing 1 trillion of the old Marks. While the inflation years had made life difficult for most of the population, their abrupt end ruined those who had been speculating.

Gradually life came back to normal in our town, as it did all over Germany. Extensive building activity started and with it came a big demand for household goods, clothing and food. The quality of manufactured goods improved, as materials previously dedicated to the war became plentiful. Imported goods also became available. Because we had little competition in our trade, we were not greatly affected by the dreadful years of the deflation from 1924 to 1930.

12

In March 1925 a *Purim* ball was held in Gütersloh to which Jewish families from surrounding towns were invited. Leopold and I, together with the Meinbergs and Hopes, took part in a play we had written. As I entered the dance hall, Änne Sommer (née Mendels, of Harsewinkel) from Lünen beckoned, 'Fräulein Herzberg, I'd like to introduce you to my brother and sister, and to my friends.'

I had met Änne through my sister Helene, as both lived in Lünen. Our parents had been friends years before, but had drifted apart. She introduced me to her brother Karl. When we were little girls I knew Änne's sister Ella, but had no idea she had a brother. Änne was there with her husband, Emil, and their business partners, Willi and Ella Seligman.

As the band started to play Karl asked me to dance. He was not the only young man with whom I danced, but he was very charming. I just fell for him. I noticed Mother waving to me, 'Why leave our table and sit with strangers?'

'Mother, they're not strangers; they're the Mendels from Harsewinkel. You remember them?' We moved and joined them.

That evening Leopold and Ella also met for the first time. During the summer the four of us socialised, sometimes the Mendels coming to our home or we visiting them. In January 1926 we two couples announced our engagements and on 14 February had a combined celebration in Harsewinkel.

Leopold and Ella were married on 8 August 1926. As was family tradition, a 'newspaper' was published and several table songs composed. I wrote lyrics set to a variety of popular songs.

Detail of the two young couples at their engagement.
Left: Ella and Leopold; Right: Käthe and Karl.

Group photo at the engagements of Ella and Leopold, and Käthe and Karl.

Rosenblätter

zur Vermählung von Frl. Ella Mendels mit Herrn Leopold Herzberg

Einmalige Ausgabe

Erster Jahrgang

Ohne Verantwortung der Redaktion.

Nummer 1 — Harsewinkel, den 8. August 1926 — Nächste Ausg. in 25 Jahren

Dem jungen Paare!

(Melodie: „Strömt herbei, ihr Völkerscharen")

Stimmet an, Ihr Festgenossen,
Stimmet an den Jubelklang,
Heil dem Bund, der heut' geschlossen,
Fest steh' er in Sturm und Drang.
Dieses Tages helle Sonne
Lächle hold ihm immerdar.
:: Segen blüh' ihm, Glück und Wonne!
Grüß' Dich Gott, Du junges Paar! ::

Laßt Gesanges Wogen rauschen,
Laßt sie schwellen mächtig an,
Lasset Lied um Lied uns tauschen,
Jubelnd brech' die Lust sich Bahn.
Froh dann in die Becher klingen
Aller bangen Sorgen bar.
:: Laßt aus vollem Herzen singen:
Grüß' Dich Gott, Du junges Paar! ::

Was in ernster Weihestunde,
Ihr Euch feierlich gelobt,
Euch gelobt mit Herz und Munde,
Sei in Wahrheit stets erprobt.
Was Ihr Euch habt zugeschworen,
Haltet es im Leben wahr.
:: Ewig bleibt Euch unverloren
Gott zum Gruß, Du junges Paar ::

Wandelbar ist unser Leben,
Singet ja schon der Psalmist,
Ew'gem Wechsel preisgegeben
Stets der Mensch hienieden ist.
Dunkel in der Zukunft Schoße,
Der enthüllt noch keinem war,
:: Ruhen Eures Lebens Lose —
Schütz Dich Gott, Du junges Paar! ::

Frischen Mutes froh und heiter,
Hell die Augen, rein der Sinn,
Sei Gesundheit Eu'r Begleiter,
Euer Schaffen bring' Gewinn.
Reich an Liebe, reich an Treue,
Eins im Glück, wie in Gefahr,
:: Euer Bund sich stets erneue,
Gott mit Dir, Du junges Paar! ::

Aus der Gesellschaft.

Eine Mitarbeiterin schreibt uns:

Die Hochzeit des Herrn Leopold Herzberg mit Frl. Ella Mendels macht viel von sich reden. Die Gäste entstammen den ersten Familien Deutschlands. Wir bemerkten mehrere führende Wurstfabrikanten, Großkaufleute, Pferdeexporteure sowie die imposante Gestalt eines jetzt schon berüchtigten, angehenden Lappenfabrikanten, der nach Urteil von Fachleuten einer unserer Großen werden wird. Das Gebahren des Brautvaters war von einer vornehmen Würde, und die Art, wie sein Gehrock saß, bewies, daß er gewohnt ist, dieses anspruchsvolle Kleidungsstück oft zu tragen. Die Mutter der Braut erschien in einer hocheleganten, schwarzen Robe (für unseren Geschmack allerdings etwas zu weit ausgeschnitten.) Imponierend wirkte die Mutter des Bräutigams in ihrem kniefreien Gewand nach dem neuesten Schnitt, das sie mit Würde einer Frau von Welt trug. Sehr gute Figur machte das Brautpaar. Die Braut wirkte jungfräulich-lieblich in einem schneeweißen Crepe-Georgettekleid, nur war die Schleppe entschieden zu lang. (Einige

Festteilnehmer behaupteten, feststellen zu können, daß das Kleid mindestens 5 cm zu kurz wäre). Der Bräutigam wirkte einfach fürstlich in full dress. Aparte, extravagante Toiletten trugen die diversen Verwandten. Frau Levy aus Lünen erschien in einer schwarzen Gesellschaftstoilette, die bezaubernd schön war. Aus dem Rahmen der Gesellschaft fiel noch besonders das Ehepaar Neugarten aus Rüdinghausen auf, dessen fabelhaftes Redetalent dazu beitrug, daß die Unterhaltung nicht ins Stocken geriet. Ganz entzückend nahm sich der ondulierte Kopf von Frau Paula aus Schüren aus, deren künstlerische Frisur von Herrn Dagobert, wie man hörte, entworfen war. Die Damen und Herren aus Lünen in apart-einfachen Toiletten fielen durch vornehmes, distinguiertes Gebaren auf. Der selten schöne Schnitt der Crawatte des Herrn Emil Sommer wird das Entzücken der modischen Herrenwelt für die kommende Wintersaison bilden.

Es war ein herzquickender Anblick, wie zweien der Gesellschaft das bräutliche Glück aus den Augen strahlte. Die Festteilnehmer unter 18 Jahren waren in den verschiedenen Toiletten anmutig und liebreizend anzuschauen. Der Gesellschaft wohnte

Rosenblätter, the 'Newspaper' composed for Ella and Leopold's wedding.

Leaves of Roses

Marriage of Miss Ella Herzberg to Mr Leopold Herzberg

Single edition

Year one

No editorial responsibility taken

Number 1   *Harsewinkel, 8 August 1926*   *Next edition in 25 years*

To the Young Couple

The five verses are not included in the translation

Guests attending.

From a freelancer.

There is much to report from the wedding of Mr Leopold Herzberg to Miss Ella Mendels. The guests were from the top families of Germany. We noticed several leading small goods manufacturers; big businessmen; horse-dealers, as well as the imposing figure of a notorious, prospective rag-dealer, who according to experts will become one of our Big Guys. The bearing of the father of the bride was very dignified and the fit of his frock-coat demonstrated that he wears this fastidious garment regularly. The mother of the bride wore a black gown (in our opinion too low cut). The mother of the bridegroom was most impressive in the latest 'above the knee' gown which she wore with dignity, as a woman of the world. The bridal couple cut a fine figure. The bride, of virginal charm, wore a snow white crèpe georgette dress, but everyone agreed that the train was decidedly too long. (A number of the guests maintained that the dress was at least 5 cm too short). The bridegroom bore himself regally in formal dress. Divers relatives wore select extravagant outfits. Mrs Levy from Lünen appeared in a black dinner gown bewitching and stunning. The Neugartens of Rüdinghausen stood out from the crowd; their amazing conversational talents attracted great attention and made sure that the hubbub of voices did not falter. The wavy coiffure of Mrs Paula of Schüren was positively and charmingly styled after the artistic hair-do of her husband Mr Dagobert. (Editor's note; Dagobert was totally bald!) While the ladies and gentlemen from Lünen were so simply attired, they were notable for their dignified bearing. The unusual fine cut of the bow-tie of Mr Emil Sommer will be the delight of the fashionable male world this coming winter season. *et seq. et seq.*

Translation of upper and lower sections from preceeding page 102.

Cuttings from Rosenblätter,
the 'Newspaper' composed for Ella and Leopold's wedding.

Amtliches.

In das standesamtliche Register wurde heute aufgenommen, daß die Verlobung zwischen Fräulein Ella Mendels und Herrn Leopold Herzberg aufgehoben ist, angeblich, weil sie in den Ehestand getreten sind.

Polizeiliche Verordnung.

§ 597. Das Rauchen bei Tisch ist nur den warmen Speisen gestattet.

§ 874. Sämtliche Damen sind gebeten, möglichst heitere Gesichter, die unverheirateten Herrn möglichst ernste Absichten mitzubringen.

§ 312. Sämtliche Liebeserklärungen, die nach 10 Uhr gemacht werden, sind nicht mehr ernst zu nehmen.

Die Ortspolizei.

Notification.

The registrar's office reported to-day, that the engagement of Miss Ella Mendels and Mr Leopold Herzberg has been annulled, as it seems they have entered the state of matrimony.

Police Regulation.

597. Smoking at table is permitted only while hot dishes are being served.
874. Ladies all, are requested to keep a happy smile on their countenance, and unmarried men to be of serious mien.
312. Declarations of love, proposed after 10 pm, are not to be taken seriously.

Local police

Tafel-Lied

zur

Vermählungs-Feier

von

Fräulein Ella Mendels mit Herrn Leopold Herzberg.

Mel.: Strömt herbei ihr Völkerscharen.

> Endlich ist es wahr geworden,
> Leopold geht in's Ehejoch,
> manche Maid aus West und Norden
> hoffet auf ihn heute noch.
> Keine andere als die Ella aber führt er heute heim,
> wenn auch manche hold ihn ansah
> niemals ging er auf den Leim.

Mel.: Das Wandern ist des Müllers Lust.

> Das Reisen ist der Ella Lust,
> das haben wir schon lang gewußt,
> das Reisen,
> sie reist so gern nach Elberfeld,
> doch jetzt mit Poldi in die Welt
> doch jetzt mit Poldi in die Welt
> die Ella.

In schwesterlicher Liebe gewidmet von

Käthe.

Two verses selected from the Tablesong.

Tablesong

for

The wedding

Of

Miss Ella Mendels to Mr Leopold Herzberg

Finally, it's true. No joke!
Leo's taken marriage yoke.
Many a maid from far and wide
Hoped to lure him to her side.
He takes only Ella's hand
From all the girls around the land.
Maids admire this handsome chap
Who's avoided their en-trap.

Ella's passion is to travel,
That's not hard for us t'unravel,
To travel.
To Elberfeld she loves to go,
And now with Poldi in her tow,
And now with Poldi in her tow,
Our Ella.

With love from your sister
Käthe

Our wedding was to be on 27 September 1926 but was postponed as I had severe tonsillitis, fainting during a fitting for my bridal dress. While the civil ceremony had to take place as arranged on 26 September, the ceremony in the synagogue was celebrated on 3 October. The *Schul* was crowded. The whole congregation attended, as did many of our non-Jewish friends. The *Chuppe* was followed by a beautiful reception at the Hotel Kaiserhof. My brothers and sisters had written a play, table songs and produced a special newspaper, as had been done for Ella and Leopold. We left for a wonderful honeymoon to Bavaria, the Tyrol and northern Italy, following the route Leopold and Ella had taken. Merano was the place we liked best.

Then home, via Gütersloh, to Harsewinkel, where a new life began for me. It was nice to know that I was no further than thirteen kilometres from Gütersloh, a half-hour ride in the little steam train that went four times daily in each direction. Karl was already the proud owner of a car, an old Mercedes Benz which he soon exchanged for a brand new Opel.

We were overjoyed when on 28 June 1927 our first child, a boy, was born. We named him Paulhermann, after my two brothers who had died in the war. We waited another five years before our beautiful little daughter, Erika, was born on 5 August 1932.

Masthead from: G.Z. am Mittag
(Gütersloher Zeitung, The Gütersloh News - Mid-day Edition),
'Newspaper' composed for Karl and Käthe's wedding.

Mendels house and shop in Harsewinkel, 1908.
(The two lads on left are onlookers.) (l-r): Willi and Gustav Mendels, Paula, Ella,
Leon (in maids arms), Lina Bock, Riekchen in doorway.

13

From 1926 monetary inflation developed worldwide and became extreme in Germany. Having lost the war, Germany was made to pay 132 billion Marks in reparation imposed by the Treaty of Versailles. Unemployment rose from week to week. The coalmines in the Ruhr District had been one of Germany's greatest sources of wealth, but now worked shorter hours. Many closed as there was no demand for coal. Business was going from bad to worse. The only things growing were the queues at the employment offices! People had suffered during the war as a result of the food blockade. Now they had new reason to grumble. They didn't have money for bare essentials. Many turned to communism. There were also many who listened to Hitler's Nazi Party. In 1923 Hitler and his small gang had unsuccessfully tried to start a *Putsch* against the government and been imprisoned. While in jail he wrote his infamous book, *Mein Kampf* (My Struggle). It was no best-seller and had no immediate impact. Most Jews would not have read that book.

During the years 1924 to 1927, the Nazis organised frequent meetings, even in small townships. The Social Democratic Labour Party and the communists busied themselves disrupting those gatherings. With increasing unemployment there was growing discontent in all classes of the population. Since the peace treaty had limited the previously substantial military forces, many soldiers, especially among the nobility, could not find work even if they had suitable skills. The Nazi Party attracted these men.

From 1927 onwards more and more was heard of the Nazis, whose political party was growing. First, not so much was said against Jews. Many who joined the Nazi Party didn't know about the anti-Jew program, which for a time was soft-pedalled. To increase their appeal the Nazis promised much for those in need. As conditions made unemployment worse, the Party grew larger and Hitler made promises to every faction. His speeches fascinated and hypnotised the masses until even the reasonable and tolerant citizen said, 'If he thinks he can really change things for the better, let him have a go.' In January 1933 Hitler was appointed *Reichskanzler*. As long as the old war hero Hindenburg was still *Reichspräsident*, people believed democracy was safe, not realising that the old man was no more than a senile figurehead. He was soon made irrelevant by the tactics of Hitler, Göring, Göbbels and accomplices.

On 1 April 1933 Hitler declared his boycott against the Jews. Throughout the Reich, the *Sturmabteilung* (SA, 'Brown Shirts', Storm Troopers, the party militia), were posted at the entrance of each Jewish shop and office to intimidate the general population from entering.

One of the Brown Shirts posted outside our house had once been Karl's business partner, buying and selling horses. This man had defrauded us of substantial moneys. It was common knowledge he had also cheated some of the farmers. He blustered, 'Don't go in and buy from the Jew.'

'You can't stop us. Dealing with Mendels means you're in honest hands. You ought to pay Karl what you owe him.'

Demonstrating their opposition to Hitler's decree, many of the locals came into our drapery shop, located in the front of our house. The same thing happened in Gütersloh at L & K Herzberg. Our shop and business and those of our relatives and friends were not disadvantaged by this boycott. We had retained the trust and respect of our customers, but throughout Germany many Jewish shops closed that day.

Threatening speeches over the radio by Göring or Göbbels caused us concern. Some days they were continuous so we just switched off the set.

Slowly but surely the Nazis became more and more powerful. They established the *Winterhilfe* (Winter Relief). So that no Aryan should be without fuel or food during winter, on one Sunday every month donations were collected from every household. On that day, every household was to have a one-course dinner so that the money saved could be donated to the fund. Hotels and restaurants could serve only a one-course meal. Those savings also went to the so-called *Winterhilfe*.

Hitler captured the masses with his many promises. His *Kraft durch*

Freude Kampagne (Strength Through Joy Campaign) offered the people cheap subsidised fares for vacations.

After Hindenburg's death, Hitler also became Commander in Chief of the Armed Forces. He was now Supreme Leader, in fact Dictator – empowered to make any law. Soon Nazi laws influenced every aspect of life throughout Germany.

On 15 September 1935 the Nüremberg Laws were declared, establishing two distinct categories of civil status: the *Reichsbürger* of Aryan blood and the non-Aryan *Staatsangehöriger* – subject, not citizen. Marriage across this divide became illegal. Ostensibly, this was to prevent *Rassenschande*, race defilement. Another clause stated that non-Jewish domestics under the age of forty-five could not be employed by Jews. If an actor were Jewish, or even if only one of his grandparents were Jewish, he could not get a contract. A member of the Party was installed in every factory large or small and the owner was compelled to follow the dictates of this man. Every government official had to belong to the Party and was monitored to see whether he bought from Jews. Many of them sent friends to buy goods on their behalf from Jewish shops. At the beginning of 1936 many big Jewish department stores were taken over by Aryans. Their Jewish employees then had to look for jobs elsewhere and were able to apply only at the dwindling number of Jewish firms.

We always had maids working in our house in Harsewinkel, young peasant girls who lived in. We needed help because we lived in a large three-storey house with water available in the kitchen only, and that from a hand pump. Water for the bath was heated on the kitchen stove using wood and coal, as there was no gas. As the bathroom was upstairs, hot or cold water had to be carried up in buckets.[36] The Herzberg family home in Gütersloh had gas, as well as hot and cold running water.

Besides housework, there was much else to be done. I looked after the drapery shop and, if Oma Riekchen, Karl's mother, was busy, I would chat to farmers waiting for Karl, who was often away on the road. Oma supervised the work in our fields and garden and liked to do the shopping. And, of course, Paulhermann and Erika needed care and attention.

---

[36] People throughout the whole of Europe used to bathe only once a week. In our house only the adults used the upstairs bathroom. Erica and visiting little children had their bath in a metal tub in the kitchen. The older children (including visiting nephews) bathed in a metal tub in the laundry. The laundry, toilets and stalls for a few animals were in a separate building behind the house. There were no indoor toilets.

The Nürnberg Laws, which now redefined German citizenship and set out regulations 'for the protection of German blood and German honour', should have made us realise the need to leave the country. On the other hand, our customers and friends constantly assured us of their confidence and friendship. We couldn't make up our mind to leave. We believed we had every right to stay in Germany. After all, our ancestors had settled in Germany centuries before. Two of my brothers had died on the battlefields during the war. All the men of the family under the age of forty-five had been in the army, Karl and Leopold having served in France throughout the war.

Emigration was challenge enough for the young and single but for a family of two generations – and in our case three – migrating was far more difficult. Among the great problems would be the wrench of leaving family, friends and familiar surroundings, disposing of home and business and resettling in a country with an unfamiliar culture and different language.

Most countries required affidavits or permits. It was helpful to have a friend or relative already there who could apply for permits and visas and act as guarantor. Most were without such help. An affidavit might be given by a sponsor, yet a visa be refused without explanation. There were quotas in most countries, including Australia, America and even Palestine under British Mandate. One had to be numbered on a list and wait to be called from a queue, a fact of which many were unaware. There were so many difficulties.

Hitler assumed more and more dictatorial powers. He banned all political opposition and enforced his control by systematic terror and the establishment of concentration camps. He destroyed the power of labour progressively by seizing independent trade union funds, imprisoning union leaders and thereafter forbidding all strikes. In 1933 when he came to power, six million wage earners had been out of work. Through development of the country's infrastructure, such as the Reichs-Autobahn, the freeway road system, the average Aryan man now had a job and the assurance of keeping it. Germans came to believe that Hitler would fulfil his promise and bring glorious times.

4268 - 71

Leopold Herzberg

Gütersloh
Moltkestr. 1

Zentralnachweiseamt   Gütersloh, den 15./10. 33
Eing.   16 OKT. 1933
Anl.:   Abt.   Vordr. 581 abgej.
An das   №

Zentralnachweiseamt für Kriegsverluste

Berlin - Spandau

Bei meinem Ausscheiden aus dem Heeresdienst
habe ich keinen Pass sondern nur einen Entlassungsschein erhalten. Im Jahre 1919 habe ich um Zustellung meines Passes
gebeten, erhalten habe ich jedoch nicht etwa den Original-
Pass sondern eine Zweitschrift. In dieser sind die Zeitangaben,
ferner die Angaben über Beförderungen, Auszeichnung und die
Zugehörigkeit zu den verschiedenen Truppenteilen richtig ange-
geben, es fehlen jedoch die Angaben über Führung und Strafen
und über die mitgemachten Gefechte.
        Ich bitte daher ergebenst, mir eine Beschei-
nigung über die in meinem Pass fehlenden Angaben über Führung
& Strafen und über die mitgemachten Gefechte auszustellen.
        In den Heeresdienst eingetreten bin ich
am 29./10. 14, bei der 2. Eskadron Train Ers. Abtlg. No. 18
in Darmstadt, zum Schluss des Krieges war ich bei der 2. Komp.
Feld Rekr. Dep. 21. R.D., mein Entlassungsschein ist ausge-
stellt von der 12. Komp. R.I.R. 87.

Leopold Herzberg

Request by Leopold for official documentation of his war record.
Note: application made on 15.10.1933, six months after Hitler came to power.
(Translation below)

When leaving military service I didn't receive a Military Paybook but only a Discharge Certificate. In the year 1919 I applied for consignment of my Paybook, but actually received not the original Paybook, instead a duplicate. In this document the dates of Promotions, Awards and Assignments to the various military units are correctly stated, yet the details about Deportment, Penalties and Campaigns in which I took part are missing.

I therefore respectfully request certification of the Deportment and Penalties sections missing from my Paybook and a listing of the campaigns in which I saw active service.

I entered Army service on 29. 10. 1914, with the 2nd Squadron, Army Service Corps Reserve, Division 18, in Darmstadt 21 R.D.; my Discharge Certificate is issued by the 12th Company R. I. R 87.

Bescheinigung

Der Unteroffizier

Leopold Herzberg,

geboren am 22. 9. 1891 in Gütersloh

gehörte im Weltkriege der 12.Komp.Res.Jnf.Regt.87 an und hat bei

dieser an den Stellungskämpfen in der Champagne und westl.

der Argonnen,bei Verdun und im Chapitre-Wald vom 21.8.15-

18.10.1916 teilgenommen.E.K.zweiter Kl.5.4.1917 ----------

Vorstehende Angaben stimmen mit den Eintragungen in der Kriegs-Stammrolle

Bd.1o32/874 XVIII.

und anderen amtlichen Unterlagen überein.

Gemäß Erlaß des Herrn Reichsministers des Innern vom 5. Juli 1933 (Reichsministerialblatt Nr. 26, S. 370, vom 7. Juli 1933) dient vorstehende Bescheinigung als ausreichende Unterlage zur Nachprüfung der Frontkämpfereigenschaft.

Herrn

Leopold Herzberg

in Gütersloh

Moltkestr.1.

Certificate of War Service for Leopold Herzberg.
(Translation below)

Certificate

The Non Commissioned Officer

Leopold Herzberg

Born on 22.9.1891 *in* Gütersloh

During the World War served with the 12th Comp. Res.Inf.Reg't 87 and while with this Regiment participated in the battles in the Champagne and the western Argonne, in Verdun and the Chapitre Wood from 21.8.15 – 18.10.1916. Iron Cross Second Class on 5.4.1917

The above data are in accord with entries in the War-Time Personnel Roster.

File: Bd.1o32/874 XV111.

and consistent with other official documents

Pursuant to the decree of the Minister of the Interior, 5 July 1933 (Ministerial Document26, S.370. 7 July 1933) the foregoing certificate serves as definitive documentary proof of first class active service in the Front Line.

Signed and sealed

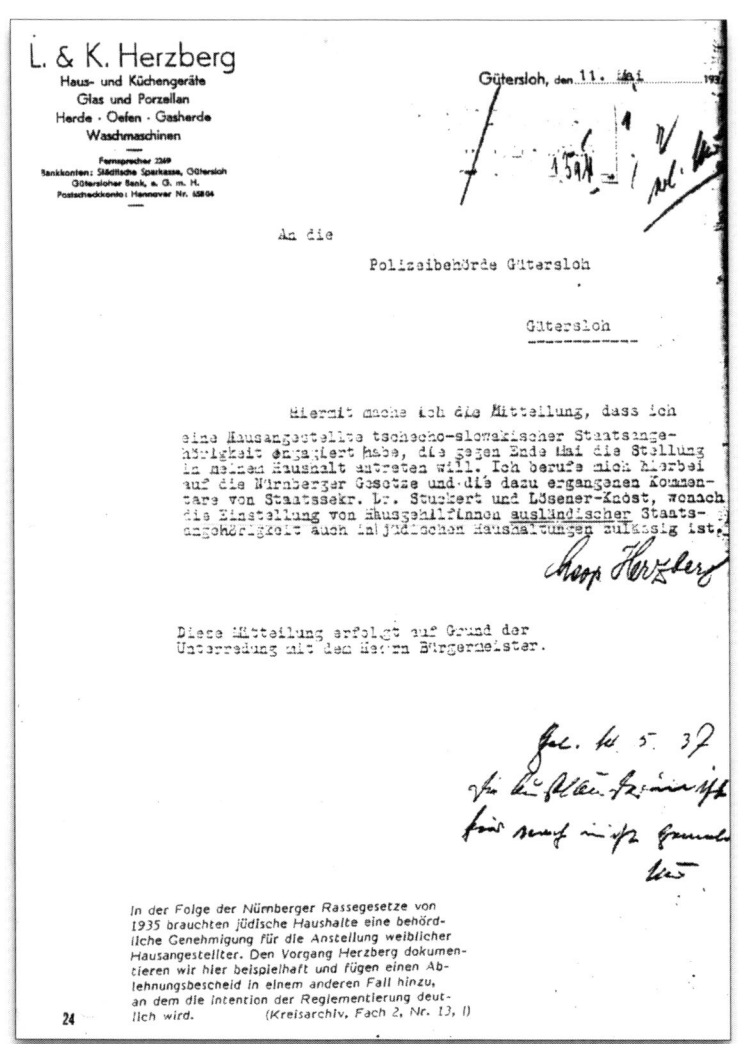

Application for employment of a maid, by Leopold Herzberg.
(Translation below)

To the
Police Department
Gütersloh

Herewith I want to inform you that I have employed a maid of Czechoslovak nationality who will commence employment towards the end of May. I make reference hereby to the Nürnberg Laws and the relevant comments of Secretary of State, Drs. Stuckert and Lösener-Knost whereby the employment of home help of foreign nationality is allowed also in Jewish homes.

Leopold Herzberg

This communication follows from the discussion with His Honour the Mayor.

Tthe Nürnberg Racial Laws of 1935, require Jewish households to obtain official permission for the employment of female household help. We document here the Herzberg example and enclose a rejected application of another case in which the intention of the ruling is clear.

(District Archive Section 2, No13, 1)

Our family wanted to be together in Harsewinkel on 22 May 1936 to celebrate the seventy-fifth birthday of my mother-in-law, Oma Riekchen. We waited in vain for Karl's younger brother Ludwig, at that time an employee of a large Jewish firm in Berlin. A few days later he notified us that he would be delayed for a few weeks as the store where he was working had been 'burgled'. The fact was he had lost his job, the firm having been taken over by an Aryan businessman.

Ludwig came to Harsewinkel as promised. He told us he had decided to emigrate. This news was a bombshell, especially to Oma, his elderly mother. Where would he go? Only enthusiastic Zionists thought of going to Palestine, where the climate was difficult for Europeans; a neglected barren land, much as it had been at the time of the Crusades!

My wealthy uncle Ben Levisohn of New York, Mother's brother, had already given affidavits to two of my cousins and my niece Paula Levy.[37] I was going to write to Uncle Ben about Ludwig when I found a new travel book about Australia, titled *Der Unbekannte Continent* (The Unknown Continent), which I drew to Ludwig's attention. At about the same time, Ludwig happened to meet Cousin Alfred Bock's well-to-do father-in-law, Jack Sander, who had recently been to Australia. He painted an attractive picture of the country: the temperate climate of Sydney, the people casual and friendly, the advantages of a young country with many opportunities.

In August 1936 Ludwig and his Berlin friend Hans Weissbrehm (Hans Whitman) left for Sydney, knowing not a soul there. They had to obtain travel permits and buy return tickets, hoping to sell the return sectors of their tickets after arriving in Sydney. It was hard for us, particularly for Oma, to farewell Ludwig, her youngest child. It seemed unreal when he said to me,

'I think it won't be long before you'll follow.'

'No, we can't just leave. We've Oma and the children to consider. How would we be able to make a living there for a family? We don't know the language or the customs.'

'I believe you'll send your children over soon. There's no future for them here.'

I took several deep breaths and prayed that I would never have to part from my children.

---

[37] My sister Helene's younger daughter. At various separate times in the second half of the 1930s, Helene, Emil and their three children, Inge, Paula and Hans, migrated to the United States. There they changed the family name to Lind. Helene became Helen and Hans became John.

Ludwig wrote he'd had a pleasant trip, made friends on the boat and was improving his English. The Jewish community of Sydney had been helpful to him on his arrival. He had found a job as salesman with the large department store Grace Bros, on Broadway, and was earning the basic wage. After a few months he changed jobs, receiving a higher salary. He wrote contented letters and told us that he was no longer Ludwig but Leon.

Mendels Family.
Back row (l-r): Karl, David, Ludwig.
Front row (l-r): Ella, Änne, Riekchen, Paula.

14

In our little township of Harsewinkel lived a man called Herbrink. He, and especially his wife, had always been good friends of the Mendels family, so it was surprising that he was one of the first in the locality to become a member of the Nazi Party. One day during a Party meeting Herbrink opposed the branch leader on several issues. We found out later that it was mainly in relation to the anti-Jew program. The branch leader, actually his brother-in-law, reported him to the hierarchy. Herbrink was thrown out of the Party, arrested and taken to Papenburg concentration camp. Nobody ever learned what was done to him there. There were rumours that many of the inmates of the camp had died in the surrounding swamps or were shot while escaping, an impossibility as the camp was surrounded by electrified barbed wire. After nine months, Herbrink came back. He looked old and thin and spoke hardly a word. Now he would have to be more careful than ever. None of the Herbrinks ever spoke to us or acknowledged us again. To them, as to many others, we were now just 'thin air'.

The betrayal that caused us greater hurt was the breaking of friendship by Frau Hedwig Blanke-Brommelmeier!

When I came to live in Harsewinkel she was Fräulein Blanke and had been in the Mendels house for about thirteen years. Not only was she an excellent dressmaker, making dresses for our customers from our materials, but also doing alterations on ready-made clothes that we sold. She was familiar with all aspects of the shop, knew many of our customers and how to deal with them. As she lived in, she understood the family, knew about *Kaschrus*, Jewish customs and Jewish holidays. Fräulein Blanke was really part of the household. My parents-in-law, David[38] and Riekchen Mendels, thought very highly of her and gave her substantial presents for Christmas and birthdays. After she had been with them for ten years they gave her a diamond ring.

At first it had been difficult for me to get on well with her, but after a while we became good friends. She was very fond of Paulhermann and would look after him any time, often spoiling him with sweets. The child also liked her and called her 'Hetta'.

In 1931, when Blanke was in her late thirties, she met and married a widower named Brommelmeier, who had been a long-time friend of Karl's sister Paula and her husband, Dagobert Schöneberg, in Schüren-Dortmund. When Brommelmeier was out of work during the difficult economic times, we found him a job in Gütersloh. Later, through Karl, he came to an even better job in Harsewinkel, at Claas & Co., manufacturers of agricultural machinery. The Brommelmeiers moved to Harsewinkel and Blanke again worked for us a few hours a day.

It was not long before she tried to take over management of the shop. At the beginning of 1933 when Hitler first came to power, she was already suggesting we sell the business to her on the grounds that people would no longer buy from Jews. As she didn't have the money, this was a 'bit rich'.

One day when both Brommelmeiers were sick I took a fine meal over to them. I was taken aback by the sign on the front door:

Grüss Gott, tritt ein, es muss nur nicht ein Jude sein.

(G-d bless, and enter too, so long as you are not a Jew.)

Silly me, I left the food for them. As I was about to leave, that beast of a Nazi, Brommelmeier, said disdainfully, 'Oh, don't forget to bring us more of your wonderful food.'

I was stunned and speechless. I rushed home to tell Oma and Karl what had just happened. We couldn't believe that our Hedwig Blanke, treated almost as one of the family for so many years, could have turned against us. In 1937 we learned that her husband had secured a top job in the Nazi Party, as a manager in *Winterhilfe*.

---

[38] David Mendels was a cattle and horse dealer. He died in 1929. The shop was run by the women of the house.

'Family train' (l-r): Annelore (sister of Kurt and Werner), Clara, Käthe, Bertha, Hedwig Blanke (Brommelmeier), Werner, Leopold, Kurt, Ludwig.

* * *

After the Treaty of Versailles in 1918, Germany was allowed no more than 100,000 men in its armed forces. The general population did not know that Hitler had trebled the size of the army and had secretly ordered the manufacture of arms, battleships, submarines and aeroplanes. Even though under the Versailles Treaty the region was demilitarised, in March 1936 German forces re-entered the Rhineland, the area between the Rhine River and the French border. This challenge elicited no protest from France or Britain. Hitler was on his way. Many Germans previously antagonistic now said, 'He gets things done.' Recruiting accelerated for the *Sturmabteilung* (*SA*), the Storm Troopers or Brown Shirts, and for the *Schutzstaffel* (*SS*) and for the Gestapo, Hitler's elite security service, prominent in their black uniforms with (of all symbols) skull and crossbones on their caps.

Getting a job went something like this: 'You want a job? If you join the Party, the answer is yes. But your wife will have to join the Nazi *Frauenschaft*, the Women's Organisation; your son has to join the Nazi *Hitlerjugend*, the Hitler Youth; your daughter, the Nazi BDN, *Bund Deutscher Mädchen*, the League of German Girls. People came to us apologising that 'Circumstances force us to join the party and wear the swastika. Underneath, we're still the same. We're like an underdone steak: brown on the outside (the colour of the SA uniform), red on the inside (the colour of Democratic Labour).'

We felt firmly rooted in Germany, part of the German people. Many Germans led us to believe that we still belonged. This blinded us to what was happening around us. Hitler once stated he wouldn't harm anyone so long as they didn't oppose him. Many Jews thought this included them and they could stay on in their familiar surroundings, even if in reduced circumstances.

One day a commercial traveller said to Leopold,

'A man like you has to join the Nazi Party.'

'I don't want to join the Party.'

'But why? You told me you're a war veteran whose brothers gave their lives for the Fatherland. You're one of us.'

'The Party's anti-Jew policy has sawn off the branch on which I perched,' was Leopold's pointed reply.

Life for the Jews of Germany was becoming ever more difficult. During 1937 we heard of more people emigrating. An early case in point was the discrimination against Jewish professionals from April 1933. Denied the right to draw payments from the *Krankenkasse*, the government medical fund, Jewish doctors were finding it hard to maintain their practices. Membership of the *Krankenkasse* was compulsory for every employee of government, large firm or small business, even the maid in a household. Each member contributed a small amount out of their wages, the employer a larger amount. Doctors and chemists were paid directly by the fund without additional charges to patients for treatment or medicines. As Jewish doctors lost work, migration became a more attractive option, even though they would have to repeat some years of training and pass examinations to requalify in their destination country.

For lawyers it was even more difficult. As law differs from country to country, immigrant lawyers would be required to complete a full law course or turn their skills to some other vocation.

Unpleasant incidents multiplied throughout Germany. If Jews went to a café or hotel it was not unusual for the waiter to hand them a card: 'Leave this place! Jews are not wanted here.'

Once people joined the Nazi Party, they were afraid to be seen going into Jewish shops, hence these shops lost substantial business. We began to notice this to some extent in our drapery shop. On the other hand, our cattle-dealing business was doing better than ever. The party then threatened that farmers continuing to deal with Jews would not get fertiliser or imported fodder such as soy beans, which owners of small farms needed to fatten their pigs. Large farms in Harsewinkel and surrounding villages didn't need imported fodder and fertiliser. Anyway, most were not pro-Nazi. We kept their custom.

By the end of 1937 the world economy had not yet recovered from the Great Depression and in many countries unemployment was still high, making immigrants unwelcome. While the German economy was being boosted by Hitler's expenditure on armaments and autobahns, the Nazis made business and trading harder for Jews day by day. When we sent fat cattle to the markets, the non-Jewish butchers would not buy from us. Then the Nazi authorities took control of marketing, limiting the number and quality of animals Jewish butchers could buy.

15

These pressures finally convinced us that we would have to leave Germany in the near future. Our first thought was to migrate to Holland. Karl and my brother Leopold went there for a few days' vacation[39] and were enthusiastic about the country, but realised it was not far enough away from Nazi Germany. Jews who migrated to the Netherlands, thinking they had escaped the Nazis, were later caught during the German occupation and sent to the ghettos, concentration camps and gas chambers. As it turned out, this applied to any European country. Most countries wanted financial and security guarantees for new migrants. Switzerland took an anti-immigrant initiative, approaching Germany with the demand that German Jews be identified by having the letter 'J' displayed in their German passports.

We submitted applications for migration to both the United States and Australia. On reaching the first Australian port one had to show £200 'landing money' per family. Jewish emigrants were allowed to take only 10 Marks per person out of Germany. Therefore it was necessary to get money out of the country. Sending money out by couriers was dangerous and cost a substantial percentage. There was also the risk of a total loss, which we eventually experienced. When we sent out the final package, our courier claimed he'd had a car accident, been assaulted and lost all the money. We didn't believe his story but couldn't disprove it and couldn't complain to any authority.[40] At that

---

[39] Most probably, the purpose for this journey was to set up a means of transferring money out of Germany, for the future. (See appendix 3)

[40] The Mendels and Herzbergs succeeded in transferring money to Holland. The above incident refers only to the final transfer. The Schönebergs also transferred some money out successfully, but after the war their son Lutz was able to retrieve only a few Marks.

time the Nazis weren't in a position to punish a Dutchman who was a courier. A German Jew caught smuggling money would be shot instantly.

In early 1938 we set in motion arrangements to leave Germany. Together with the Herzbergs, we wrote to Karl's brother, Leon, in Sydney, to seek nine permits for Karl, myself and our two children, Erika and Paulhermann, as well as Leopold, Ella and their two children, Walter and Ursula, and Oma Bertha Herzberg. Feeling confident we could get permits for the United States with help from relatives there, we put our names on the American quota list also. Oma Riekchen feared the long sea voyage. She wanted to go to Holland, stay with her sister Jenny Bock or go into an old age home there, but, as it turned out later, none could be found that could take her.

We regretted that our sister-in-law Clara, whose husband, Salomon, had died in 1931, didn't want to come with us to Australia. She had applied for a permit to Palestine, where her eldest son, Kurt, now known as Jehuda Barlev, and wife, Liesel, already lived. Palestine, mandated to Britain by the League of Nations in light of the Balfour Declaration's support of a Jewish national home, also had a restrictive quota. Once her younger son, Werner, had reached New York, Clara also put her name down for the United States.

Karl's sister Paula and husband, Dagobert Schöneberg, with son, Lutz, procrastinated but finally agreed to migrate to Australia, provided we also arranged permits for Dagobert's sister and family, the Ahrenbergs of Dortmund; six permits instead of three. We encouraged them to begin making arrangements to leave and undertook to write to Leon asking him to apply for the additional permits.

We believed that if Oma Riekchen later changed her mind we would be granted a permit for her as a parent and she would be able to travel with the Schönebergs. Now Ella Weinberg, Oma Riekchen's youngest sister, her husband, Gustav, and their twenty-seven year old son, Walter[41] decided they also wanted permits. We tried to help them as well, but sadly those latter applications did not succeed.

Our nephew Ralph Sommer, son of the late Änne and Emil, and orphaned at the age of nine, had been in the Jewish orphanage in Paderborn for four years.[42] Shortly

---

[41] Walter Weinberg lived underground in Holland, posing as a Christian during the war. He was an excellent soccer player and played for one of Holland's best teams during that time! He later migrated to Montevideo, Uruguay.

[42] Ralph's parents, together with their business partners, ran a high-fashion dress shop. His mother, Änne, always wore the latest fashions. She often wore slacks and was a heavy cigarette smoker, both practices daring at the time, for a woman. When Paulhermann, as a little four-year-old, saw her, he wanted to know 'ob die Frau ein Mann war' (if the woman was a man). Ralph's mother, Änne, died of consumption, or possibly lung cancer, due to

after his *Barmizwo* in August 1937 he sailed for Australia to join his uncle Leon.

As things eventuated, we felt it was a pity that other youngsters in the family, namely Lutz Schöneberg, as well as Ilse and Rolf Neugarten (children of my sister Rosa and husband Louis), didn't follow Ralph's example. Lutz was an only child, his parents having lost Fritz and Dieter, twins born in 1930 who lived for a few months only. Understandably, the parents did not want to be separated from him. The Neugartens faced a similar problem. Married for thirteen years before their first child, Ilse, was born, they couldn't bear to have their children leave Germany on their own. Their late application as a family for American visas was not successful. Had those young people reached Australia early, they well might have been granted permits for their parents. Rolf eventually reached London with the *Kindertransport*, the Children's Transport.[43] Ilse[44] followed later, working as a live-in maid during the war. Both sets of parents, as well as Lutz, were left behind, trapped in Germany.

Jews could employ Aryan women under the age of forty-five as maids,

---

her heavy smoking. Diagnosis at that time was not as accurate as today. His father, Emil, committed suicide three months after her death.

[43] On 15 November 1938 eminent British Jews met Prime Minister Chamberlain seeking temporary admission of children and teenagers, who after vocational training might migrate on. The Jewish community promised guarantees. They specifically mentioned teenagers in concentration camps and asked that some be allowed to go to Palestine. This was discussed in Cabinet the next day and it was subsequently decided that Britain could accept unaccompanied children under the age of seventeen.

On 21 November the Home Secretary met a large delegation of Jewish and non-Jewish bodies, including Quakers and Inter Aid. These now combined as The Movement for the Care of Children from Germany. To speed up the process, travel documents were issued for group lists rather than individuals. The refugee agencies offered funding. For every child, there would be a £50 guarantee (in the year 2002, equivalent to US$5000), for the subsequent emigration. On 25 November, Viscount Samuels appealed on the BBC for foster homes, and received 500 offers. There was no insistence that these should be only Jewish homes. The homes were judged on their cleanliness and seeming respectability. Within a short time, representatives were sent to Germany and Austria to interview children and organise transport. Volunteers worked to list the most imperilled: teenagers in concentration camps or in danger of arrest; Polish children or teenagers threatened with deportation; those whose parents were too impoverished; and whose parents were in concentration camps. Parents who believed their chances of emigrating were very slim approached the organisation to take their children. About seventy volunteers in Bloomsbury House, London, processed several hundred applications a week. Once they were listed, parents were given travel dates. For those children and parents, the last hours together were unimaginably stressful. On 1 December 1938, the first *Kindertransport* left by train from Berlin, and the first from Vienna nine days later, passing through Germany to the Hook of Holland and then by ferry to England. About 10,000 infants and teenagers were saved.

[44] Ilse got to London with one of the last *Kindertransport*s to leave Germany.

provided they were foreigners. The coal mines of Hamm, a nearby town, had many Czech workers and we had employed girls from the miners' families. At the end of October 1938, just before *Kristallnacht*, our current maid got a letter from her mother: 'Would Herr Mendels please come to Hamm.' She said she had something important to tell him. Perhaps the woman meant well and wanted to warn us about something, but since two of the girl's brothers, though foreigners,[45] had become Storm Troopers, we feared a trap. Karl did not go to Hamm! A few days later, the girl received another letter, burst into tears and left immediately.

* * *

In October 1938, our six-year-old daughter, Erika, came down with scarlet fever, an infectious disease that can be serious. I first kept her home but with my many responsibilities, including shop and household duties, it proved impossible for me to give her the care and attention she needed. She had to be isolated and stay in bed. All the bedrooms were upstairs. After a few days she was admitted to the small local hospital. Erika happily settled into a ward shared with a mother and her little son, both with scarlet fever. Suddenly our doctor, Dr Heinrich Pieke, no Nazi, asked us to take Erika home as the other two patients had left and we were told it wasn't efficient for the Sisters to nurse just one patient in quarantine. The doctor had obviously been intimidated by the local Nazis. When she was discharged her skin was still peeling and we understood she was still infectious, so kept Paul away from her. I will always remember the date: Monday 7 November 1938.

On Tuesday 8 November 1938, the newspaper reported that an official at the German Embassy in Paris, Ernst vom Rath, had been shot by a young Polish Jew, Herschel Grynszpan.[46] We had no doubt that Hitler would use this event to increase restrictions on the Jews.

On that very day Paulhermann went by train to Gütersloh around mid-day for Hebrew lessons, as he did every Tuesday. He wasn't home by the usual time of seven o'clock. We were greatly worried, especially Oma. I phoned Gütersloh. The Herzbergs told me that our young man, who was very fond of

---

[45] It is likely that for foreigners to be admitted to the SA, they would have been ethnic Sudeten-Germans from northwest Czechoslovakia.

[46] The shooting took place on 6 November and Vom Rath died in the afternoon of 9 November. Within hours of his death, throughout the Nazi-controlled areas of Germany and Austria, the *Kristallnacht* pogrom was unleashed.

his cousin Walter, wanted to stay a little longer, but would be on the next train home. I went to the station just as the train pulled in. A very upset Paulhermann ran into my arms. 'Oh Mum,' he sobbed, 'there were lots of men in uniform getting on the train in Gütersloh, but in my compartment were only Hetta (Hedwig Blanke-Brommelmeier) and me. She didn't speak. Just stared at me.' The eleven-year-old just couldn't believe that someone who'd been so fond of him could have changed so. Once home, I helped him to bed and stayed with him a while, to calm him.

Two days later, on Thursday 10 November, we were up early. Karl had promised to take Farmer Wessel to the market in Soest, two hours away by car, to help him buy a draft horse to work his fields. Wessel came to our place at seven. When the two men left I went on with my housework, made breakfast for Oma and the children and sent Paulhermann off to school. Once Oma was dressed I went to the post office as usual to get our mail. The woman behind the counter greeted me in an unusual way, rather sadly I thought. On my short way home, I was thinking about her. The phone was ringing as I walked in and I ran to answer it. To my great surprise I heard the distressed voice of my niece, Ilse Neugarten. Between sobs she asked,

'Is Uncle Karl at home? Can he come straight away to our place?'

'No. What's happened? Have you rung Uncle Leopold?'

'Something terrible has happened. Our shop has been turned upside down. Kerosene and paint have been splashed on dress materials and many other things are damaged. Father has fled and I can't reach Uncle Leopold. No one is answering their phone.'

I was stunned. 'I'm sorry I don't know what I can do to help. Karl may not be home before evening. But do you know whether the same has happened in Gütersloh?

'Could be, but I don't really know.'

That phone call frightened me. I couldn't think of anything else. I didn't want to upset Oma, who had been very edgy lately. I went upstairs to get Erika dressed and then brought her down to the lounge room where Oma could look after her. It occurred to me that if the Nazis were taking action against Jews, they might cut our phone line or listen in on our conversations. So I decided to go to our good friend and neighbour, Bernhard Brinkmann. He had a grocery and gift store and was for many years in the same bowling club as Karl. I asked to use his phone.

As I couldn't reach the Herzbergs, I rang their neighbour Osthus, but it was his young nephew who came on the line. When I asked about the previous night he said, 'Well, the synagogue, the adjoining school building and several Jewish homes are burning. Your brother's shop was ransacked. They smashed the shop windows with rubber truncheons. There are truckloads of broken china, crystal and porcelain on the street. They didn't spare Mrs Clara Herzberg's home either. They smashed the furniture, even levering a heating stove off the wall while it was burning, tossing it on the carpet in the living room. Nothing happened to the house where your mother and brother Leopold and family live. And I don't know why not,' he said arrogantly.

'What's happened to my brother Leopold?'

'The SA gave him a hiding then put him against a wall. I don't know whether they shot him. Perhaps he was only arrested like all the other Jewish men.'

The receiver fell out of my hand. I had to steady myself. I nearly fainted. How could I find out what had really happened? I took a few deep breaths, calmed myself and went to speak to Mr Brinkmann. I related what I had just been told, then asked, 'Would you drive me to the outskirts of Gütersloh, to see if I can help my family?'

'No!' said our presumed friend. 'I certainly will not. Just get out. Don't ever come back!'

I couldn't keep all this to myself. I had to share some of it with Oma.

I now decided to ask for help from our other neighbours, Heinrich and Gertrud (née Feldhaus) Austermann, usually and quaintly called Feldhaus, for they lived in the old Feldhaus family home. They were about our age, good-hearted, unpretentious country folk who had a bakery. Tonius, their eldest son, was very fond of Paulhermann and the two boys were almost inseparable. Heinrich's spinster sister, Liesbeth, lived with them. When I told them what had occurred they immediately showed their concern. Gertrud's young sister, Katherine, who happened to be visiting said, 'Don't worry, Käthe. I've got my motorbike here. Liesbeth and I will ride to Gütersloh to see what's happened and what can be done to help.'

Heinrich, who started in his bakery in the early morning hours, always rested during the day and was sleeping at the time. He was a harmless fellow who liked his drink. Gertrud said, 'I'm glad Heinrich's asleep. He's fond of all of you. He hates the Nazis. If he knew what's going on he'd do something rash and that wouldn't help. So I put a bottle of brandy next to his bed. He'll stay asleep for quite a while.'

Knowing that there was still one family whose friendship we could rely on, I felt a little calmer and quickly went home. I hadn't been there long when the front door opened. A stranger entered. 'Could I speak to Mr Mendels?' he asked, handing me his card which read: Inspector ... (I don't recall his name.), Taxation Department, Warendorf. I was shocked when he insisted on seeing our business books even though I told him my husband wasn't home. Was he looking for a pretext to arrest Karl?

I showed him into our office, gave him all the books connected with the drapery store and said, 'Sorry, the books of the cattle business are kept by my husband. I believe he took them to our accountant.'

'Mrs Mendels, your books are in order. I want you to trust me. If your husband is really not home, can you get in touch with him and warn him? He needs to go into hiding. In Warendorf this morning, I saw the Nazis ill-treat and beat up all the Jewish men before arresting them. Some Jewish homes were burned. In others furniture was severely damaged. Heavy pianos were thrown onto the streets and shops were smashed.'

'My husband drove to the Soest market this morning. I don't know when he plans to be back or how I could contact him.'

I thanked the man for his advice as I showed him out. My head was spinning. I was trembling.

I went into the lounge to see Erika and Oma. A moment later, Liesbeth Feldhaus came in, having just returned from Gütersloh. She told me that the reports I had heard were true. My mother, my two sisters-in-law and the two children were safe. She had seen them but couldn't speak to them. Leopold had not been shot but had been arrested, together with all the Jewish men in the town.

I thanked Liesbeth for her help. Without saying a word, she took silver and crystal from the sideboard and china cabinet and carried the items to her home in her apron. She came back a second and a third time until she had everything of value. At first I thought she might be robbing us, but soon realised she was taking the items to keep them safe for us. In Gütersloh she had seen what happened to Jewish property.

Our phone rang. Miss Steinfeld from Versmold, a small town nearby, asked for Karl. 'Please, can your husband come over to help us? Our house and furniture have been smashed and every window shattered. I am so frightened.' Karl had previously given advice not only to her, but also to her sister and her widowed mother. Knowing they were already under stress before this latest episode, I was sorry I could do nothing for her. When Miss Steinfeld heard that Karl was not home, she burst out crying. Her diabetic brother, a cattle dealer, had been arrested by the Nazis some time earlier and was still in prison, falsely accused by Aryan competitors of having starved cattle. Actually the animals had foot-and-mouth disease.

It was now after one o'clock and Paulhermann came home from school. We told him Uncle Leopold had been mistreated and arrested, that similar events had occurred in other towns and might happen here in Harsewinkel. He began to cry. He calmed down when I said, 'I really need your help as Daddy isn't home.'

Our phone rang again. Thank goodness, it was Karl.

'I'm in Gütersloh. Is everyone alright?'

'We're managing. I've heard what happened. Where's Leopold now and how's the rest of the family? Ilse rang early this morning; she wanted your help. I found out from her about the dreadful things that happened in Rüdinghausen. She also tried to phone the Herzbergs but couldn't get through.'

'Leopold, together with the other men of the community, is still held at the police station.'

'I've been warned that it isn't safe for you to come home.'

'For the moment I have to stay here anyway. I have to nail boards over the broken windows of the two shops and Clara's home. There's plenty for me to do here. Thank G-d Leopold and Ella's home was not damaged. Clara is staying with Ella, her two children and your mother.'

'Just don't come home till I let you know it's safe.'

Oma and little Erika were kept busy being hospitable to Salli Lorch, who visited us in the early afternoon. A widower in his sixties, he was the only other Jew living in Harsewinkel, his two married daughters living in other towns. Since the death of his wife he often came on weekends, joining us for meals.

Liesbeth Feldhaus dropped in to tell us what she had just heard: 'The Nazis who are attacking Jews, damaging and destroying property are always from out of town. Their leader is always a local, so he can point out the Jewish homes and synagogues. They were going to set fire to your house yesterday but August Claas protested. He told them he's buying your properties. The Herzbergs' houses in Gütersloh were also to have been burned, but apparently Mrs Frederich told the SA her husband had bought the Herzbergs' properties.

Käthe, you'll have to expect they'll do something here. They'll probably smash windows. I've told them that you have allowed us to use your stable for our sow and piglets, because our sty is too small and if they burn down your place it will be our pigs they are killing.'

I didn't tell any of this to Oma. Paulhermann suddenly remembered that four of our cows were still in our paddock. He was to have brought them home, as the November nights were too cold for cattle to be left outside. He went by bicycle to the paddock and as usual rode behind them shepherding them home. They were docile and knew the way.

He had just left when I heard our front door pushed open and a man say in a loud and commanding voice, 'Open the other half of the door Mrs Mendels!'

I ran down the hallway.

'You'd better do that yourself. I'm not tall enough to reach the bolt. What do you want?'

'Where's your husband?'

'He's not home. You can't touch this house. It's been sold to the directors of Claas Brothers. Any damage you might do will be done to them. You can use the telephone in our office[47] and confirm this at Claas.'

'I wouldn't use a Jew's telephone. Show me the contract.'

As I was getting the contract I heard the noise of smashing glass at the front of the house. How fortunate that I had closed the wooden shutters, which were on the inside of the lounge room where Oma and Erika were sitting. Mr Lorch panicked and ran home.

The official was convinced when he saw the contract, but thank goodness didn't realise that it had not yet been signed. I then heard the noise of stones crashing into our shop and upstairs windows. Several Nazis entered our house wanting to smash the furniture. 'Stop!' I shouted. 'This furniture doesn't belong to us anymore; it's been sold.'

Outside there was terrific noise. Men and women were shouting, some wanting to loot the shop, but they were held back. Amidst all this, I suddenly heard the frightened bellowing of the cows Paulhermann was bringing home, the noise of the crowd causing the animals to panic and run towards the gates of our yard. Unfortunately, these were locked. Some kind friends opened them

---

47   The 'office' contained a writing desk, a safe and the telephone; as well as a couch, a table and the only radio in the house. It was used as an office on weekends when farmers came on business and where they would enjoy a drink. For the rest of the time it was for family use.

and helped Paulhermann bring the animals into our stable. He was still shaking when he came running, to stand with me.

Suddenly a woman shouted out, 'You must stop! It's just been announced that the *Aktion* is over. Stop immediately!' It was Gertrud Feldhaus, our friendly neighbour, her two brothers by her side to protect her.

We heard angry voices, 'Grab that woman! She's worse than a Jew!'

'Nobody touches her or we'll do something worse to you,' said others, who then overturned the truck in which the Storm Troopers had come to Harsewinkel.

Police Sergeant Arnold arrived. He too had heard the official command on the radio that the *Aktion* should cease. He immediately told the Nazis to stop. In reality, as a civil policeman he was now actually powerless against them. As a true friend he was trying to help. He told me to let down the iron shutters that covered the shop windows to prevent looting by the wild mob. We found we couldn't get into the shop, the Nazi leader having confiscated the key.

By now it was seven and a dark November evening. There was a lot of glass and rubbish in front of our house. Police Sergeant Arnold asked me to clear it immediately, without calling on anyone other than family to help. Paulhermann and I took the big wire baskets used to gather potatoes at harvest time, as they were easy to handle. Again and again we filled them with the stones and the broken glass. While we were working I felt a light touch on my shoulder. It was Clara, who had come from Gütersloh. She whispered, 'Karl drove me over. He's on the outskirts of Harsewinkel, hiding with his car behind some trees. We just had to see for ourselves that you're alright.'

With Clara's help, we quickly cleared the footpath. As we were going into the house via the back door I saw our cleaning lady digging in our garden. We were still able to employ her as she was over the age of forty-five. I called out to her, 'Frau Buchmann, what are you doing here so late at night? Please come inside.'

She came in sobbing, 'The Nazis wanted to burn down your house, so I wanted to be nearby and save little Erika. It's all so dreadful!' I calmed her and told her that the *Aktion* was finished and we would now be safe. She left for home greatly relieved.

Oma had set the table in our living room-cum-office. She had prepared the evening meal of bread, meat and delicious *Wurst*, which we had recently made. Despite the tensions it was important for us to eat. During the meal we told Clara about all that had occurred. I asked her to assure Karl and the family in

Gütersloh that we were alright, but most importantly, that it was unsafe for him to come home.

Clara then told us about events in Gütersloh:

At about three this morning, Leopold and Ella were wakened by the night watchman they'd employed. He told them the shop windows had been smeared with the word *JUDE*, painted in large red letters.

They threw gowns over their nightwear and raced downstairs from their first-floor apartment. It was hard work to get the sticky paint off and they had not quite finished when Storm Troopers arrived, shouting, 'Hey, just look at these Jews!' Using their truncheons they smashed the shop windows as well as everything inside, all the precious china and crystal. They then threw stones into all the upstairs windows, including our bedrooms, missing Walter's head by inches.[48]

Storm Troopers came into my bedroom, led by a young man whose parents had for years been customers and enjoyed many favours in my butcher shop. He told me to get dressed and get out quickly, or else they would let me burn with the house. I refused to change in front of them. Once they had left, Walter and I quickly dressed. As we ran out of the house I saw that my sideboard was knocked over and smashed. The noise of glass and furniture being shattered was ringing in my ears as the two of us ran to Leopold and Ella's house.

Suddenly everything came to a halt. Mrs Frederich came and shouted at the top of her voice, 'All the Herzberg properties now belong to us. Don't set fire to them!'

This infuriated the Nazis. Prevented from torching the houses, they turned to search Leopold's home, saying, 'The Jew must have money and probably weapons.' They searched every corner and cupboard. They confiscated Paul's elegant blue military dress coat. (He had worn it as *Einjährig Freiwilliger,* a one-year volunteer, before the war. Mother had kept the coat in his memory.)

Leopold was arrested, still in pyjamas and thin dressing gown. As he was taken from the house, Mother cried out, 'I sacrificed two sons in the war. Why take this son from me also?'

---

[48] Since her son Werner had left for the USA, ten-year-old Walter had been sleeping at Clara's place so she would not be in the house alone.

Ella could not utter a word.

Later Ella packed a case with a suit, coat, hat and toiletries and took it to the police station. She was assured Leopold would be given his things.

Some time earlier in the evening, we had seen the SS giving Leopold a terrific hiding, then standing him up against the wall as though to shoot him.

The synagogue, the adjoining school building, the houses of the Löwenbachs, Daltrops, Meinbergs and Gartys have gone up in flames. All the men under the age of sixty have been arrested. Mrs Bernard Daltrop took some pyjamas out of the burning house for her sick husband, who was also arrested, but the Nazis tore the parcel out of her hands and threw it back into the flames. Old Ernst Löwenbach went to save his pet dog from the fire and nearly died in it himself. All who now have no home went to the Steinberg's, which was not burned because of Aryan tenants.

'I must hurry back now; Karl is waiting for me,' Clara said. We all kissed her, thanked her for coming and asked her to ring us as soon as she knew what had happened to the Neugartens in Rüdinghausen.

* * *

During the night it occurred to me that I should take all the valuables out of the house. As we had been planning to emigrate we had put a lot of our good things into the storeroom. I now packed some into a case, went through our yard to the hedge which separated our garden from Feldhaus's and was surprised to find Gertrud already waiting on the other side. I told her I would bring other items for her to store.

In Oma's living room was a gun that had belonged to my late father-in-law. In my time in Harsewinkel nobody had ever used it. There were also some rifles, which were used during the town's annual shooting festival. I was glad to get rid of them. If the Nazis found we had guns we would surely be punished.

Every time I crossed the yard I thought it strange that it was so bright outside even though there was no moon, until I realised that the front of our house was lit up with spotlights, particularly the entrance. The Nazis were still waiting for Karl to come home so they could arrest him.

I couldn't sleep. I was too anxious. Thank goodness Oma, Paulhermann and Erika were now soundly asleep. Nothing further happened during that Thursday night.

As it had been decreed some months earlier that Jewish children were banned from government schools, I had to keep them home, so couldn't totally prevent their being together. I told Paulhermann not to get too close to Erika, as she might still be infectious.

In Gütersloh the following morning, Friday, Karl made enquiries as to whether Jews were still being arrested. He learned that the *Aktion* was over, and concentration camps all over Germany were 'full', so he decided it would be safe to come home.

Before leaving the Herzbergs, he made arrangements by phone to meet one of the directors of Claas & Co. in Warendorf, the town where Harsewinkel properties were registered. There they signed the sale documents already prepared by the solicitor. Everything was settled very quickly.

Karl drove home and on coming into Harsewinkel passed the offices of the mayor and town clerk at mid-day, just as the employees, of whom some were Nazis, were going home for lunch. He couldn't escape their notice.

As soon as Karl was home I made him a nice fish meal. Our doorbell rang while he was eating. Opening the door, I was confronted by Policeman Kruse. He told me he had to arrest Karl. I should pack a small case with pyjamas, toothbrush and shaving gear. Although Kruse's wife was supposed to cook for prisoners in the little jail, he suggested I supply Karl's food so I would have an excuse for frequent visits. Kruse then came into the dining room and in Oma's presence said,

'Karl, I have to take you to the mayor's office to sign something.'

'You won't keep him there, will you?' Oma cried out.

'No, he'll be back soon.'

Shortly after they left, I packed pillows and blankets in lots of clean paper, a washbasin, some food, a bottle of drinking water and a few pieces of cutlery. I asked Paulhermann to help me, as he could transport most of these things on his bike. Before leaving I said to Oma, 'It seems they've arrested Karl, so I'd better bring him food and pyjamas.'

Yes, they had arrested Karl. He was in the little local police cell. When the thick, heavy door opened it was weird to see Karl in that tiny cell with room only for a narrow stretcher and a little low table, which actually contained a commode toilet. Near the ceiling was a small window with iron bars, which let in a little light. Luckily, I brought him plenty of wrapping paper and also the newspaper for him to read. Karl used all the paper to cover everything in the room. As I left I thought, 'He'll be home tomorrow.' That didn't happen!

My thoughts drifted to our families in Lünen and Schüren and to the family in Gütersloh whom we couldn't contact; the Nazis had broken their phones. As I entered our house I heard Oma's voice, 'O G-d, what are they doing to us?'

While I had been at the police station, Karl's sister, Paula Schöneberg, had managed to phone from Schüren-Dortmund and told Oma, 'They've arrested Dagobert and our fourteen-year-old Lutz. We'd been warned by non-Jewish friends that something ominous was brewing, so went into hiding after dark on Wednesday night. By Thursday morning we thought the *Aktion* must be over, so decided to go home. We found that a mob of Storm Troopers had invaded our home and smashed windows and fittings in our butcher shop while we'd been away. Knowing we had returned, they came and arrested Dagobert and Lutz. Who would have thought they would take a youngster?'

Oma cried for hours. I didn't know how to console her.

That afternoon when we all had to have our fingerprints[49] taken, Oma was again very upset. 'We're not criminals,' she shouted.

Later, we learned that in Lünen, where Helen and Emil Levy had lived before they moved to Essen, two Jewish men were shot in the presence of their wives while still in bed. Two other Jewish men were taken from their beds and thrown into the river Lippe. One of the men could swim, but the other, Waldemar Elsoffer, drowned. (His son Walter now lives in Melbourne and has changed his surname to Eltham.) Mr and Mrs Rosenthal of Annen, who later came out on the same ship with us to Australia, were taken from their bed and marched out of town. They were both severely beaten on head and body, then told to dig their own graves. Their lives were saved by some passing miners going to their early shift. They were hospitalised for months while recovering from their injuries.

We were all the more shocked by these events considering that we Jews, living in Germany for centuries, had contributed to the high standards of art and culture, science and trade and had fought in its wars. We had been respected citizens of our towns and in the eyes of many we still were. Yet

---

[49] This fingerprinting of Jewish citizens seemed a gross affront at the time, but compared with what lay ahead during the Nazi period, it was barely significant.

the Nazi propaganda proclaimed: *Die Juden sind unser Unglück* (The Jews are our misfortune). However terrible were the days of late 1938, they gave no warning of the horrors that awaited the Jews of Europe.

Early on Saturday I went again to the police station to bring Karl food and newspapers. It was heartbreaking to see him in his poky cell, restless as a wild animal in a narrow cage. He wanted additional news and asked me to go to Gottemeiers' Newsagent to buy *Die Glocke* (The Bell), a more informative paper. It had become pro-Nazi, our reason for having cancelled our subscription. When the Gottemeiers, close neighbours, had been in financial difficulties, my late father-in-law and Karl had for years given them credit, helping them build up a good business. Therefore, I felt comfortable entering their shop.

I was hardly in the door when Gottemeier shouted, 'How dare you come in here. Get out or I'll throw you out!' I was stunned. People were now showing their real character. I went home, realising that one doesn't always get thanks for good deeds done.

Most inhabitants of Harsewinkel and its surrounding villages were strict Catholics and went to church every Sunday. Many of our customers would come in after church to discuss a cattle trade or horse deal, or to buy goods in the drapery store. They might stay and talk; the men enjoying Schnapps and cigars; the women, coffee and cake.

After the events of the past week I didn't expect anyone to drop in that Sunday. I was surprised. Quite a number came to say how sorry and angry they were about all that had happened, in particular about Karl's arrest. One man brought two chickens for me to cook for Karl. Others brought fresh lettuce and fresh peas, rare delicacies in winter. These were families without their own chicken farms or hot-houses.

In the days that followed I was asked if I wanted to sell any of our household goods and furniture. Not knowing exact market values, nor having time to consult Karl, I sold many items right away, even the car, the trailer and some farming equipment. These sales were helpful, as we no longer had any income. Clearing the decks also helped us organise our emigration.

Our papers applying for landing permits to Australia had already been sent to Leon seven months earlier. Now the need for the permits was critically urgent.

In the afternoon Ella brought Walter to stay with us for a few days. Her expression reflected her worries about Leopold and her voice was affected by the stress. She could hardly make herself understood. On the one occasion when she saw Leopold in the Gütersloh police cell, he told her to cable Leon in Sydney, prepaying the reply:

Leopold and Karl not at home. We must leave. Ella. Käthe.

Just after her visit to the jail a big truck had arrived and taken all the Jewish men to Bielefeld. They had left Bielefeld and no one knew their destination.

Ella also told us that Clara had been to Rüdinghausen and had reported:

Long before I entered the house I saw feathers floating down the street. The Nazi mob had slashed the eiderdown bedding in Louis's shop and poured kerosene and liquid soap over dress materials. They didn't set fire to the house because of Aryan tenants. Next morning, Louis, Rosa, Ilse and Rolf had gone to Witten to be with friends and family and that's where I found Rosa and Ilse.[50] Louis had been arrested and taken to concentration camp. Rolf had fled to his uncle, Paul Neugarten, in Dortmund.

In the evening Ella returned home by train.

It was good to have the children around during those terrible days. Walter, Paulhermann and Erika played nicely together. Oma sent Walter out to buy some groceries. She neglected to tell him not to go to Brinkmanns. Of course that's where he went! It was the nearest shop. He was greeted with: 'Get out! We don't sell to Jews!' The boy came home, shaking.

It became routine for me to visit Karl in prison before daybreak, bringing him food, drinking water and anything he needed. Every morning as I was setting out I could hear Oma sobbing. It frightened me that this woman who had always been so strong had lost her nerve.

The days were distressing enough. The nights were unbearable.

Several days after Leopold's arrest, Ella received a postcard, stamped Buchenwald. '*Wir sitzen hier gut ein. Gruss Leopold.*' (We have settled in well. Regards Leopold.) It was good to see his handwriting despite knowing the words had obviously been dictated.

---

[50] The Neugarten family spent the night of 9–10 November in the attic of their house. Louis was apparently arrested in Witten, sent to the police lock-up in Bochum and then to the Oranienburg concentration camp. Rolf and his uncle, Paul Neugarten, were both arrested in Dortmund and sent to Dachau. Even though only seventeen, Rolf was held for some weeks.

FEE.—£1 (One Pound.)   Form No. 41.

COMMONWEALTH OF AUSTRALIA.

Permit   № 27032   DEPARTMENT OF THE INTERIOR,
CANBERRA, A.C.T.,

24th November, 19 38

LANDING PERMIT.

To whom it may concern:

THIS IS TO CERTIFY that permission has been granted for the admission to Australia of the undermentioned person or persons (four   in number), said to be of   German   nationality, at present residing in   Germany   whose maintenance on arrival in Australia has been guaranteed by Mr. Ludwig Mendels of   Waverley, New South Wales.

This authority has been granted subject to the conditions that such person or persons shall be in sound health, of good character, and in possession of a   German   Passport or Certificate of Identity, bearing photograph of the holder , ~~and duly viséed (if not issued) by a British Consular or Passport Officer~~ and subject to any further conditions which may be stated below.

This Permit is valid until   24th November, 1939.

NAME.	AGE.	RELATIONSHIP (if any) TO GUARANTOR.
HERTZBERG, Leopold	44 years	brother-in-law
HERTZBERG, Ella	40 years	sister
HERTZBERG, Walter	10 years	nephew
HERTZBERG, Ursula	8 years	niece

NOTE:- Mr. L. Hertzberg must satisfy the Customs Authorities on arrival in Australia that he is in possession of at least £200 (Australian currency) capital.

Transmitted per   Mr. Ludwig Mendels,
"Telrah,"
Waverley Street,
Waverley, N.S.W.

By authority of the Minister for the Interior.

NOTE.—This Permit should be forwarded to the person in whose favour it has been issued (or to the chief member of the party if more than one person is included in the Permit) for production when applying for passport facilities or steamer passage tickets, and for production and surrender to the Examining Officer of Customs at the Australian port of disembarkation.

If an extension of this Permit is desired, application should be addressed to the Department of the Interior. A fee of 10/- (ten shillings) is payable for each year's extension authorized.

By Authority: L. F. JOHNSTON, Commonwealth Government Printer, Canberra.

Australian Landing Permit for the Herzberg family.
(Herzberg name misspelled in document)

In 1938 we had no idea Buchenwald was a concentration camp, nor were we aware of the suffering of the inmates. A blessing that we didn't know.

Karl had at first been fearful he might be sent away. He was lucky to have been arrested late, the concentration camps by then being filled beyond capacity. On 24 November, when Karl had been in the tiny police cell[51] thirteen days and fourteen nights, a telegram arrived from Sydney confirming that both families had been granted landing permits and stating permit numbers.

Ella told us this good news by phone. I went immediately to our town's mayor asking for Karl's release. He wanted the permit number but I had been so excited, I hadn't asked Ella that detail. 'I would like to free your husband, but I should really see the telegram or at least have the permit numbers. Without proof I could be in big trouble!' The mayor was no Nazi, but was expected to follow Nazi rules.

'Frau Mendels, I know you're an honest woman. Is it really true that the permit has been approved?'

'I give you my word of honour, Herr *Bürgermeister*.'

'Your husband will be home soon.'

* * *

Yes, Karl did come home soon. It was wonderful to have him back. There was a different mood in the house, even though Karl himself was rather withdrawn. He now focussed on getting Leopold home. As soon as he had bathed and changed into other clothes he phoned Ella telling her that he would go with her by train to the Gestapo District Office in Bielefeld to apply for Leopold's release.

When Karl and Ella arrived at the Gestapo headquarters a Nazi official shouted, 'What do you want?'

'We have our permits for Australia. You want us to leave and we're ready to go. This is my sister. What can we do to get her husband, Leopold Herzberg, released from Buchenwald? Can I go there myself to bring him home?'

'Sure! Go! They'll keep you there!'

---

[51] Compared to other arrested Jews, particularly those in concentration camps, Karl's imprisonment did not involve great suffering. For exercise, he was daily taken for a walk by the friendly local policeman Kruse, whom he knew well. Karl, with his special charm, would suggest that they take a different route each day, allowing him to complete outstanding business matters!

Just then the well-known Aryan lawyer, *Herr Justizrat*[52] Meyer of Bielefeld, arrived. 'Good Morning, *Herr Justizrat*', said the official. 'Please take a seat.' The *Justizrat* said, looking at Ella, 'I'll come back later in the day' and walked out. There stood Ella, tense and shivering, a bundle of nerves, barely able to stay on her feet, but the official hadn't offered her a seat. After a series of further questions, Karl and Ella were told to come back for a decision after lunch.

Exhausted, they went to a little coffee shop nearby. Several uniformed Nazis were there relaxing, but seemed not to notice them. Refreshed by their coffee, Ella and Karl went back to Gestapo headquarters for their appointment.

As they came in, the Nazi official shouted, 'You dirty Jews. How dare you enter an Aryan restaurant. If that happens again you'll be sent to concentration camp.' Then, calming down he told them what they had come to hear:

'If you undertake to leave Germany within months, Herzberg will be set free.'

---

[52] The equivalent of the Queen's or Special Counsel in England.

BOOK TWO

Lest We Forget
Damit Wir Es Nie Vergessen

Leopold Herzberg

Translated by
Ursula Cher (née Herzberg)

If, drunk with sight of power, we loose
Wild tongues that have not thee in awe
Such boasting as the Gentiles use
Or lesser breeds without the law
Lord G-d of Hosts, be with us yet
LEST WE FORGET. LEST WE FORGET.

'Recessional'
by Rudyard Kipling

1

L e s t w e f o r g e t

Damit wir es nie Vergessen , was den deutschen Juden in der Nacht
vom 9. auf den 10. November von Adolf Hitler und seinen Trabanten angetan
worden ist, will ich das, was ich selbst erlebt habe, aufzeichnen. Diese
Aufzeichnungen koennen nur einen ganz kleinen Ausschnitt aus dem riesengrossen
Judenprogrom geben, der eine ewige Schmach fuer unser frueher so schoenes

LEST WE FORGET what was done by Adolph Hitler and his hooligans to the Jews of Germany on the night of 9–10 of November 1938, I, Leopold Herzberg, want to record my own experiences. My story covers only a small segment of the enormous nationwide pogrom mounted against the Jews, a pogrom forever a disgrace to our former beautiful Germany. In retrospect, I didn't believe it possible that the criminals holding Germany by the throat would dare to unleash their sadistic instincts openly before all the world, and in such a vehement way.

The attempt on the life of an official of the German Embassy in Paris, Ernst vom Rath, shot by Herschel Grynszpan, would prove to be an added pretext for the German government and media to engage in further incitement against the Jews. Clearly this act would be used as the basis for new foul deeds. Two days after the event, in the evening of 9 November, we hear the announcement that the German diplomat has died as a result of the attack. I now expect that measures already in force against us will be intensified. I anticipate that they will take the form of harsher government regulations and discriminatory laws.

We go to bed relatively unworried.[53]

About three o'clock in the morning, we are awakened by a night watchman, who tells us that our shop windows are besmeared. *JUDE* is written with oil paint in huge letters on every one of our shop windows. My wife, Ella, and I go to work straight away to remove the daubing. Not an easy task. At intervals we try to ring our friends, the Daltrops, to alert them, but can't get through. This doesn't particularly disturb us.

The two shop windows on the Königstrasse are the last to be cleaned. We have just started on these when a large group of men rounds the corner of the Town Hall into the Königstrasse. What now follows, occurs ever so quickly. Before we realise what is happening, heavily armed men in SS uniform arrive. Instantly, and with unbelievable speed, the six shop windows and the glass in the other windows and front doors of the corner house on the Königstrasse are smashed. Around us there is such a clinking and clanking, crashing and smashing that occasionally, even years later, I can hear the cacophony ringing in my ears. Windows and doors are forced open; the house is stormed through every opening and from all sides. And then begins destruction such as I have never before witnessed, not even during the war.

Meanwhile, we are pushed aside and both ordered to report to the police station across the road for protective custody. We go only a few steps when I hear my wife call out, 'No, I won't desert my children!'

'What! There are still people in the houses? Get them all out quickly. I warn you. Get a move on.'

As though pursued, we race back and as we do so we can see the swine smashing everything. We hurry upstairs into my sister-in-law's house. Clara is standing by her bed in her nightgown, hair loosened, sobbing. She is surrounded by four SS men and by Klostius, a stuck-up prig in civilian clothes, whose father has been a bookkeeper at Steinberg's for more than twenty years. Our son, Walter, aged ten, comes out of the adjoining room, crying and shaking. A heavy stone crashing through the window has just missed his head.

Leaving Ella there, I run next door to our place to waken my mother, Bertha Herzberg, aged seventy-five, my daughter, Ursula, aged eight, and the

---

[53] The first order concerning the *Aktion-Jude* was sent out by Heinrich Müller, Head of the Gestapo, at 11.55 pm on 9 November and *inter alia* stated 'Preparations are to be made for the arrest of about 20,000 to 30,000 Jews in the Reich. Above all, well-to-do Jews are to be selected'. An hour and a half later Reinhard Heydrich, Chief of Security Police, sent out his notorious instructions for the pogrom. (See Appendix 4)

young Jewish housemaid, with us for only a few days. An SS man shadows me constantly. I find Mother in a dreadful state, sitting in bed crying. She had left her bed, but fear has driven her back. There is no time for lengthy explanations: 'Get dressed as quickly as possible.'

I go to the top floor, 'escort' in tow, to the room where Ursula and the maid sleep, urging them also to dress quickly. As I return to our level, I realise that the terrible crashing and clinking has stopped. I presume the vandalism has ceased; there is probably nothing left to destroy.

Suddenly everything seems to spin, and all is black before my eyes. When I come to, I'm sitting in the kitchen, 'my SS man' supporting me and pressing a glass of water to my mouth. Water is running down my throat without my having to swallow. The SS man doesn't say a word, but from the way he's looking at us we can see he hates having to help me, a Jew. I ask permission to go back to Clara's. He accompanies me as far as the front door, from which I see a scene I can describe but whose true 'colour' I just cannot convey.

The lights are on throughout her whole house. The lampshades have been smashed, the globes not. In the living room both the lamp and cord have been ripped out of the ceiling. Where there had been windows, there are now gaping cavities. The curtains hang in shreds. It is barely possible to enter the rooms, as all the furniture is strewn about in total chaos. The writing desk is upside down; papers and books wildly scattered throughout the whole room. The piano is overturned, as are the table, the sewing table, and the telephone stand. The broken phone is under the rubble. In the middle of the room lies the safe, weighing hundreds of pounds, simply torn off its base with crowbars.

All pictures on the walls have been battered and ruined; chairs reduced to firewood. The lounge-dining room in the front of the house is in a similar state. The burning heater is overturned on the carpet. No one has noticed that it is still alight. (Clara will find it still smouldering two days later.) Next to it, in chaotic disarray, are table, remnants of chairs, upper section of the sideboard, and all that had been on it and in it. The glass in the new front door of the former butcher shop is gone, as are the mirror and doors of the beautiful wooden linen cabinet standing in the hall. The icebox and the small-goods slicing machine are lying in the middle of the floor. Likewise in the kitchen, the cupboards[54] and their contents are tipped over, as is the shoe cupboard in the small hallway.

The new show windows on the Moltkestrasse, modernised a few years

---

[54] Tall, free-standing cupboards as in country style kitchens of today.

earlier, the showcase, and both our shops present the same dreadful picture. With so much glass, porcelain and crockery at hand, the hoons had really let themselves go. Few items remain in one piece. Everything that could be knocked over lies on the floor. They have simply tilted the shelves so that the goods have slid off. Where that didn't work quickly enough, they've used long staves to clear the shelves. The former butcher shop, into which our business extended some time before, has received the same treatment.

On the other hand, with the exception of the large glass entrance door, the section of the shop containing heaters and cooking stoves has been spared by the sudden order to stop. After all, one must not spend too much time on just a single property when there are still many other 'Jewish jobs' to be done in Gütersloh.

As I enter the house I see Clara and Ella coming down the stairs, Clara completely distraught. Whereas in our case only the shops and stock are smashed, in Clara's home all her possessions, loved and valued throughout her marriage, are lost and destroyed.

We then all go next door to our place and sit around the table, not knowing what might happen next, what might follow. After approximately half an hour of helpless waiting, the doorbell rings. A uniformed police officer is there, politely asking me to clear the footpath covered with broken glass. Clara and our maid go downstairs with me. The lights are still on in all the rooms and shop windows. It is eerie to see the violated building brightly illuminated, yet with no one inside. Stationed across the street silently watching us as we work, are eight to ten SS men. Clara and the maid are in the Moltkestrasse. I am in the Königstrasse. We have almost finished and are about to go back upstairs when a car drives up. Three members of the SS and one from the SA jump out. One runs towards me and hits me directly across my left eye with a type of horsewhip, a baton with a loop of leather attached. I react by muttering, 'Leave me alone.'

He swings round and strikes me on the same spot, shouting, 'You shit! D'you want to make something of it?' I shudder. I know what it means to defy the SS, but I also know he is shouting loudly to impress the neighbours.

As I try to go round the corner into the Moltkestrasse, a horde of ten to fifteen men assaults me with a hail of kicks and blows. An SA man twists my arm behind my back, so that I am no longer able to move. He takes me across to the Court House; forces me to stand face against the wall. On letting go of my arm he threatens, 'You shit, if you move so much as a finger, you'll be sorry.' Then he steps back and commands, 'Stand still! 'Stand at attention!' A short pause, then, 'Get yourself back to your *Bude*[55].

Shattered to hear our home referred to in this way, I finally get upstairs and again meet terrified faces. I can't talk very much. It must be evident I've been through a tough time.

Two and a half hours after it all began, at about five-thirty in the morning, the doorbell rings again. It's Detective Grüschow, whom I know by sight, flanked by four SS. 'Have you weapons in the house?'

I explain that I have a French bayonet, which I brought back from Fort Faux, near Verdun. The bayonet is confiscated and after one of the SS men 'stands guard' at the entrance door of our house, a very careful search for weapons in all the rooms begins – carried out, however, in the most correct and polite manner. This lasts till about seven. The detective then says, 'Now you just have to come with us to the police station.'

While Ella goes to fetch hat and coat for me, Mother, tears streaming, comes down the stairs crying out, 'I sacrificed two sons in the war. Why take this one from me also?'

I see to it that I get away quickly. The police station is crammed with SS. I have to surrender everything in my pockets, as well as braces and shoelaces. There is no shortage of sarcastic remarks and curses as I am searched once again and led away. As the door of the cell opens, Josef Steinberg appears from the semi-darkness inside and asks to go to the toilet. 'You've sure got big ideas, you pig,' comes the answer. 'That sort of comfort is over. Shit in the box in your cell.' The cell door is slammed shut.

I had assumed the whole operation had for some unknown reason been directed against me and my family only. I am therefore amazed to see that most of the men of the Jewish community have also been arrested. I am told that besides those in my cell, the other Jewish men are imprisoned in the cell next door. I learn that old Mr Meinberg and Mr Löwenbach have been spared, due to their age.

I learn several other things too. It seems likely that we are facing a pre-organised, large-scale pogrom against Jews throughout Germany.

Our synagogue and its schoolrooms have been burned to the ground. Though the fire brigade has been alerted, it has been ordered to restrict activities only to protecting neighbouring buildings.[56] The Daltrops' building, living quarters

---

[55] Dump, hovel or shack.
[56] See Appendix 5

151

and shop, the Löwenbachs', Meinbergs', and the homes of both Josef Steinberg and Karl Steinberg, with all contents, have been totally destroyed.

In hushed voices, one after the other of my cellmates recounts what has happened to him, what he's been through. Eventually we realise that nothing we can do will alter our situation.

It is our good fortune that in no time Paul Meinberg regains his customary humour. Those who know him can picture him kindly inviting Josef Steinberg not to let our presence restrain him from his 'business'. That's the business recommended by the SA man just as I arrived. Actually Paul's motive is to avoid the embarrassment of being the first, but is keen to be the next to use the 'box'. Josef apologises repeatedly, 'You must forgive me, but really I can't help it. You know I have a complaint.'

Paul Meinberg tells us that at his place a fire had actually been set, but that he had been able to extinguish it. Willi Garty[57] interjects, 'But Paul, as I came round the corner at Tigge's place, I could see a number of lights burning throughout your house.'

Paul is sure the power had been cut off just before the destruction began at his place. The opinions of the two men clash. As Willi Garty defends his view, it finally dawns on Paul: 'Well then, it couldn't be lights you saw, but a *Sereifo*.[58] There won't be anything left of our venerable villa, weighed down by mortgage and all.'

And he is right. As he speaks, all that remains of the Meinbergs' house is a heap of smoking ruins. All their furniture, beds, linen, clothes, jewellery, paintings and food have been burned, the stables behind the house remaining untouched. I learn later that a new bicycle and an old motorbike were taken from the back stables to the house, and so burned. Paul's wife, Ilse Meinberg, and their ten-year-old daughter fled to our place, both dressed only in nightgown, slippers and coat. As soon as they arrived, both were given stockings and underwear; they had not been allowed to put on their own or take anything with them.

Fortunately, the two older Meinbergs had been in the Catholic hospital for the past few days, thus safe and well cared for.

---

[57] Of the Jewish families living in Gütersloh during this period, Willi Garty and family, Paul Meinberg and family and our Herzberg-Mendels family were the first to emigrate. Gerda Steinberg, Josef Steinberg with daughter and son-in-law were able to escape later.
[58] German *Jiddisch* from the Hebrew for 'an inferno'.

Long after we were released from the concentration camp, the following conversation unfolded, with Paul Meinberg ribbing Detective Himmelhaus:

Paul: 'Tell me Mr Himmelhaus, could you give me some idea where my bicycle is, the one that was out the back?

Himmelhaus: 'Yes, it was burned in the front.'

Paul: Thank G-d, then I'll need only a new front tyre.'

Himmelhaus: 'Why a new tyre? What do you want with a new tyre?'

Paul: 'Because it's burned at the front.'

Himmelhaus: 'But I'm telling you it was totally burned in the front.'

Paul: 'What, the whole front wheel? Blast! Then it'll be an expensive repair.'

Himmelhaus: 'For goodness sake, don't you understand? The bike was totally burned in the front.'

Paul: 'Yes of course, but the front wheel can be replaced.'

Himmelhaus: (Now shouting) 'No, the whole bike was burnt, lock stock and barrel with the house up front.'

Paul: 'Really, you mean in the house at the front? Naturally I couldn't know that. But how did the bike get into the house in front?'

This brought the discussion to an end. Himmelhaus wasn't going to answer Paul's last question.

But in our police cell we're in no mood for jokes. We can hear there is far more activity in town than usual; constant shouting by traffic policemen stationed nearby, on the street corner of my shop and at the intersection of Königstrasse and Berliner Strasse. In the midst of this, fire engines race through the streets. Our hearts are pounding, as we wonder whether the arson will continue. Already we hear people outside, yelling, 'Now Daltrops' is burning.'

The events of this fire were later described to me as follows:

The two Daltrop wives are sitting in their living room on the first floor after the arrest of their husbands. Suddenly they hear a noise. When they check at the door, they are confronted by a member of the

SS, who at once callously orders them back into the room. They have time enough to see people rushing around in the rooms downstairs, piling tables and chairs on top of each other. Bauer, former clerk of the Simons Werke Rheda, now Nazi-appointed Mayor of Gütersloh, joins in the destruction. A few moments later the two anxious and terrified women smell smoke. Despite having been told to stay in the room, they leave to avoid being trapped in the fire, only to find tall flames already advancing towards them. It seems everything has been doused with petrol or other flammable liquid, which explains the rapid spread of fire.

They cannot rescue anything, not even the cash in the house. Paula Daltrop manages to take only a small suitcase, into which she has crammed nightwear for herself and her husband. Both women then rush through the flames to be greeted with the brutal, sarcastic remark, 'What! Still trying to smuggle out your fortune?' The little suitcase is roughly torn from her hands and tossed high into the flames. The SS then force them back into the burning house. They escape being burnt alive by slipping out through an unguarded side door.

The Daltrops have lost everything in the fire, without exception. Even the account books of the business are destroyed by the conflagration. Whether the safe wasn't totally fireproof or whether by unfortunate coincidence it wasn't securely locked, I don't know. How will they ever prove what customers owe them. Many will later use the absence of records to evade payment. By contrast, the Daltrops will be required to meet every one of their obligations.

The fire brigade has its hands full, having been ordered to protect Aryan premises. When the neighbouring Löwenbach house is set alight[59] at each corner simultaneously, access for the fire brigade to two Aryan homes in the adjoining building is obstructed.

With all the furniture and furnishings inherited from their parents totally destroyed and still in shock from the terror of the previous evening, the two elderly Löwenbach siblings now face the new calamity, fire. They completely lose their heads, running back and forth as though possessed, trying to salvage

---

[59] The arson team setting fire to Jewish properties was later found to be two SS men and Justice Secretary Schmidt.

a few items, even though forbidden to do so. When they are finally outside, Ernst suddenly realises that his much-loved dog, Pussi, is still in the burning house. He rushes back through the flames, disregarding his own safety and saves the dog.

Of the beautiful old Löwenbach Heritage Trust home with all its contents, only a smouldering ruin remains. With one exception. Untouched by the flames there lies on the ruins the decoratively carved beam from above the front door, still ironically displaying the inscription:

Cast thy burden upon the Lord, and He will sustain thee.
He will never suffer the righteous to be moved.
(Psalm 55, verse 23)

That only this beam carrying the biblical quotation escapes the flames makes an immensely powerful impression on all who see it.

2

We sit in our prison cell. Time and again I clamber up to the window and look across the road to our house, to see whether it is also engulfed in smoke. It is already sold, but the documents have yet to be exchanged. I later heard from many sources that our house had also been listed for destruction by fire. Only the persuasive efforts of the buyers changed the minds of the officially appointed arsonists.

Gütersloh Town Hall. This also housed the jail (below street level) from which Leopold could see the old family home and shop directly across the road (encircled). Local announcement of the outbreak of the 1914 War was made on the square in front of the Town Hall.

Isn't it remarkable that precisely those houses that the town had previously decided to purchase for traffic adjustments and other civic purposes were the ones razed? After the houses were gone, the town acquired the sites very cheaply, and indeed picked up the Daltrops' and Löwenbachs' for 7.50 Marks per square metre. Three weeks earlier the municipality had offered the Daltrops 22,500 Marks for their house. The town ultimately paid them 3,000 Marks, which did not even cover the 5,000 Marks mortgage. Moreover, the unfortunate victims of the fires were 'permitted' to pay not only for destroyed gas and electricity meters, but also for removal of the ruins. These costs for the Daltrops amounted to 900 Marks. Charges imposed on the Jewish community for the lost synagogue were 400 Marks.

All this is the work of the good old honourable Nazis, so unjustly maligned by the whole world. No angel is so pure; burning down of houses is a thoroughly justifiable, righteous and worthwhile exercise. Why? Because, as rumour has it, 250,000 Marks in cash, a mere quarter million, were found at Leopold Herzberg's home, together with valuables worth 2 million Marks and five or six heavy machine guns. Actually a few too many for just one man to handle; perhaps Oma was expected 'to man the guns' or operate at least a few of them! And at the synagogue a complete arsenal of hand grenades and dozens of machine guns with ammunition were found.

Are these fantasies believed? My word they are!

Time and again in the following months I am asked by innumerable old, close friends whether there is any truth in these allegations. Of course the stories are difficult to believe; but, after all, they have been asserted time and again with such certainty.

* * *

Again I've been rushing somewhat ahead of events and will now continue to report what happened on 10 November. We are taken one by one into the courtyard of the gaol and photographed from front, right and left, all full length. Then fingerprinted forty-four times, four of every finger, two of each hand. Then interrogated. Extremely detailed records are taken. The whole course of our life, our overseas interests, our business and financial circumstances with exact figures have to be declared, all from memory of course.

In the evening at about seven, I'm called up to the guardroom. There to my surprise I find my wife, who is allowed to speak to me for a few minutes in the presence of the commissioner. Her emotional state is beyond description. In our short conversation she tells me that everyone is more or less alright and, very quietly, that her brother, Karl Mendels, is with them and for the time being wants to stay. A sandwich she has brought is first carefully examined before I am allowed to accept it. I ask Ella to send cables to America and Australia as soon as possible. This she does, together with Karl, late that same evening. As it turns out, this telegram to Australia will save my life.[60]

After only a tin bowl of pea soup at noon, we are now each given a small mug of coffee and a piece of bread for the evening meal. Then we try to sleep. The following morning finds us considerably calmer. In the early hours, sounds of loud hammering can be heard coming from our shop. I have been put into another cell, from which I can just see the corner of our property. Karl and Ella are boarding up all the windows, including the shop windows – a job they had been unable to complete the previous day.

Interrogations and record-taking continue today and take up the whole morning. I am now in the same cell as Bernard Daltrop, who, unlike his brother Julius, hasn't heard the shout 'Now Daltrops' is burning'. I can't bring myself to tell the truth to this very sick man, but I try repeatedly to hint at it in various ways, unfortunately without success, as later becomes clear.

---

[60] Because of the urgency of the request the Australian visas were granted within days, leading to Leopold's release after fifteen days in Buchenwald. He was sure he would not have survived had he been imprisoned a few more days.

3

At this point, I want to record the experiences of my extended family during and after *Kristallnacht*.

In Harsewinkel nothing occurs during the night of 9–10 November. About 5 am the following morning, Karl leaves by car for the market in Soest. He passes through Oelde and sees that houses belonging to Jews are in ruins. He has promised to pick up cattle dealer Steinberg. He finds his colleague in his partially demolished house, bleeding from many wounds. Thinking these are local incidents, Karl drives on. By the time he reaches Soest he has seen enough to realise what's happening. He heads back home, stopping on the way to ring the Schönebergs in Schüren, but can't make contact. He can't get through to Rüdinghausen or Gütersloh either. He reaches Gütersloh about nine the same morning.

My niece from Rüdinghausen, Ilse Neugarten, after a vain attempt to make contact with Gütersloh, rings my sister Käthe, in Harsewinkel, who is completely unaware of what's going on and at first can't understand why Ilse is repeatedly asking for Karl, while emphasising that no one has been hurt, thank G-d, but their shop has been vandalisead.

Käthe, now really concerned, phones Gütersloh but can't get through, so rings our neighbour Osthus. Father-in-law Roggenkamp takes the message but, fearful of Nazi reprisals, won't deliver it to the Herzberg household. Käthe runs to her neighbours. Liesbeth Austermann readily volunteers to go on her motorbike to Gütersloh. She returns with details of the devastation.

Then a kindly official of the taxation department comes to Käthe, ostensibly to check the books. This is, however, only a pretext; he has actually come to warn Karl to disappear. Towards evening, a truckload of SS men arrives from Warendorf. They smash the shop windows and force their way into the house, where Käthe explains that everything has been sold. The bookwork concluding the sale has not yet been completed. Mrs Feldhaus-Austermann bursts in, shouting that suspension of all anti-Jewish operations has just been ordered over the radio. There is a standoff. While all this is happening, the buyer of the house, the well-to-do manufacturer Mr Claas[61] has managed to bring the vandalism to a halt.

Karl stays the night in Gütersloh and on the Friday morning drives to Warendorf to exchange contracts and formalise his deal with Claas. In answer to his many inquiries he is assured that he can safely go home; there are to be no further arrests. This turns out to be incorrect. Within hours of his return a policeman arrives with a warrant.

For thirteen days he remains in solitary in the Harsewinkel police station. Käthe is allowed to bring all his meals, books, blankets, anything he wants. On one occasion the policeman who takes him out daily for some fresh air allows him to call in at home! In the dark of night, of course.

As my Gütersloh family is anxious about the Neugartens, with whom they can't get in touch, Clara goes by train to Rüdinghausen on the Sunday morning, 13 November.[62] Here too, the 'mob' has done a pretty complete job. As she approaches the house she is greeted by bed feathers dancing towards her in the breeze. None of the family is home. From the house tenants she learns that my sister Rosa and her daughter, Ilse, are most probably somewhere in the nearby town of Witten, where Clara eventually finds them at the home of a Jewish family, known friends of theirs, together with a number of other women. Rosa has not yet regained enough courage to return to her own home.

During the horrific night of 9–10, they had experienced hours of terrible fear hiding in their attic to escape the menaces of the Hitler gang. The tenants sharing the house were too frightened to give them refuge. My brother-in-law Louis had been arrested shortly thereafter in Witten, I believe, and taken to the police lock-up in Bochum. His son, Rolf, had fled to his uncle Paul Neugarten in Dortmund. There, they were arrested and taken to Dachau concentration

---

[61] Claas & Co, the largest business in Harsewinkel, were manufacturers of agricultural machinery, still producing and exporting today.

[62] By train, as she did not own a car, nor could she drive one.

camp, Rolf being released much later than me, even though a youngster, not yet eighteen.

My brother-in-law Emil Levy was arrested while visiting a friend whom the police were just coming to pick up, using the opportunity to take Emil as well. However, he sat out his time in the police lock-up in Essen.

In Schüren, my brother-in-law Dagobert Schöneberg and family are warned by Christian friends that something is going to happen, so after dark on the night of 9 November they flee to Dortmund. When they return home the following morning they find their house and shop thoroughly and systematically smashed. Next day Dagobert and his fourteen-year-old son, Lutz, are arrested.

Throughout the whole of Germany the Nazis raged: 'From the Maas to the Memel, From the Etsch to the Belt',[63] missing not even the smallest village; committing robbery, destruction, arson and murder.

In Lünen there are two instances in which Jews are shot in their beds, their wives next to them. Two others are thrown into the river Lippe. Of these, only one, Mr Aronstein, Aunt Julie's cousin from Barsinghausen, manages to save himself.

Mr and Mrs Rosenthal, from Annen near Witten, who later come on the same ship with us to Australia, are taken from their beds to be brutally and inhumanly beaten, leaving many scars on head and body. Bleeding profusely, they are chased through the streets till far out of town. Then, on arriving in a field, they are handed spades and forced to dig their own graves. They are saved, literally at the edge of the grave, due to threats made against their captors by a group of coal miners on their way to the morning shift.

Such are the ways of THE THIRD REICH.

---

[63] From the anthem 'Deutschland, Deutschland Über Alles' by August Hoffmann von Fallersleben. This quotation outlines the borders of the German Confederation in 1864. It originally reflected the over-riding wish for national unity felt by German liberals. It later acquired the additional meaning of the dominance of Germany and thus became the national anthem.

4

Now to come back to my personal experiences. It is midday Friday 11 November. Everyone is given a bowl of potato soup and at about two o'clock we are ordered to the front of the police station. The various articles taken from us on arrival are returned, giving the impression that we are about to be released. But no! We are each now handed a loaf of bread and a piece of cheese. For this, plus our 'board and lodging' (twice soup and twice coffee with bread), we are 'allowed' to pay 6.75 Marks, leaving me only 1.75 Marks in my pocket.

Outside, a bus has already pulled up, but I am once again ordered to the inspector's office, this time to finalise the conveyance of our house. There is a delay, as Clara, who has not been notified, is not home. The purchaser, Eugen Frederich, taking Ella with him, rushes round town. They find Clara at Jenny Daltrop's place. In great haste the formalities are concluded. My fellow victims are already sitting, waiting in the bus. Outside in the town square, more and more townspeople are gathering. I say my farewells quickly, not only because Detective Schmidt, who has to accompany the transport, has become nervous and is hustling me, but also because Ella and Clara are so distressed. I can't bear it.

Once I'm in the bus the journey begins towards Blessenstätte. After only a few moments we glimpse the still-smouldering ruins of the Daltrop and Löwenbach properties. A scream resounds through the bus. Bernhard Daltrop, who till then had no idea that his house had been razed, shouts and sobs, 'Oh G-d, our house; Oh G-d, our house, our house,' and then this very sick man collapses. The journey jolts on to Herzebrock and soon, passing Jacob Rollman's burnt property, we head for the police station, where we pick up Julius, Hugo and Bruno Brill. Our next stop is at the Town Hall in Rheda, where we wait for about half an hour while an unruly crowd gathers. In contrast to the Güterslohers, they behave in a surly and threatening manner. Louis Stern, face beaten black and blue, leads the Jews of Rheda on to the bus.

We breathe a sigh of relief as we pull away.

Already in Wiedenbrück we have had to cram uncomfortably close together to make room for Schnurmann, Egon Hoffmann, Theodor Hirsch with his youngest son, and others of the community. We drive on to Verl, where we pick up Government Auditor A D Hope, who by chance happened to be visiting his mother. Then, via Neuenkirchen, past the sad remains of its synagogue, to Rietberg, where we pack in Dr Goldschmidt, Carl Löwenstein and Wilhelm Dreyer, my business colleague for many years. Now we head for Bielefeld, arriving there at about seven in the evening. Driving down Turnerstrasse we are confronted with a ghastly sight. The large synagogue of Bielefeld, renowned for its beauty, lies in ruin, the dome collapsed, the massive outer walls rearing up in the dark November night – 'in the desolate window sockets dwells the horror'.[64]

Through a side street we are driven into the grounds of a large school and unloaded. Here SS swarm. With swearing and shoving they herd us into the gym hall. About 500 Jewish prisoners from the Bielefeld Gestapo district[65] are already there. I see many familiar faces: my cousins Moritz Herzberg, Max Werthauer and Moritz Isenberg,[66] and further away also Hugo Oppenheim from Rhaden.

As there isn't enough room, we are taken up to the physics hall. Most have small suitcases with a change of clothing, having been told at the time of arrest where they would be going. We from Gütersloh have only our bread under our arm and a piece of cheese in our hand. Pocketknives, scissors, razor blades, pencils, fountain pens and such have to be surrendered. Something akin to the death penalty is threatened should any of these later be found on us.

Hour after hour goes by. If occasionally someone rests head on hand, the

---

[64] 'Das Lied von der Glocke' lines 214-215, by Friederich von Schiller.
[65] Government district Minden and both Lippe districts.
[66] According to the document from the Buchenwald Foundation, Moritz Isenberg was not released from Buchenwald till 16.12.38, nineteen days after Leopold Herzberg. See official Buchenwald record of numbers allocated to inmates, page 171.

whole group has to stand. 'Liven up' comes the command. Yet cruelly we are not allowed to stand unless ordered to do so. Bernhard Daltrop, who had persistently but without success requested a doctor while still in Gütersloh, can no longer sit or lie. He begs to be allowed to stand. This is denied him. His brother Julius finally promises to try to find a doctor, despite the late hour.

At two in the morning, the first transport marches off; at half past three the second; and then those of us who remain are organised for a roll call. A miracle occurs. Bernhard Daltrop is medically examined and released, together with the young boy Hirsch from Rheda, who is not yet fifteen.

At exactly five o'clock, our column marches off, hemmed in on both sides by SS, wielding rubber truncheons. And now begins a rowdy pageant of ceaseless screaming, shouting and herding. 'Keep up, keep up' is heard constantly. Despite that, gaps still form. Without keeping in step, it isn't possible to stay close together in a column. A gap in the ranks brings down a rain of blows on offenders.

A little out of breath we arrive at the railway station. Instantly the order is given: 'Stand still'. For the next three quarters of an hour, till our departure, we stand at attention, not allowed to move – an enormous strain for those holding luggage and for the many older and more frail among us. We are loaded onto carriages, which are then hitched to the regular Hannover express. We steam out on the stroke of six.

Around this time Bernhard Daltrop arrives back in Gütersloh. Instead of going directly to his sister-in-law's he makes his way to the Kirchstrasse, where his house once stood. Here, where he had been happy in his work and in his family circle, all that he had lived for is now thoroughly destroyed at the hands of those criminals. A workman on his way to an early shift takes pity on him: 'Come on Daltrop, this is not for you.'

Taking him by the arm, he brings him to the sister-in-law's home, where his wife has sheltered since the fire. Three months later, in February 1939, Bernhard Daltrop dies, his last words: 'Those damned louts. They're to blame.'

In Hannover we have a two-hour layover before being hooked up to the Leipzig express. In my compartment are Ruben, a manufacturer from Lübeck, the two brothers Fränkel, from Lemgo, and a further three men from Lippe. In every carriage a compartment is reserved for the accompanying SS men, one always patrolling the corridor. Apart from smoking, we are allowed to do whatever we like, even go to the toilet – naturally only with prior official permission. Poor foolish me – when I go, I close the door behind me. The outburst of swearing that descends leaves me, old soldier that I am, quite unmoved. Other than this incident the atmosphere is reasonably cosy. With congenial conversation we almost forget our predicament!

In Halle we are again reshunted and then, via Merseburg and Apolda, head towards Weimar, the city in which the German spirit found its finest expression. The first lines of Goethe's famous poem spring to mind:

'Noble is Man to be/ Helpful and good …'

Slowly the day slips away. As we have seen or heard little from our group of guards since Halle, and after three days of baiting and anxiety, a feeling of peace washes over us. It is already dark as we reach Weimar, stiff from the long journey.

Greeting us on the platform are men in grey-green uniforms armed with rifles, SS Verfügungstruppe 'K'.[67] At the time I was yet to learn who those 'noble' fellows were. The platform meantime is cleared of civilians. The order is given: 'Fall in four abreast. Move it now, four at a time, or we'll help you find your legs.'

Four men run towards a designated spot about fifty metres away. Dreadful screams yank me back to reality. I don't know what's going on, but then once again I hear: 'Next four, let's go. Go.'

Again four men run off and I can now see how one after the other they trip and fall, to be beaten with rifles and sticks in the most mean and brutal way. The screams of those beaten and the ranting and raving of the SS make the blood freeze. I pull myself together and observe SS standing along the right and left of the platform extending leg or rifle to trip the oncoming runners. Now it's my turn. I run like a hare, jump over legs and rifles, evading the traps. When I realise that one of the SS is blocking my path, I simply run at him full force so that he stumbles backwards, then line up breathless in rank and file, as required.

That was Act One. The interval doesn't last long.

After we've been counted, it begins again. This time down the stairs to the underpass, four at a time, clobbered as though we were inanimate pieces of

---

[67] The SS Verfügungstruppe 'K' (SS unit for special tasks) was originally a ready reserve at the disposal of, and controlled by, Himmler. It was the nucleus of the later Waffen SS (Armed SS). The term 'K' indicates that in the circumstances described above, this military unit was being employed in herding the prisoners to the camps. SS camp guards came from the ranks of the elite SS Totenkopf-Verbände (Death's Heads Unit), which controlled the camps.

A very fit Leopold (left) on holiday with his nephew, Kurt Herzberg, in 1934.

wood. Again I get by untouched, but for the less agile and the old it is cruel. Downstairs in the tunnel we have to line up, this time in groups of five, but facing the wall. Behind us and around us the SS scurry like a pack of wild furies. 'Hats off, hats off!' they shout, indiscriminately beating the victims, always on their heads. No one knows what to do. Some take their hats off, and wooden staves come whistling down squarely on bare heads.

'What does it matter if you perish? That's why you were sent here, you swindlers.' With hat pulled down to eye level, I plant elbows and knees against the wall, not to be crushed by the frightened men standing behind me.

Already another order: 'Seven men go. Get a move on, you dogs!' We have been standing in rows of five! So, as the men start running there are always too many or too few in the line to form sevens; the many 'extras' get the 'treatment', especially those who are not fleet of foot.

This time we get as far as the front of the railway station, where a line of personnel trucks is standing. With one leap I'm on, grabbing a seat more or less in the middle, from which I won't let myself be pushed, even though more and more people are cudgeled into the vehicle. The frenzy of the 'pack of hounds' continues. We are pressed together more and more.

'Keep those heads down! Will you get your heads down!' And where a head is not pulled down onto the chest, blows rain from all sides. We are bathed in perspiration, panting from exertion and agitation.

Suddenly all is quiet. A single voice is heard: 'So, tonight is your Sabbath! Well then, one of you can say a prayer.'

Silence! One hears only the laboured breathing of people driven harder than cattle. Then someone from the middle of our group declares loudly, voice tense and trembling:

'Shema yisroel adoschem elokeinu adoschem echod. Boruch schem kewaud malchussau ...' (Deuteronomy 6:4/5)

'And what does that mean in German?'

'Hear, O Israel: the Lord our G-d, the Lord is One. Blessed be the name of His glorious kingdom for ever and ever.'

'So now, somebody tell us something from that fine Talmud of yours.'
The reply comes in a flash:
'Weohafto lereiacho komaucho' (Leviticus19:18)
'And what's the German for that?'
'Thou shalt love thy neighbour as thyself.'
A short surprised silence.
'Oh, no! No way. It's *Der Stürmer*[68] you should read. That's where you'll find the truth.'

Did the biblical quotations make any impact on these dehumanised people? Who knows? At least there is now peace and quiet.

Several more minutes elapse before the convoy moves off.

In just under half an hour we reach our destination. Even before our truck is opened I already hear the ranting and raving of the SS above the screams of defenceless victims. As the flap of our truck is let down I see a building about forty metres ahead with a central entrance way: *Das Tor* (The Gate). It has a divided latticed grill. Only one half of the grill is open. Towards the narrow gap, rush frightened men. A few have fallen while leaving our truck; they are

---

[68]   The Nazi anti-Semitic newspaper.

writing on the ground. With a broad jump I leap over them and run; run through *Das Tor*, across a wide square and then hear someone say, 'Easy boys, just take it easy. We won't harm you. The main thing is you've got past those brutes at the gate.'[69]

The person speaking is wearing a sort of uniform: forage cap, prewar Uhlan brigade jacket shorn of the red trimmings and buttons, black breeches and high cavalry boots. There are several men similarly dressed whose armbands say either 'Block Senior' or '*Kapo*'. They organise us into ranks of ten, one row behind the other, forming squares. They calm us with their words, speaking to men totally exhausted from days of unceasing tension. After the harried run, men are now collapsing like flies.

'We are prisoners just like you. We've survived in camps like this for several years.' It seems like a ray of hope. Could there also be real human beings in this camp, not just beasts of human appearance?

A few snowflakes dance in the air and it's wonderfully refreshing to catch one in your mouth. Slowly we calm down and look around. We are standing in a large square illuminated by a number of searchlights from the direction of *Das Tor*. To the right, to the left and behind us stand other blocs of prisoners, some having arrived hours before us. From somewhere in the dark there is a continuous sound of hammering and banging. Prisoners in blue-grey striped prison garb are carrying piles of planks and beams; apparently more barracks are being built.

Next to me is my friend Wilhelm Dreyer from Rietberg. We promise one another to stay together if possible. I am somewhat worried about my cousin Moritz Herzberg, from Detmold. Finally having asked around, I learn that he has a gash at least five centimetres long, with blood crusting from the top of his head to his brow. The area around the injury is now very swollen. He also has a cut on one hand. He is generally alright, but the pain is severe.

Will there be anything to eat or, better still, to drink? The traumatic turmoil has made us very thirsty; we've had no fluids since early yesterday morning. Hour after hour passes. For many of the elderly among us, standing still for such a long time is indescribably difficult. The bright beams of the searchlights become unbearable. The air is also becoming chilly. Buchenwald is about 2,000 feet above sea level. We are not permitted to wear hats. Only days later do I learn the reason for this restriction. It seems that hats are inappropriate for

---

[69] See Appendix 6

168

people of a lower race. It is actually regarded as an outrageous provocation to keep one's head covered within range or view of people of the higher race. Therefore, in the camp we are allowed to wear hats only in the barracks and in the narrow paths between barracks, where we can't be seen by guards. If, however, someone from the SS approaches, then there will be loud warning: 'Attention!' Whoever does not remove his hat quickly can expect to have it knocked off his head with a riding whip.

We stand, we wait, we wonder about things to come. Then everyone receives a chit of paper with a number on it. We are ordered: 'Keep your piece of paper in your pocket so that you are always identifiable, no matter what.'

I am now 28978.[70]

Kommandantenhaus (Headquarters) and watchtower over *Das Tor* (Entrance Gate) – approach to Buchenwald concentration camp.

---

[70] This numbering of concentration camp inmates merely on paper foreshadowed the notorious tattooing of numbers on the forearms of inmates at Auschwitz.

The latticed gate carrying the ancient slogan
Jedem Das Seine (To Each What He Deserves).

Day long assembly for roll-call in Buchenwald concentration camp of the men
arrested during *Kristallnacht*. (Source: US Holocaust Memorial Museum)

28	961	Jacobs	Adolf	19.12. entl
	2	Hauschner	Hans	16.1. entl
	3	Silberbach	Walter	12.12. a.18
	4	Arensberg	Hermann	12.12. entl
	5	Kleinstrass	Karl	6.12. entl
	6	Frenkel	Walter	12.12. entl.
	7	~	neue Nr.	30 349
	8	Kaudors	Eduard	12.12. entl
	9	~	neue Nr.	30 332
28	970	Steinberg	Nathan	29.11. entl
	1	Katz	Alfred	27.11. entl
	2	Steinberg	Josef	8.12. entl
	3	Arensberg	Gustav	12.12. entl
	4	Frankenthal	Bruno	23.12. entl
	5	Heinberg	Fritz	19.1. entl
	6	Rosenbaum	Ernst	15.11. verst.
	7	Drojer	Wilhelm	24.12. entl
	8	Herzberg	Leopold	27.11. entl
	9	Herz	Heinrich	24.11. entl
28.	980	Eichmann	Hans	12.12. entl
	1	Jonas	Herbert	26.1. entl
	2	Davidsohn	Otto	24.12. entl
	3	Spanier	Arnold	6.12. entl
	4	Heinberg	Leopold	26.1. entl
	5	Steinweg	Leo	23.11. entl
	6	Valk	Samuel	12.12. entl
	7	Isenberg	Moritz	16.12. entl
	8	Bähr	Philipp	27.11. entl
	9	Löwenstein	Leopold	21.11. entl
28	990	Bachrach	Gustav	29.11.38 entl

1 7841

Page copied from the original handwritten Buchenwald register recording the
numbers given to inmates, their date of release (*entl*), or death (*verst*).
Leopold Herzberg became number 28978; released on 27.11.38.

Page copied from the book recording daily changes in numbers of prisoners in Buchenwald concentration camp. (Translation below)

Administrator of Belongings   K.L.Buchenwald, 12.11.38

Update Report

Inmate numbers on 11.11.1938 - - - - 13992

Departures: 15

Arrivals   4683

_____

Inmate Numbers on 12.11.1938 - - - - 18660

Numbers allocated: Corporal

Numbers available used: 515,581,603,615,832,852,955,1455,1943.
Consecutive numbers (allocated to arrivals) : 24561 to 29243 inclusive.

_____

: 399 numbers: Additionally 480, 624, 844, 2038, 2123, 2938, 6563, 6689, 6853, 8852,. Total 410 free numbers

Finally, half an hour after midnight, we are off to the barracks. Thank goodness! Down from the large asphalted square we first encounter soggy clay soil, into which our feet sink, past Barracks 1, 2, 3, 4, and into Barracks 5. Our hope of rest and sleep is short lived. The barracks are as yet no more than four walls with a very incomplete roof. What is worse – no floor boards; just bare damp clay with puddles here and there from rain earlier that day. But the real heartbreak is that the intended multiple levels of sleeping bunks have not yet been assembled. Five levels of bunks would later prove to be insufficient for the number of prisoners forced into Barracks 5. On this night, all those men had to find space for themselves on the wet clay ground, on one level only!

Everyone is seeking a somewhat dry spot. More men keep coming, trying to squeeze in somewhere – kneeling, squatting, lying every which way. It is not possible to get any rest. From time to time sleep overcomes us, but if you are lying with your back across somebody else, with your head hanging unsupported, or if someone else weighing at least 200 pounds lies across your feet, sleep is unattainable. We torture ourselves thus for a few hours. At five we are ordered back on our feet.

Again we stand and wait. For what? Will there be coffee? Will we be split up into groups? Fitted out with prison garb? Will orderly camp life begin, however harsh?

In this way hours drag by. Come dawn, I have managed to worm my way to the doorway. We are allowed to go to the toilet in small groups. On return, I see a curled-up figure on the ground, covered by a tarpaulin, just a hand poking out. A dead hand. 'This is the first,' I think to myself, and am shocked to realise how unmoved this leaves me.

We are soon ordered outside. At eight thirty 12,000 Jews of the November *Aktion*, the full complement of the five barracks, stand on the large assembly square, grouped according to the Gestapo districts from which they've come. And there we have to stand till evening, a full eleven hours.

It is more than a test of patience. It is a physically fatiguing, emotionally unnerving struggle.

But heaven is kinder to us than humanity, sending us a beautiful sunny, warm day, rarely the case in November. Throughout the day, names stream out from the loudspeaker at *Das Tor*, identifying all inmates, listing and numbering them to finalise the roll.

Around eleven in the morning there is coffee. Can this be real? Yes!

Cauldrons of coffee are dragged out. Thank G-d!

Small bowls are handed round. Now the shock. Each bowl is to be shared by five prisoners. This proves to be almost worse than if there'd been nothing at all. It needs absolute self-control to stop after one mouthful, not to swill down everything in that bowl.

Time passes terribly slowly, but pass it does. In the afternoon we get a meal of potatoes and goulash, a thick white sauce in which swim shreds of reddish meat. Prisoners lug the containers of food over to us and dish it out. As it's 'first come first served', around every pot there is crush and chaos as the starving men descend upon those doling out the food. Everyone wants to be first in line. Strangely, neither the SS nor the *Kapos* are bothered by the confusion. I finally manage to get a couple of dry potatoes, but can't get near the pots of meat. My disappointment is extreme, as is my hunger. That I have missed out on the fine goulash turns out to be fortunate, as will become evident twelve hours later.

For the time being we still have to stand. This eternal standing and waiting, the need to sleep, the hunger, the thirst, the recurring horrific visions of the past few days and concern for our families – all this is fraying our nerves.

A shout reverberates across the wide square, so loud that it reaches the farthest corners: 'A great miracle is taking place. A great miracle is taking place. A great mirac …' But now the SS and the *Kapos* have swung into action. Off they race. I see the person who is shouting, see how he is knocked down, how they forcibly hold closed his nose and mouth. He struggles as people do who suddenly go mad. When his mouth is momentarily freed, snatches resound again: '… miracle … taking place …'

From *Das Tor* the Adjutant's voice comes over the loudspeaker: 'Can't you silence that swine?' Yes! They can do that. A few blows across the head with a wooden baton have the same effect as an anaesthetic, but quicker and cheaper. A Jew after all is worth about twelve *Pfennig*, – the cost of a bullet. We had been repeatedly assured of this during the 'reception' at the Weimar railway station.

What is to become of us? What are they actually planning? Such questions dominate our thoughts.

The most incredible rumours are circulating: 'England and the United States have lodged a protest with the German government over its treatment of Jews. They have decided to change their immigration laws, allowing immediate entry of all Jews who have been taken to concentration camps. Until this can be achieved, Jews are to be transferred to Luxembourg and Belgium, which will accept and house the Jews in camps. The whole world is enraged by the uncivilised and inhuman treatment meted out. In the past few days enormous amounts of money have already been raised to facilitate the release from their tormentors. Transport out is imminent; perhaps already tomorrow.'

Once again, someone quite nearby has become disturbed. It's Levy from Rheda, the painter's brother. He is already talking loudly, just absolute nonsense. There is madness in his eyes. Again and again we manage to calm him to avoid attracting attention.

It has long since grown dark. Our hopes fade that before this day ends we will be given something more to drink, be able to have a wash, be fitted out in camp gear, be grouped to occupy the barracks visible behind the parade ground.

We are told there is virtually no water up here in Buchenwald. The little that is available, and only at certain times, is said to be contaminated by typhoid. An attempt to obtain and drink the water would anyway be punishable by death. Some in our section approach a *Kapo*, who promises to get us coffee if we make a donation 'to a good cause'. In no time 60 Marks are collected. Now we should be alright, at least that's what we think. However, no coffee eventuates. As a result our sense of thirst increases.

* * *

Shortly before eight in the evening we finally move off, our group once again to Barracks 5, no closer to completion than on the previous evening. For a while I remain in the pathway between the barracks, partly because one can't really lie down anyway, but also in the hope of somehow getting something to drink. I meet Hugo Brill, who has bought a bottle of 'typhoid-free water' for 5 Marks. He gives me a thimble-full, but won't divulge its source.

At about ten, Wilhelm Dreyer and I go into the barracks and squeeze ourselves in, somewhere near the entrance. He sits on his small suitcase and I lie in front of him, the last of my bread under my arm, my head in his lap. How long has it been since I last slept? On the night from Tuesday to Wednesday, I was awakened at three in the morning. The following night in gaol I also didn't get much sleep. The last two nights I have spent totally without sleep. I am lying very uncomfortably. Moreover, someone is now sitting on my right leg. Someone next to me constantly supports himself with his hand on my left foot. Despite all this, I'm hoping to be able to sleep. I desperately need sleep.

However, the commotion is much too great. Approximately 2,600 men are in our barracks, which is about eighty metres long and ten metres wide. A hum buzzes as in a beehive, interrupted every so often by the shouts of the two or three men who are the supervisors and are supposed to ensure law and order. Unfortunately, the men chosen are those least suited for the job. They are more nervous than those in their care. By their continual yelling and screaming they are aggravating the unrest, which swells increasingly. I don't want to hear a thing. I want to sleep. But that is impossible.

Now there is a loud call from somewhere in a far corner: 'Doctor, doctor, doctor.' One of the many doctors among us works his way towards the area from which the call came. Someone has fainted. This recurs several times and I quickly realise this will be another night without sleep. It will be a night of horror. If only we were able to sleep for a few hours we might be free from reliving the terrors of past days. It might help us tolerate the hunger or, worse, the thirst.

Nerves are being tested to breaking point. Many among us are unable to cope. It happens, as it had to happen. No! As is being provoked by those beasts in uniform. Through planned deprivation of sleep, hunger, thirst and constant threats, those with weak nerves become frantic and are driven to bouts of madness.

It starts with one person whose hysterical shouting draws a pair of *Kapos* into the barracks. After a few attempts to calm and pacify the man, they drag him outside into the night, where he is 'doctored' as was the 'miracle man'. Before long, another. Restlessness is spreading progressively throughout the barracks. It is as if the first case has been infectious. More *Kapos* come in and finally beat anyone who screams. Between the shouts and yells are heard the pleadings of the circumspect among us who urge peace and quiet. This is set against the hollering of the supervisors until finally SS guards appear, threatening the most severe measures unless there is instant quiet.

But there is no peace and no quiet. Suddenly someone next to me yells out he wants his shoe; he screams non-stop. He is quickly given any shoe just to calm him, but he becomes quite wild. A *Kapo* crawls towards him and holds his mouth and nose shut, but to no avail. He throws himself on top of the man and then twists each one of his fingers out of joint. The ranting and raving become worse and the victim suffers the same fate as the others: dragged out into the night and beaten senseless.

I feel a prickling and crawling sensation in my veins, as though I have swallowed a thousand ants. I know that in this place I must not become agitated. Lose your nerve and you are unlikely ever to see family again. I force myself to appear calm, suppressing my feelings about the dread happenings around me. Everything leaves me quite cold, even when I see Willi Garty, friend from Gütersloh, eyes staring, froth at the mouth, raving and thrashing about, now also carted to the exit. Happen to him what may, there is no way I can help him.

I … must … remain … calm.

I would like to sleep, but more and more people are stepping over me, heading for the toilet. At first I have no idea why, even though among 2,600 people there must always be quite a number needing to go. However, the pace increases constantly; the rush towards the exit accelerates. Outside, frightening scenes are being played out between the supervisors and the people with urgency. Ten men only from each of the barracks are allowed out to the toilet at any one time.

What's happening? It seems an epidemic has broken out. Once again rumours buzz from ear to ear; first it's dysentery, then typhoid. Yes, typhoid. Many drank from the supposedly typhoid-free water. Apparently they have infected everyone else.

There is a strange mood in the large semi-dark barracks, now bubbling like a witch's cauldron. Suddenly, from the entrance there is a call of 'Attention!' In camp this means SS are approaching and it calls for complete immobility and silence. This time, however, the order is ineffectual, even though repeated four or five times. In no time, the Camp Adjutant himself appears at the entrance with a large bloodhound on leash and accompanied by two guards. He picks his way deliberately and slowly to the centre of the barracks and with the gradual onset of silence, declares in an ugly, arrogant voice: 'Every disturbance in camp will be treated as mutiny. Rioting will be very quickly and effectively put down with machine-gun fire. Aside from the guns on the watchtower, a further twelve have been set up in readiness!'

He brandishes his long elephant whip and departs.

However, the quiet doesn't last, can't last. More and more people are becoming ill. As we learn later it's not from typhoid in the water. The small amount of water made available in Buchenwald is actually pure as can be. Were it even possible to get some, drinking it would be forbidden. No! The people have been made ill by the 'good food' served in the afternoon. The goulash made from whale meat, rancid fat and excess soda has caused the frightful epidemic of diarrhoea. The bouts are more sudden and severe than I have ever observed or believed possible. Whoever needs the toilets climbs painstakingly over comrades on the ground. But in haste and need, they frequently step on bodies or limbs, as there isn't enough free space on the barrack's floor. This can't happen quietly!

Now we hear: tak, tak, tak, tak, tak, tak. I know right away that those shots are not coming into, nor even over the barracks; it's a ploy to frighten and torment us further. The shooting makes me calmer and has a similar effect on many others. But there are still a large number whose fear and anxiety have taken what remained of their sanity. The fits of raving increase.

Willi Garty, recovered from his first attack and returned to the barracks, starts to rave again. I call to him, but neither I nor anyone else manages to calm him. He shouts and yells that he wants water. Out he goes again, grabbed, dragged and beaten so horribly and brutally, as in all G-d's wide world is possible only in a Nazi concentration camp. After only a few minutes he is brought back, but in what a state. He is now wearing only trousers and shirt, the latter hanging in tatters. His arms dangle as though disconnected from his shoulders. He is being wrapped in a blanket and laid on the ground near the entrance. I hope that at last he will be calm and quiet but he continues to moan and whimper.

Now surprise, surprise – a supervisor offers him a sip of water, which only enrages him.

'You dogs! Now you have water? Before, when I begged for one mouthful, just one mouthful for G-d's sake, you had none. I would rather die than drink that water.'

'What? You want to die, you stupid fellow? Here, we can arrange that very quickly.'

Already he is dragged to his feet. 'Yes, I want to die, but first let me pray once more.'

This unhappy man rises to his knees and prays in a voice reaching every corner of the barracks. He prays for his old, sick mother, about whom he's been fantasising these past days. Witnessing this stresses me anew; my limbs are shaking. I feel I should intervene, but I force myself to hang back. No one can help him. One can only bring harm upon oneself.

But scarcely have his first terrible screams penetrated the barracks when a young man leaps out of the semi-darkness, near the entrance. 'Jews,' he shouts, 'are you still Jews or not? How can you watch while your brothers are butchered one after the other?' He gets no further before being grabbed and also dragged outside. I've realised who he is; he is the younger of the two brothers Fränkel from Lemgo. Willi Garty is his sister's fiancé. The older brother, not wanting to desert his sibling and future brother-in-law, pushes his way forward, intending to follow.

His way is barred and he is threatened with the same fate if he dares to step out. 'I don't care,' he replies. 'I was in the trenches for four years. I have severe war injuries; I am certainly not afraid of you.'

'So, you're not afraid? Well then, take your courage outside with you.' Before he can exit, he is hurled through the doorway. The drama proceeds outside, unseen but not unheard.

While these are isolated incidents in an enormous *Tauhu wovauhu*[71] occurring in the large hall, they distress me all the more because I know the people involved. Given the virulence of the diarrhoea epidemic and the erupting fits of madness, it is as if all order has been abolished.

* * *

Many hours have passed since the order was given that ten men only may leave the barracks at any one time. Many hours also since I gave up my place on the ground because ever-increasing numbers of people are becoming ill. In their urgency to reach the exit they stumble with less and less consideration over their comrades. Many don't reach the goal in time. My suit is soiled with shit running out of the trouser legs of those who clambered over me. I've fled to the wall of the barracks, together with Wilhelm Dreyer and Carl Löwenstein. So far, we three have been spared this illness, and hope to avoid it.

Then Wilhelm Dreyer's face suddenly becomes ghostly pale – no, green. His lips quiver and he weaves as a drunk towards the exit. At first Carl Löwenstein makes corny jokes about him, but soon follows. It is terrible to observe that within moments this illness can make tough, strong young men listless and weak as children.

To stay on my feet, I must now marshal all my energy. Though I've eaten hardly anything for days, I don't feel hungry. Though I've hardly slept a wink, I

---

[71] *Tauhu wovauhu* (In Hebrew, *Tohu Vavohu*): the literal translation of the words is 'formless and void'. In this case the meaning is 'disorder' or 'chaos'.

don't feel tired. But I am in a fever-like state; my knees are becoming weak, my head feels hollow, everything that happens around me seems blurred and unreal.

Out of the turmoil and confusion a man comes towards me, an apparition from the heaving horde, face and neck smeared with blood. He is in a state of extreme agitation and despair, perhaps even madness: 'I have just said the *Scheimes*[72] for my son': "The blood of your brother Abel cries out to me." My son is lying outside, in front of the barracks, dead and dreadfully mutilated. Now I am going outside to take revenge on his murderers.' All attempts to calm and restrain him are to no avail. He too runs out into the night. Which of his thoughts are real and which are delusions, I don't know. Neither do I know what happened to him, but I can imagine.

Suddenly there is an announcement. The *Kommandant* is making an exception due to 'special circumstances', giving permission to leave the barracks before six in the morning. I thank G-d that this night has come to an end. I'm ready to believe that orderly running of the camp and regular distribution of food are about to begin. Anticipation works wonders, as does the truly beautiful air of the Thüringer Forest, which I now drink in, in deep draughts. Not only do I feel better, but I've also regained strength and courage. It may not seem plausible but I am now fully convinced that the truly wonderful air in the Thüringer Forest has greatly contributed to our survival during this frightful period.

We gather in a small area directly adjacent to our barracks and stand for more than two hours sinking into deep, mushy clay, without anyone bothering about us. Then it's 'at the double' to the assembly square. There we are sorted and counted and counted again, the while having nothing to do but stand. That is not easy, for it takes so long. Our craving for something to eat and drink has again been aggravated.

Gradually the emptiness in my stomach causes nausea, made worse by the stench from all directions; every third person has soiled his trousers to a greater or lesser degree. Many collapse, particularly those with heart problems or diabetes. When a member of the SS comes into view, these men are quickly stood on their feet by comrades, to avoid 'other measures'! A scene of grief and misery.

Have the hands of the clock on the headquarters tower stopped? Has time

---

[72] The three attributes of G-d recited at the conclusion of *Ne-ile* on *Jaum Kippur*: 'Hear, O Israel: the Lord our G-d, the Lord is One. / Blessed be His glorious Kingdom forever and ever. / The Lord he is G-d.' In Germany at the time this was usually recited by a member of the *Chevro Kadischo* for a person approaching death.

itself slowed? There is still nothing to eat, but we do have a lovely day, warm and sunny, like early spring, even though it's mid-November! It's very beautiful up here in the Thüringer Forest. The broad well-kept assembly square suggests a park. Several fine, tall trees have been left standing here and there. You could make believe you were at a scenic outdoor health resort. Added to this, the *Kommandantenhaus*, the camp headquarters building, is crowned by a pretty little clock tower and has two adjoining wings. It fits well into my daydream as restaurant premises similar to the coffee houses we used to visit with family and friends on Sunday afternoons. Missing are elegant people, tables and chairs and waiters rushing about.

At the camp headquarters building, *Das Tor* is the latticed gate (the *Gittertor*) which bears the slogan *JEDEM DAS SEINE* (To Each What He Deserves). The rooms above the gate serve as guardrooms for *Scharführer* and *Oberscharführer*[73] and others on duty. Besides housing the clock, the tower is ringed by powerful searchlights, which can illuminate the whole assembly square so brightly that not even a tiny mouse could hide. It is surrounded by a wide gallery from which guards on duty have an excellent view of the whole assembly square and can see down the mountain to the far-away barracks for long-term 'guests'. Several machine guns are always at hand for immediate use.

To what use the side buildings are put I have not personally experienced. I have learned that at least one contains the notorious *Bunker*, a group of cells for 'expiation of crimes' through additional punishments. I have heard from one of the long-term prisoners that these cells are completely dark and so small that one cannot lie down, but at least anyone confined there need not fear contracting diarrhea, as the amount of food provided is so meagre.

A different but equally charming punishment with which we are threatened at every opportunity is 'twenty-five across the backside'. For this, a low and somewhat curved table is used. It looks exactly like a frame for slaughtering calves. The 'delinquent's' feet are held by semi-circular iron rings fixed to one end. He is stretched over the table, arms then tied to the other end of the frame. Once he is unable to move hands or feet, two gallant young SS chosen for size and strength approach and pull down his trousers. To a rhythm of loud counting, blow follows blow with cattle whip or similar instrument. For every outcry an additional blow is added.

The mildest form of punishment for an accused is being forced to stand

---

73 Non-commissioned officers of the SS.

absolutely still 'at attention' for a set number of hours by the wall of the camp headquarters. These prisoners usually collapse unconscious before the allotted time expires.

From the left and right wings flanking the camp headquarters runs the barbed-wire fence that surrounds the enormous concentration camp. It is about five metres high with rows of live electric wire in the lower section. Inside this fence is a flat barbed-wire obstacle two to three metres wide. Any approach to within one metre of this is regarded as an attempt to escape, answered without further warning by machine-gun fire.

* * *

It is now midday and after standing for six hours we welcome the order to sit in the same rank and file in which we had been standing. After half an hour of this, we realise that the order given was not for compassionate reasons. Though standing for a long time had been stressful, sitting on the flat ground is far worse. We have to sit like this for hours; our backs ache and we can no longer find how best to sit.

My strength is slowly dwindling. How long has it been since I've had a worthwhile sleep? How long is it since I've had a proper meal? On Friday midday in the Gütersloh lock-up I had my last warm 'meal'– a tin bowl of potato soup. During the stormy 'reception' in Weimar on Saturday night I lost the remainder of the bread from Gütersloh. I was fortunate to get none of the appetising whale-meat goulash on Sunday but did manage to scavenge just two dry potatoes. Now it is Monday late in the afternoon and I can feel physical hunger pains.

A sudden whisper along our ranks: 'Food is coming'. A group of prisoners appears carrying large food vats. Coffee is handed round. Unfortunately, by the time it's our turn, the coffee has run out. To our disappointment we get a kind of clear soup: somewhat salty water to which a few soup cubes may have been added. This liquid is greedily poured down our throats. It does not quench our thirst, but heightens it. Now other groups of prisoners come, this time handing out a sixth of a loaf of bread and a piece of soft cheese. The cheese is dry and very sharp, almost bitter. I try to force it down to satisfy my craving for anything edible, but end up giving it away to avoid increasing my boundless thirst.

Once again we ask ourselves: 'Is this all there'll be?' The disappointment drives me to such a level of despair that I could do something rash. Here in this camp any foolish reaction will have most severe consequences.

But no, thank heavens! A bunch of prisoners, Jewish youth from Vienna, comes carrying large containers of food. In no time we all have a small bowl of hot soup, a kind of sweet milk soup with a little rice. It tastes just so good. After the first helping we actually get a second and a third. Never in my life, not even during the war, have I gulped down food so greedily. The first intimation of feeling satisfied has so shaken me that my body and limbs quiver and quake. Tears trickle gently down my cheeks.

My strength and confidence return. What had been done to us till now surely was intended only to intimidate us severely. Routine life in the concentration camp can hardly continue in this way. The world around us seems a little brighter.

And lo and behold! Further relief. Though the majority has not yet recovered from the effects of the food poisoning, they have not been allowed to the toilet throughout the long day. A row of drums is now set up on the edge of the assembly square and the order given: 'Step forward one at a time'. The scene that now unfolds is comedy – no, tragicomedy. From all directions men come singly as commanded. In haste they stretch their backsides over the drums, each of which has to accommodate a minimum of three men at a time. From *Das Tor*, the Adjutant and the *Scharführer* enjoy this spectacle, intended as yet another means of humiliation. In fact, it is further evidence of Nazi sadism in KZ[74] Buchenwald. Evening has arrived and with it the degrading episode comes to an end.

Finally we are released from the torture of sitting for so many hours on the flat ground and are moved off to our barracks, adjacent to the assembly square. As work on the interior of our Barracks 5 has been going on all day, everyone expects to find enough space for a reasonable night's sleep. But no, the work is still not finished, so again, from about seven to ten, we have to stand and wait, wait and stand.

At long last we storm into the barracks. Everyone wants to find a good spot. I lie next to Wilhelm Dreyer and my cousins, Moritz Herzberg and Moritz Isenberg. Now we are able to stretch out fully, but even on this night worthwhile refreshing sleep eludes us. Thirst plagues us terribly. Gums and teeth are coated with a thick and sticky layer of mucus.

---

[74] KZ = *Konzentrationslage*r (concentration camp)

Despite my enormous need, sleep will not come. I cannot stop my thoughts wandering back to recent events. All the horrific scenes come back to life – nightmarish life.

I am suddenly shocked out of half-sleep by a scream more harrowing and ghoulish than any I have ever heard. It comes from somewhere outside the barracks. It lasts only moments. In no time the whisper spreads: 'Somebody is hanging on the wire.'

Tension becomes extreme. Fear and dread constrict the breast. I can hardly breathe.

End of Leopold Herzberg's unfinished manuscript.
The further twelve days of his incarceration went unrecorded.

BOOK THREE

To A New World
1938–1956

Kate Mendels (née Herzberg)

1

The arrival of the Australian permit led to the order for Leopold's release from Buchenwald. We all waited anxiously for his return. On 27 November we received his telegram: 'Home today. 3 o'clock train from Bielefeld'. Such excitement.[75]

Karl went to the railway station to meet him, scrutinising everybody passing through the gates. But no Leopold! Finally a figure appeared, in a long overcoat and a hat much too large pulled down over the face. He was looking around warily and seemed frightened of meeting anyone. He scuttled along, every now and then hiding in a recess or doorway. Karl hurried to catch up with him.

There was silent, tearful joy when the family embraced him. He had little appetite for the wonderful meal waiting for him as he was suffering from a severely upset stomach. What a state he was in! So thin. Skin and bones. Sunken eyes. Hair once so full, shorn.

While in detention he had been given little food, and what there was, was contaminated. Worse had been the lack of drinking water. Prisoners had been catching raindrops with their mouths. Leopold was longing for a warm bath, which Ella quickly filled. In her excitement she added too much cold water giving Leopold a frigid surprise. Once this was corrected he could relax and luxuriate.

He volunteered nothing and could not be drawn about his experiences in the camp. He had been told that if he spoke of what he had endured and what he had seen, there would be reprisals against his family. On release, he had been made to sign a document stating he had been well treated.

---

[75] See Appendix 7

Leopold soon recovered mentally and physically with the care given by Ella, his mother and Clara.

After the experiences of *Kristallnacht*, Clara no longer wanted to live alone in her vandalised home, so she moved in with Ella, Leopold and family. Clara was confident that she would shortly get permission to join her elder son, Jehuda, who had migrated to Palestine in the previous year – her preferred destination. Her second son, Werner, now already in New York for some months, had managed to get a well-paying job in his trade as a butcher. She now also applied to go to America.

Long before, we had tried to encourage her to join us when we originally applied for permits for both the United States and Australia but at that time she wanted to be with one or the other of her sons: 'If I come with you to Sydney, I will never be able to see them again. I won't be able to afford it.'

The 'choice' of Australia was made for us on 24 November, when we were granted our landing permits, the basis for release from concentration camps. Permits for the States arrived six weeks later, by which time our Australian travel plans were already well underway.

We were very fond of Clara and again begged her not to close off the option of Australia. It was going to be so hard for us to part from her.

* * *

Outside cover of identity card issued by the Nazi regime.

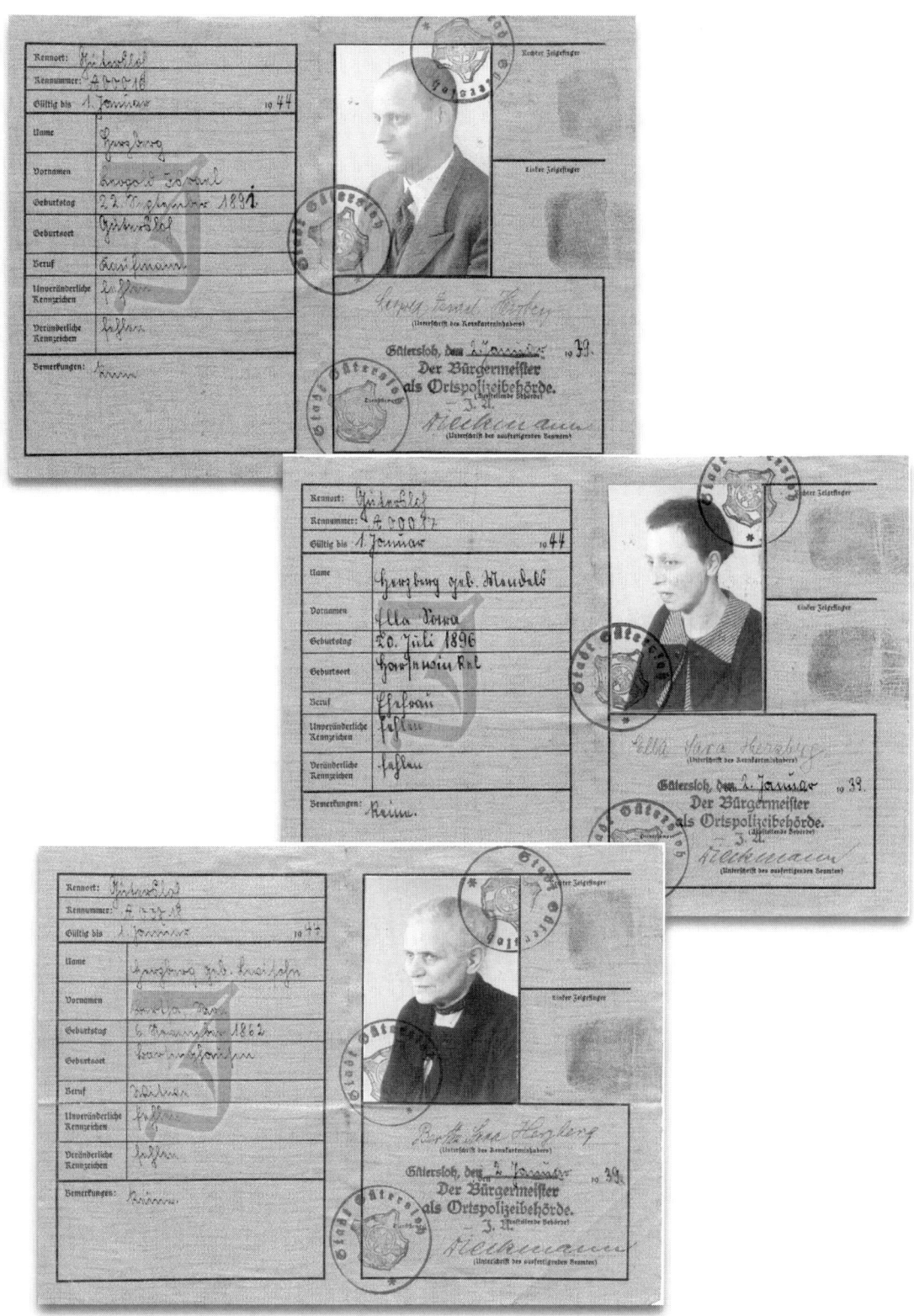

Identity cards of Leopold (Israel), Ella (Sara) and Bertha (Sara) Herzberg,
issued by the Nazi regime.

We were eager to leave the country. Our first task was to book passage by ship. Our choices were limited since we would not go to Australia on a German vessel. Next we had to make arrangements for Oma Riekchen. She could not bring herself to travel across the world. She would either stay with her sister, Jenny Bock, in Holland, or enter an old-age home nearby.

In early January 1939, Karl and Leopold hired a car and drove to Cologne. They were able to book passage on the Dutch liner *Sibajak*. It would be a long journey to Sydney via the Dutch East Indies (today Indonesia) and the coast of northern and eastern Australia.

That achieved, the two men intended to go on to Holland to find accommodation for Oma Riekchen. Though they had passports and permission, they wanted to know whether it was wise to cross the border, so they called in to the Jewish Advisory Committee in the city. The official warned against going into Holland, as they would not be allowed re-entrance. Attempts to return to Germany would likely result in arrest.

Early on the same morning after the men had left for Cologne, a member of the SA, accompanied by a young woman, arrived on our doorstep demanding to take stock in our shop. I begged them to come back the next day:

'My husband's not home. He's gone to Holland to find accommodation for my mother-in-law. He'll be returning tonight.'

'Yes, we knew your husband was planning to go to Holland. Sure, you saw him leave. You may find we won't let him come back! So you may not see him come home.'

'Oh Lord!' I thought. 'Please keep him from crossing into Holland.'

They did the stocktaking in our unheated shop and despite the cold, refused to use our little heated office for their bookwork. They had little knowledge of our goods, recording low values for those easy to sell and surprisingly high values for some old stock.

I worried all day about Karl until at last he phoned from Gütersloh with the good news that they'd managed to get tickets for us and for the Herzbergs, including Oma Herzberg.

Oma Mendels now changed her mind, wanting to follow later with the Schönebergs. Consequently we set about applying for a permit on her behalf. When it was time for us to leave she would spend the interim with her sister, Ella Weinberg, and husband, Gustav, who had moved from Vlotho to Dortmund with their son Walter.

The German government allowed each emigrant to take just 10 Marks out of the country, which would not go far in Australia so we needed to stock up on quality clothing and ample household goods. Organising this kept us busy.

We heard from a number of friends and relatives who were also leaving Germany. Sadly, many others had nowhere to go and knew no one who would arrange permits or affidavits for them. Most of the 'not-so-young' were frightened, overwhelmed at the thought of having to learn a new language and make a living in some unfamiliar land. Hence many German Jews went to Holland or Belgium, countries close by.

A young couple migrated to Holland with their baby son soon after Hitler came to power. Intending to continue in the horsehair manufacturing business, they obtained permission to take with them their truck and machinery from their factory and did well there for a few years. Shortly after Germany occupied Holland, the couple was ordered to Gestapo Headquarters where they were accused of having taken equipment out of Germany without permission. Not expecting to be detained they had left their young son, Peter, with some non-Jewish friends.

The parents never returned from that visit! They shared the fate of so many other Jews trapped by the Germans during the war. The boy came to be regarded by the childless Christian couple as their own son. After the war they wrote to an aunt of Peter's mother in New York, asking whether she wanted Peter to come to her. The aunt replied that she couldn't take the child, being now a widow and living with her daughter.

* * *

No one could know, and few would have believed, that Hitler was planning the extermination of European Jewry. Thousands were waiting for their quota number to be called or permits to come through. Many who knew they had no chance of getting permits decided to accept the very difficult climate and lack of business opportunities and go to Shanghai,[76] or to equatorial South America.

---

[76] To enter Shanghai no permits were required because it was an international city. It has a varied climate, very cold in the winter, hot and humid in the summer. In 1939 the European Jews in Shanghai were all moved into the suburb of Hongkew. Housing was very limited so families lived in just a few rooms. In December 1941, when the Japanese took over the city, the housing became even more limited, as Japanese families were also moved into the district. Although one had to get permission to leave the so-called ghetto, the Japanese treated the Jews reasonably, despite pressure to the contrary from their Nazi allies. Sephardi Jews having British passports were interned separately. In the community there were also Russian Jews from prewar days who were not affected by any restrictions, as the Japanese had a fear of the Soviets.

My sister Rosa and husband, Louis, received their affidavit for financial support guaranteed by our uncle, Meier Levisohn, of New York. They were way down on the quota list, having been reticent in applying for American visas. Their son, Rolf, had by now reached London with the *Kindertransport*. My sister, Helene Levy, and husband, Emil, received their documents for the United States and planned to leave in June to join their three children already in New York.

Jews – now without jobs or businesses, many about to leave for different countries – spent free time visiting family and friends whom they might not see again; many came to Harsewinkel. Oma grew silent and looked ill. Undoubtably she was troubled by our leaving without her. Before our main packing started Karl took her and her belongings to the Weinbergs. Erika went with them to stay in Dortmund till our departure.

In the first days of March 1939 we packed furniture, linen and household goods. There was great excitement in the small town of Harsewinkel when a big van from Bielefeld drove through the streets loaded with a *Lift*[77] labelled SYDNEY AUSTRALIA. Our niece Ilse had come from Rüdinghausen, joining our faithful cleaning lady, Frau Buchman, to help. The firm had sent three experienced men to do the packing, so everything went well. Customs had of course sent someone to supervise. Tax had to be paid on any new item taken out of the country, requiring us to list each item and state how long it had been in our possession. The customs man was good to us: 'The deadline for taking out jewellery is only a few days away. Pack it all now. I'll put my seal on the parcel and all will be well.' As the *Lift* would be arriving after us, we packed three big cabin trunks and several suitcases for the time on the ship and the first weeks in Sydney.

Many of our friends and former customers were standing on the street watching our belongings being loaded. Police Sergeant Adolphe came, 'I see your things are now packed,' and whispered, 'I wish you the best of luck.' We knew there were many who cared and understood that we were fortunate to be able to leave. A cattle dealer to whom Karl had directed a number of our customers generously gave us a gift of 50 Marks, not knowing what to buy.

There were also some who were spiteful, mainly among those who had owed us money for years. Knowing we had no remaining rights under the law, they felt, 'We no longer need to pay our debts to Jews'.

---

[77] A *Lift* is a big shipping container.

Unsere Stadt - gestern und heute

17   <u>Zum Gedenken an die Juden in Harsewinkel</u>

Bis in das 18. Jahrhundert zurück lässt sich jüdisches Leben in Harsewinkel nachweisen.
Blieben die Spuren anfangs sehr vage, so sind seit dem Beginn des 19. Jahrhunderts die beiden
Familien Ostheim und Meinberg nachweisbar. Sowohl die Ostheims als auch die Meinbergs, die
1873 nach Gütersloh übersiedelten, waren Metzger und Viehhändler und angesehene
Geschäftspartner der katholischen Landbevölkerung.

Der Kaufmann Isaac Lorch heiratete 1875 eine Tochter der Familie Ostheim. Von der Familie
Ostheim-Lorch lebte 1938 nur noch der Sohn Salomon Lorch in Harsewinkel. Salomon Lorch
wurde am 10. Dezember 1941 aus seinem Haus am Kirchplatz abgeholt, in das
Konzentrationslager Riga deportiert und ermordet.

1888 ließen sich, von Rheda kommend, die Brüder David und Albert Mendels am Marktplatz in
Harsewinkel nieder und eröffneten ein Textilgeschäft. Sie gehörten bald zu den angesehensten
Einwohnern Harsewinkels. Nachdem Albert Mendels 1911 nach Kamp Lintfort gezogen war,
betrieb David Mendels das Textilgeschäft weiter. Nach seinem Tod im Jahr 1929 übernahm sein
Sohn Karl das Geschäft. In den Abendstunden des 10. November 1938 wurde das Geschäft
überfallen und die Schaufensterscheiben wurden zertrümmert.
Am 4. März 1939 wanderte Karl Mendels zusammen mit seiner Frau Käthe
und den beiden Kindern Paul und Erika nach Australien aus.

Nach 200 Jahren erlosch damit das jüdische Leben in Harsewinkel.

This plaque is on the exterior wall of the very small Jewish cemetery in Harsewinkel. 17 denotes
that this is the seventeenth station of the town's sightseeing walk. (Translation below)

City of
Harsewinkel

Our Town – past and present

17   <u>Commemorating the Jews of Harsewinkel</u>

Jewish life in Harsewinkel can be traced back to the 18th century. Though early information is very
vague, records from the early 19th centuy confirm the presence of the two families Ostheim and
Meinberg. Both the Ostheims and the Meinbergs, who moved to Gütersloh in 1873, were butchers and
cattle dealers and well respected business colleagues of the rural Catholic population.

The merchant Isaac Lorch married a daughter of the Ostheim family in 1875. The only member of the
Family Ostheim-Lorch still in Harsewinkel in 1938 was the son, Salomon Lorch, who was taken from his
home on the Kirchplatz on 10 December 1941, deported to Riga concentration camp and murdered.

The brothers David and Albert Mendels, formerly of Rheda, settled in Harsewinkel in 1888 and opened
a textile shop on the Marktplatz. They were soon among the most respected citizens of Harsewinkel.
After Albert Mendels moved to Kamp Lintfort in 1911, David Mendels continued the business. After his
death in 1929, his son Karl took over the shop. In the evening hours of 10 November 1938 the shop was
raided and the display windows smashed. On 4 March 1939, Karl Mendels together with his wife Käthe
and children Paul and Erika emigrated to Australia.

Thus was extinguished 200 years of Jewish life in Harsewinkel.

When most of the packing was done Ilse took Paulhermann to Rüdinghausen. Our house now bare and empty, Karl and I spent our last night in Harsewinkel with our good neighbours the Feldhaus-Austermanns. Even though there were many Nazis in town, our hosts made us welcome and comfortable. As March nights are cold they gave us a hot water bottle for our bed. Next morning a good breakfast awaited us. It was a Sunday morning. We stayed until after the main Mass, so that churchgoers could make their farewells. Many said they realised how hard it would be to go to a country far away, with different language and customs. Our response to all was: 'The Nazi's *Kristallnacht* and pogroms have made it easier for us to leave. We are thankful there is a country to which we can go, where people live without fear.'

We had sent our big cabin trunks to the Dortmund railway station the day before and now had only hand luggage. We said a last goodbye to our good friends, stepped into a taxi and drove to the cemetery to take leave of the graves of Karl's father and his maternal grandparents, Daniel and Lina (née Frankenfeld) Gronsfeld. As we left town, I looked back for a final glance and said, 'Harsewinkel is history. We're off to a new world.'

2

In Gütersloh we enjoyed a hot lunch lovingly prepared by Clara. We spent time with Oma Bertha, Leopold, Ella, Walter and Ursula, who were to follow us to Holland a few days later. We had made our visit to the cemetery in Gütersloh some days earlier and had exchanged a last *Auf Wiedersehen* with most of our Jewish Gütersloh friends. Saying farewell was wrenching for us and for them, especially for those who had not found a country that would accept them. Eyes brimmed with tears.

Parting from Clara, a wonderful person,[78] was harder than expected. We had been such close friends. Our shared hope was to find some way to see each other again, even were it to take years. That was not to be. Poor Clara! How dreadful was to be your fate!

A short train ride took us to Dortmund, where we stayed till Tuesday with Oma Riekchen and Erika, at Ella and Gustav Weinberg's place. Oma was excited to see us, but upset that Paulhermann wasn't with us. We phoned the Neugartens in Rüdinghausen and Ilse brought him within the hour.

When time came to say goodbye we were hoping for a reunion in Sydney, having applied for permits for the Weinbergs also. The plan was for them to travel with the Schönebergs and Oma Riekchen. Oma did not look well, anxious over both our parting and our journey. I believe she cried for a long while after our departure.

---

[78] When we left, Erika was only five years old and so couldn't comprehend the anguish of the moment. She turned to Aunty Clara and said, 'Bye-bye Aunty Clara. We are going a long way away and we are never going to see you again.' None of the children realised what a traumatic time this was for the adults. For them, embarking on this journey was an adventure.

At the railway station in Dortmund we saw my sister Rosa and husband, Louis, for what would be the last time. Their daughter, Ilse, was soon to join her brother, Rolf, in London.

On our way to Utrecht in Holland, Karl and I were preoccupied with thoughts of the past months. As we approached the Dutch border Karl commented, 'Look children, that locomotive over there with the big brass chimney – that's Dutch.' 'Now can we spit on Germany,' said the children. They promptly did.

At the border, Nazi and Dutch officials came into our compartment for customs inspection, fortunately treating us reasonably. We had heard of people who had been body-searched or strip-searched.

Oma Mendel's sister, Jenny Bock, husband Julius, and son Ernst, lived in Utrecht. We four stayed with them the first night. When the Herzbergs arrived, Ella and Leopold, Karl and I booked into a hotel, leaving the four children and Oma Herzberg at the Bock's. After lunch on Wednesday and more farewells, the nine of us left together for Rotterdam to board the big steamship, *Sibajak*.

This was my first view of the ocean. I was forty-four years of age! What is more, since my marriage I had not taken a real holiday other than our honeymoon. I had done no more than visit family, mostly Karl's siblings or mine, for an occasional weekend.

The Herzberg family ticket from Rotterdam to Sydney for both the *Sibajak* and the *Marella*.

3

We sailed out of Rotterdam at five on the afternoon of Wednesday 8 March 1939, a rough and windy day. The North Sea was wild. Most of the women and children were soon seasick, but Leopold and Karl felt fit enough to go to the dining room. We were travelling first class, because that arrangement allowed us to take limited additional money out of Germany to spend on board. We hoped to save most of it for Sydney.

The ship was luxurious. All cabins had expensive wall-to-wall carpets. The children's cabin adjoined ours and both were spacious. We shared a bathroom with another family. The dining room was magnificent, tables laid with the finest damask tablecloths, decorated daily with fresh flowers and silk ribbons. Lunch and dinner menus offered a choice of forty dishes, individually identified by a number. An East Indies boy attended each couple. On a silver tray, he took away cards on which guests had written the numbers of the items chosen. In no time he brought and served the meal. Stewards helped us select from the menu and served drinks. The children had their separate dining room, supervised by a children's nurse.

To occupy the youngsters on the long journey a young crew member taught handicrafts, also supervising exercise classes.

On 15 March we heard over the ship's wireless that Hitler had occupied the rest of Czechoslovakia. It was frightening to realise that he was gaining power over more and more countries in Europe.

On board were many wealthy Dutch passengers – plantation owners and big businessmen returning to the Dutch East Indies from holidays in Holland.

There were also many Jewish refugees. Like us, they were enjoying life aboard ship, at the same time concerned about challenges we were all about to face and problems affecting the families left behind. At every port we looked forward to letters from them, some written and sent before our departure. Airmail was still a rarity.

Among the letters that reached us was one from Oma Riekchen saying that the Weinbergs were looking after her very well and imploring us to do our utmost to get permits for the Schönebergs and Weinbergs. Walter Weinberg had married and would now need a permit for his wife as well.

There was also a letter from my sister, Rosa Neugarten:

Dear ones all,

Perhaps you have already heard from the States but if not, I am sorry to be the bearer of sad news Mother. I have just learnt that your brother, Uncle Meyer, has passed away. We send our condolences. Despite her loss, Aunt Tillie has remembered to send our affidavits.

You'll be surprised that this letter comes to you from Cologne. We left Rüdinghausen for a number of reasons, the most important being that I could get no medical attention for my diabetes, as no Aryan doctor would treat me or even see me. Moreover, our tenants became intolerably spiteful.

Here, we are in a big apartment building with many Jewish families. We are pleased to be with people of similar views and lifestyles. I get good treatment at the Jewish hospital.

We had a happy letter from Rolf from London. Ilse will shortly be joining him. We hope our USA quota number will soon be called, leading to reunion with our London children, in New York.[79]

Helene and Emil Levy will sail in a few weeks and are looking forward to joining their three children in New York.

Louis sends regards.

Love and kisses,

Your daughter, sister and aunt,

Rosa.

---

[79] Rosa and Louis were expecting to go to America, anticipating that Ilse and Rolf would come from England to join them in New York, where there was a large circle of relatives. In England there were none.

The third letter was from my sister-in-law, Clara Herzberg:

Dear ones all,

My thoughts are with you constantly, accompanying you on your long sea voyage. The trip through the tropics must be very exhausting.

Today a letter arrived from Jehuda with unpleasant news. His wife, Liesel, has had an affair. He is divorcing her. Liesel's father had offered to guarantee £1000 for my admission to Palestine. That offer has been withdrawn; my opportunity to join Jehuda is now lost. Unfortunately my number on the USA quota list is very high. I have to accept reality!

I did not take up your offer when you begged me to go with you to Australia, a land so far from Palestine or America, because I could not see myself ever in a financial position to see my sons again.

Since having to give up my home, I am living with the two Daltrop sisters-in-law, in Karl Steinberg's house. We're getting on well together. They send regards.

Lots of love and kisses,

Clara.

Clara's letter shocked us profoundly. We immediately sent a message to Leon in Sydney, asking him to find a guarantor for Clara to come to Australia, stressing that she was a capable businesswoman and skilled housewife, willing to work as a housekeeper.

We were not always in a mood to participate in entertainment provided nearly every night: dancing, even fancy dress balls for adults and parties for children. Shortly before arriving at Colombo the captain gave an *au revoir* dinner for those refugee passengers who were to transfer to a ship taking a direct route to Australia.

* * *

Karl developed a carbuncle, which made it painful for him to sit. As antibiotics were not yet known, many uncomfortable days had to pass before the ship's doctor could lance the boil. We supplemented the dressings with sterile gauze we had brought with us, convinced that the dressings weren't being changed often enough.

At Surabaya all of us disembarked, except Karl. It was good to feel land under our feet again. The world we saw was very new and intriguing: the huts of the indigenous population, monkeys clambering up and down tall palm trees.

In our absence, while Karl was relaxing on deck, one of the Dutch plantation owners approached him, 'Are you alright?'

'I've got a carbuncle which makes walking painful for me but it's getting better. But I do have another problem.'

'Could I help?'

'Maybe. You see, by travelling first class we could increase the amount of cash we could take out of Germany for ship-board spending. We understood that what we didn't spend, we could take into Australia. Now the purser tells us that while we can buy whatever we want on board or in the various ports, money not spent has to be returned to Germany.'[80]

'Surely there must be a way round the problem. I know the purser well, because I make this journey frequently, always on the *Sibajak*. Perhaps we could work something out. Now, if while you're in Batavia you could 'buy' refrigerators, for example, in a phantom deal, that would give you the documentation you need. The purser and the barber take your left-over money back to Holland, taking a cut for themselves. Do you have someone in Holland who could pick up the money from them, then send it to you in Australia?'

'That's a marvellous idea. That would solve it. We do have friends in Batavia who could help. They're in the import-export business. And I do have relatives in Holland who will be able to do for us what you've suggested.'

Encouraged by Karl's new friend, the purser and the barber agreed to this arrangement – for the Herzbergs and us, only. When we came back on board Karl told us the good news. A great relief.

Our next port was Batavia, at the time part of the Dutch East Indies. Today the city is Indonesian Jakarta. A sizeable part of the population was European. We were greeted by our friends Mr and Mrs Paul Blumenthal, originally from Hannover. It was he who worked for the Dutch import-export firm. They took us in a chauffeur-driven car to their impressive air-conditioned home, exceptional in those days. Even the elegant *Sibajak* did not have air conditioning. It was certainly appreciated, the climate being hot and humid. All work in and around the house was done by coloured servants, of whom there were many.

---

[80] Our tickets for passage on both ships, the *Sibajak* and *Marella*, carried the stamp 'ANY REFUND TO BE MADE IN GERMANY ONLY'. (See document page 200.)

The Blumenthals presented us with several packets of *Matzo*, allowing us to celebrate echoes of a belated *Pesach*. *Jontef* had occurred during the first week of April, when we had not been able to have a *Seder*.

The *Sibajak*'s journey terminated in Batavia. There, together with a number of other passengers, we transferred to the *Marella*, an Australian ship, an old vessel captured from the Germans in the First World War. The *Marella*, a one-class boat, was plain and austere in contrast to the luxurious *Sibajak*. It made us wonder whether life might be equally basic in Australia.

We met new passengers and made new friends. Though English was the language of the crew, most stewards were Chinese. We couldn't understand their English. The sea was sometimes rough and we women were often seasick, Oma spending most of the time in her cabin. The Chinese cabin steward, feeling sorry for her, kept repeating, 'Granny sick again?'

Hearing this over and over, Oma would say, 'Granny sick again', and proudly claim, '*Ich habe schon Englisch sprechen gelernt.*' (I've already learnt to speak English.)

The closer we came to Australia the greater our apprehension. At Darwin, our first Australian port of call, we had to show our landing permits, our £200 landing money and our passports. The health authorities inspected our vaccination papers and examined us medically. We were then free to spend the rest of the day exploring the town. As the law courts were in session our men went there to test how much or how little English they could understand. We women took the children for a walk and made it back to ship just before the onset of a sudden tropical rainstorm, a dramatic new experience. Friends were caught in the rain and drenched.

At Thursday Island we also went ashore. In Brisbane we had our first ride on an Australian tram, an exciting experience for the children. Suddenly Erica said to me,

'Look there's a little girl from Germany!'

'How can you tell?'

'She's wearing such a long dress.'

We laughed. All refugees had bought their children clothing a couple of sizes too big, so they could be worn for a number of years.

4

We sailed through Sydney Heads on 24 April 1939, two days after celebrating Karl's forty-seventh birthday. We were struck by the beauty of the harbour and its iconic bridge, a magnificent view, marred for us only by the unknown challenges ahead. Waiting to greet us at Woolloomooloo dock were Karl's and Ella's brother Leon, together with cousins, Dr Willi Gronsfeld and Ken and Harold Lehman[81] and Leon's friend Hans Whitman.

Willi took us three women and four children in two taxis to Leon's flat in Bay Street, Double Bay. It was lunchtime by now and we were all very hungry. We had had an early breakfast and eaten very little, being too excited. Sylvia Hertzberg, Leon's friend, had prepared lunch, including a large platter of tasty fried fish.

Leon's fluent English was helpful to Karl and Leopold in getting the luggage off the boat speedily, so the men arrived at the flat shortly after us. After lunch, Leon took us to the butcher to buy a big roast, then to the greengrocer for fruit and vegetables. In the evening, we savoured a home-cooked meal, something we had longed for in past weeks. We washed up before being driven to Lamrock Avenue, Bondi, where Leon had rented furnished flats, one for each family. We were happy the Herzbergs lived close by, in the flat above. Early next morning, without hesitating and with only minimal English, Karl went to a grocer's shop to buy supplies for breakfast. Cousins Hermann and Helen Lehmann, also new arrivals, called in during the morning.

---

[81] Kurt and Helmut had anglicised their names to Ken and Harold.

It being a public holiday, Anzac Day, we were all invited to Helen and Willi Gronsfeld's flat for afternoon tea, where we met Sylvia,[82] Leon's wife to be. As she spoke no German, he tried to encourage conversation in English. Whilst I understood, I was too unsure of myself to speak.

Leon brought two letters, sent to us via his address. Oma Riekchen had written to Paul[83] and Walter, thanking them for their greetings mailed from the ship. Again she urged us to do our utmost to get permits for the Weinbergs and Schönebergs. Leon had applied for these six permits but had just been notified the applications were rejected. After a discussion, we decided to re-apply for permits for Oma Riekchen and the three Schönebergs. Having no idea how much money they would be permitted to take out of Germany, Karl and Leopold would guarantee £1000 landing money, instead of the usual £200, so there would be sufficient funds when they reached the first Australian port.[84]

We thought the Weinberg's migration could be assisted by Karl and Leopold recruiting Eric Meyer, who had been a cattle dealer known to Karl in Germany. Having the store-cum-post office in the rural district of Nattai, near Sydney, Eric might be able to interest a local farmer to give a guarantee and apply for a permit for Walter Weinberg, a fit young man in his twenties, and one for his wife. The hope was that once in Australia, Walter could then bring out his parents.

The second letter was from Clara. She had been to Barsinghausen to visit Josef Levisohn, Oma Herzberg's oldest brother, and his wife, Julie. Though his brother Ben in New York had organised affidavits for the United States, Josef and Julie would not be able to migrate in the foreseeable future, their number on the American quota list being so high. The eighty-two year old Josef had always been healthy but the stress of the past months had aged him.

The letter continued: 'Uncle Josef has become frail and unhappy. The Nazis have confiscated some of his property as *Judensteuer.*' [85] A late postscript closed the letter: 'I've just received word that Uncle Josef has died. I'm off now to Barsinghausen for the funeral and will stay with Aunt Julie for a few days.'

Oma stoically accepted the sad news.

---

[82]   Remarkably, another Hertzberg-Mendels link up. There was no family connection to the Herzbergs of Gütersloh. Note the different spelling. That Hertzberg family came to Australia via England in the 1920s. The father, Louis Hertzberg, was born in Riga.

[83]   After arrival in Australia, Paulhermann was known as Paul.

[84]   See Appendix 8

[85]   In the aftermath of the *Kristallnacht*, German Jewry was 'fined' one thousand million Marks, levied by confiscation of twenty percent of the property of every German Jew. (Source: Gilbert, Martin, *The Holocaust*)

* * *

Leopold took the four children to Bondi Public School. I was worried about our little six-year-old Erica, as she couldn't speak English and hadn't been to school in Germany. Ursula, Walter and Paul knew only a few words[86]. It was helpful that the two boys were placed in the same class. After a few days I went to see Erica's teacher to ask how she was coping. 'Oh she's doing fine. We understand each other perfectly. I can now count up to ten in German!' she replied.

A few days later I noticed our boys playing marbles with some Australian lads. We really didn't need to worry – the children were picking up the language easily.

We adults put a lot of effort into learning English, going to night classes twice a week. Ella and Karl were in the beginners' class. Both took private lessons as well. Leopold and I were in the advanced class. I had learned English at school for two years. Leopold had learned classical and romance languages and spoke French and Italian fluently. He had taken lessons in English before leaving Germany, writing well, but not keen to speak.

Karl soon found he was not one to sit and learn from books, being too impatient. He found work with a removalist firm and expected to pick up the language more quickly by mixing with people. Carrying heavy furniture was physically demanding, particularly in the warm humid climate he had not previously experienced. Karl's employer paid him under the basic wage, and at one point borrowed from us – money he never repaid.

We had lived in Bondi for about three weeks when we got word that our *Lifts* of household goods and furniture had arrived at the port. With the help of Irma Krug we were now ready to look for unfurnished accommodation. Irma, whose sister was married to our cousin Alfred Bock in Holland, had been in Australia for some time and spoke good English. She took us to several agents. We looked at flats, but the rooms were too small for our European furniture. We were then shown houses, but the rooms were no bigger and the rents were high. Finally, we viewed a semi-detached cottage in Randwick, which had large rooms. The rent was high, but Irma suggested sharing with the Herzbergs at least until our financial situation was more secure, and dividing expenses for rent, gas and electricity. We took her good advice and immediately settled with the agent.

---

[86] Ursula knew two words, 'yes' and 'no'.

During the May school holidays we moved into 16 Arthur Street, Randwick. The furniture of both families fitted in and we soon felt at home in our new surroundings.[87] The 'semi' had a little front veranda, which we enjoyed in leisure hours. In fine weather it was Oma's favourite spot while preparing vegetables or doing needlework. Keeping house for five adults and four children was quite a task, with much washing, ironing, cooking and cleaning, plus shopping and carrying home. As we had brought clothing for our growing children for several years ahead, there were always hems to be taken up or let down. There was also a little garden to look after. The children now attended Randwick Public School, soon making friends at school and in the neighbourhood, using the park opposite our house for ball games.

* * *

One afternoon our doorbell rang. I opened the door to a youngish woman accompanied by two boys. 'I'm Mrs North. These are my sons, Ian and Richard. Ian is in the same class as your boys. He tells me you're recent newcomers from Europe.'

'I'm Kate[88] Mendels. Please come in. I'll just call my brother and sister-in-law.' Leopold came, but Ella was too nervous, fearing she might have to chat.

After a few pleasantries Mrs North said, 'Our newspapers have been telling us about disturbing events in Germany, such as the *Kristallnacht*. Were the reports really true? It's hard to imagine something like that occurring in a country so proud of its culture.'

Leopold told her what had happened to us and to our relatives and friends: that he had been beaten up before being imprisoned in Buchenwald concentration camp, where the meagre rations the inmates were given to eat and drink were often contaminated; that he was released only when permits for Australia were granted and only after signing a statement that he had been well

---

[87]   The 'semi' had five rooms. Each couple had one room that housed their lounge and dining-room furniture. Each couple had a bedroom. At first Oma and the girls shared the third bedroom, Erica and Ursula in a single bed. There was also a kitchen and family room, and one small bathroom/toilet. The laundry and a separate toilet were accessed from the backyard. The latter space was used only as a smokehouse for curing *Wurst* we made for ourselves, sharing some with the extended family. The front entrance hall was divided by swinging glass doors. Ursula later slept in the section by the front door, on a couch-bed. Paul and Walter slept in the other section, one also on a couch-bed and the other on a bed that folded against the wall during the day. In the small garden at the back we sometimes kept chickens.

[88]   In Australia Käthe becomes Kate.

treated. He had been warned that if he divulged the truth to anyone, reprisals would be taken against relatives still in Germany.

Hearing the details stunned Mrs North.

Her husband, Dr North,[89] a general practitioner in Randwick, wanted to meet us. Karl and I, as well as Leopold and Ella, were invited for the following Wednesday night, when we enjoyed an interesting evening. We maintained the friendship, socialising from time to time.

Months later Ella and I went with Mrs North to the Young Women's Christian Association, YWCA, where we subsequently spent many pleasant evenings, meeting interesting women who made us feel welcome. The Norths helped us understand the language and customs of the country and took us on weekend family outings. Their assurance that they would help us whenever needed bolstered our sense of security.

---

[89] The Norths had been Christian medical missionaries in China.

5

The international political scene was deteriorating. In September 1938, there had been hope that war might be prevented by the meeting of Hitler and Chamberlain in Munich, but Hitler's urge for power was insatiable. While his propaganda broadcasts claimed that the Jews controlled the world, it was he who wanted the world at his feet.

During the middle of June a letter arrived from the Schönebergs with the sad news that Oma Riekchen Mendels had died peacefully on 26 May, four days after her seventy-eighth birthday. The Weinbergs had been very good to her. From the moment we left, she had been longing for us and had lost the will to live. She died at the very time we were resubmitting her permit application, which was granted on 26 June, exactly one month later.

The same notice granted permits for the Schönebergs. We forwarded these to Germany immediately by registered mail, not airmail, which was rarely used at the time. How could we have known war was imminent? The permits did not reach the Schönebergs till the first days of the war. To save themselves, they would have had to leave everything then and there, walk out of Schüren, escape through France to Portugal, where they might have managed to take a ship for Australia. How could anyone know what the future held for European Jewry?

Herman Ahrenberg, his wife, Liesel (Dagobert Schöneberg's sister), and son, Kurt, originally intended to migrate with the Schönebergs to Australia, but at first neither family was granted permits. The Ahrenbergs then applied successfully for permits to Chile, not including Dagobert's family, a factor in the latter's ultimate fate.

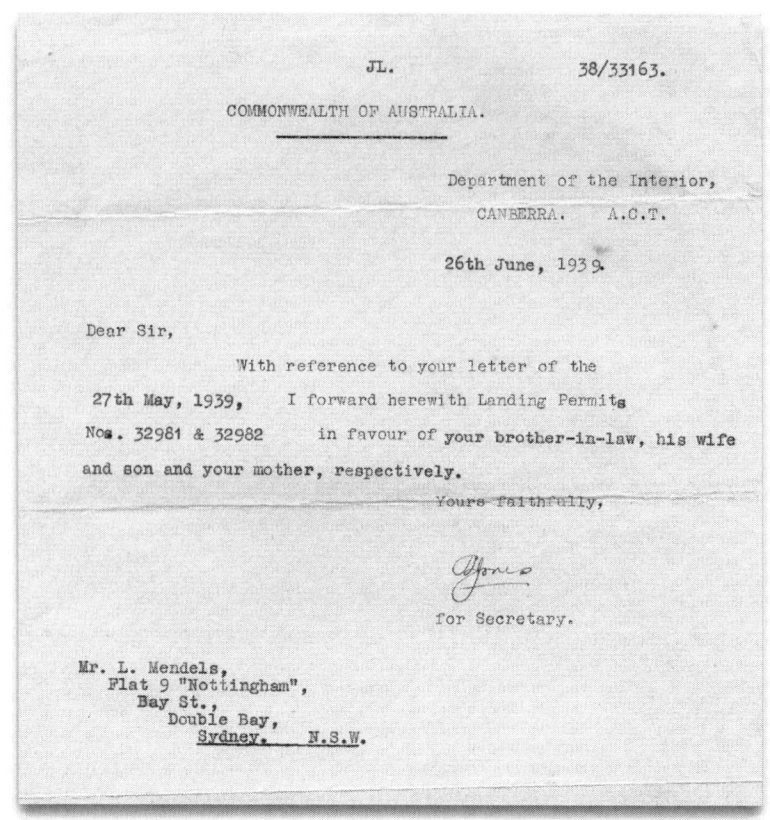

Landing permit for Paula and Dagobert Schöneberg and Oma Riekchen Mendels received too late for them to organise their emigration.

On 1 September 1939, German forces marched into Poland after a supposed attack on the German radio station[90] in Gleiwitz, allegedly by the Polish army. In actual fact, Hitler had put prisoners into Polish uniforms for this 'raid', his pretext for war.

Because of treaty obligations, once Poland was attacked, France and England mobilised and declared war on Germany, drawing in the British Empire – Australia and New Zealand included. Knowing that the German army was superbly trained and motivated, we were not surprised at their speedy successes, over-running Poland, Belgium, Holland and France. The world faced a great threat.

---

[90]   Hitler and his army chiefs concocted an incident as a pretext for the planned aggression against Poland. The Gestapo staged a faked attack on the German radio station at Gleiwitz on the Polish border using condemned concentration camp inmates outfitted in Polish army uniforms. Some of these were shot and the bodies left behind as evidence. (Source: Shirer, William L. *The Rise and Fall of the Third Reich*.)

How would the outbreak of war across Europe affect the chances of emigration for the remnants of our family still in Germany?

Direct correspondence between us and family and friends in Germany ceased. As America had not yet entered the war, we received their mail via the family in New York, Emil and Helen Lind and Oma Herzberg's sisters, Elise and Rosa. They would enclose that mail with their own letters to us and send them surface mail, the whole sequence taking many weeks.

During the first months of the war our family wrote of no new incidents. Jews were apparently not a priority, the Nazis being pre-occupied with war.

In Australia it was not wise to mention we were from Germany being now regarded as 'enemy aliens'. At first we had to report to the Coogee police station daily, then weekly and later monthly. Quite a walk from our home. We were not allowed to leave our suburb without permission, but were granted permanent travel permits between home and work. As soon as Paul and Walter turned thirteen, they also had to report. As enemy aliens we were not permitted cameras or radios.

December exposed us to the heat and humidity of a Sydney summer for the first time. I was sorry for Karl, who worked so hard and earned so little in his removalist job. He was looking for something else, less strenuous and more rewarding.

Through Leon we heard of a confectionery shop for sale called Maison de Klein in the city's Strand Arcade. The vendor, Mr de Klein, a refugee from Germany, was not well and, besides, had quarrelled with relatives who worked for him. The uniqueness of the business lay in their Vienna almonds (almonds covered with a very thin layer of toffee) and Tasmanian almonds (almonds covered in a thicker layer of red candy). All sweets were processed in the big shop window in full view of passers-by, attracting them as customers. Karl was very interested, so I went to observe the shop. Having checked the accounts, we bought the business with all fixtures and utensils, despite the high rent. Mrs de Klein agreed to work on with us for a period.

The premises repainted, the copper boilers scrubbed, additional equipment purchased, we reopened a more attractive-looking shop on 1 January 1940. In no time Karl picked up the secrets of the trade and improved the cooking techniques. Vienna almonds were cooked in a copper boiler, stirred with a large wooden spatula and when ready, tipped onto aluminium trays to cool. They were then separated with a pair of forks first dipped in water. The sweet aroma spiced with vanilla wafted through the arcade, drawing in customers.

Mrs de Klein volunteered that they had not been able to produce sweets with such a fine finish.

I worked in the shop from 'day one', either behind the counter selling, or making sure everything was spic and span. It was a blessing that we lived together with the Herzbergs. I appreciated that Erica, just a seven-year-old, and Paul, were well cared for by Mother and Ella. The two women shared the housework: Oma doing most of the cooking and baking, Ella looking after the cleaning, shopping, washing and ironing for the household of nine. Every morning I made our beds, cut our lunches and left for the city.

The business did well from the very beginning. Karl was able to double the amount of Vienna almonds cooked in each batch, but the manual work was physically demanding. We were in our first Sydney summer, exhausted by the hot, humid climate, made worse by the heat and steam of cooking, done all day without the advantage of air conditioning. Behind the counter at the back of the shop were two high, wide, sash windows, which had to be open summer and winter to allow heat to escape. Standing at the counter, I was exposed to the heat of the boiler at the front of the shop and cool or cold air drawn in by the fan through the windows behind me. Being on my feet for long hours under these conditions caused me constant backache. I didn't take a lunch break, just gobbled my sandwiches. Mrs de Klein helped Karl by weighing ingredients and separating the hot almonds.

During the first two years Leopold came every Thursday after work, when he and Karl would prepare stock for Friday's late-night shopping. For Mother's Day and pre-Christmas he came late on Friday afternoons as well; Mrs de Klein could then help me serve customers. The long Friday was very tiring as closing time was not until nine o'clock, after which utensils had to be cleaned and the shop tidied. It was always late when we started for home. There were long intervals between trams and rarely were we able to get taxis. When we finally arrived home, we were often too tired to enjoy the meal Oma had ready for us.

Paul and Walter were soon also recruited to work in the shop, Paul coming in several times a week after school. Leopold assisted us also with bookkeeping. Although he was paid, money alone could not make up for all he did. Later, when Karl bought a car, both families had the benefit.

We increased the variety of sweets we made, including chocolate almonds, marzipan and candied hazelnuts. The business was renamed The Nut Shop and became well known in the city.

* * *

We came to Australia towards the end of the Depression era. Job opportunities were almost non-existent, especially for middle-aged men with limited or no English, so each of our relatives and friends had to find some independent way to make a living. Julius and Emmy Mendels made doormats from used car-tyres. Later, when the army requisitioned all used tyres, they had to find an alternative and made camouflage nets for the army. Willi Gronsfeld had to go back to university for the final three years of Medicine at Sydney University before being registered to practise. Most refugee lawyers did not return to law, for they would have had to do the full law course. Some studied accountancy. Some went into business. Hermann and Helen Lehmann bought a grocery shop in Glenayr Avenue, Bondi. Leopold looked around for a period before going into business with Leon. They bought Langford & Company, making loose covers and curtains. Our sister Helen in New York sent apron samples which were copied or modified. Later they also manufactured house frocks and children's wear.

During the war there were occasional incidents against foreigners in which Italian and German shops were vandalised. Mrs North assured us that if we were ever targeted she and her influential friends would always be there for us. We were very careful to speak only English in public.

These were minor issues relative to those faced by our people in Nazi Europe. Would they ever be able to contact us for help? Could they escape? Would they even survive?

6

The first of our *Simches* in Australia were the *Barmizwos* of Paul on 6 July 1940, and Walter on 11 January 1941, at the Central Synagogue in Grosvenor Street, Bondi Junction. Both boys were taught by Reverend Wolff, also from Germany. We were proud of their renditions in the synagogue on the *Schabbes* morning. For each *Simcho* we had a celebratory dinner in our Randwick home for all the family and new friends. In keeping with family tradition, there were speeches and songs performed by a number of guests. Our nephew, Ralph Sommer, who was working on a farm at Dunedoo, wasn't able to come for either occasion. We tried to encourage him to return and live in Sydney with the option of a job as a motor mechanic in a workshop, but he wanted to stay in the country.

For Paul's *Barmizwo*, with letters from the Linds and aunts Elise and Rosa, came a letter forwarded from Clara in Germany sending congratulatory wishes. There was no letter from the Neugartens in Cologne. I was sure my sister Rosa would have written. Perhaps the mail was delayed and would come later. A letter arrived from the Schönebergs through the Red Cross, saying they were well but that Dagobert and Lutz were being forced to work as road labourers.

A few weeks later I happened to delay going to work, intending to clean some of my cupboards. As usual, Oma was looking out for the postman and came in waving a letter. 'It's from the aunts; from my sisters,' she said. 'They write that Rosa died on 17 June 1940. But how strange! The letter is written by Rosa herself.'

Oma's sister Rosa, in New York, was a frail seventy-four year old. We all

The two Rosas.
Left: Rosa Levisohn, Oma Bertha's sister, who lived till age 93; Right: Rosa Neugarten, Oma Bertha's daughter.

16 Arthur St, Randwick with its happy joint family.
Back row (l-r):Paul, Karl, Walter.
Middle row (l-r): Ella, Leopold, Kate.
Front row (l-r): Erica, Oma (Bertha), Ursula.

knew she had had a heart condition since her late forties. Because of this, Oma had jumped to the conclusion that it was this elderly sister who had died. In reality, it was her daughter, my sister. We were all numb with pain at this unexpected news. Bereft, Louis Neugarten had been too traumatised to notify anyone of the sad news. Clara, who had travelled from Gütersloh to Cologne for the funeral, had sent the message to the aunts in New York.

I wonder whether also in Rosa's case, the tensions of the past years had aggravated her diabetes and contributed to her death. In particular, could separation from her children, Ilse and Rolf, now in wartime London, have been a factor?

Wiping tears from my eyes, I left for work, crying during the whole tram ride to the city. As I came into the shop Karl immediately asked,

'Whatever's wrong?'

'Rosa. My sister Rosa has died.'

Again, a flood of tears. Given the overriding needs of the business, I contained my grief and managed to get through the working day. Months passed before I could acknowledge that my sister was gone forever.

Rosa's children wrote, 'Mother's death makes us despondent and distressed for our father, now all alone.' We would have liked to have brought the two young people to Australia, but that was impossible during the war. They would soon have to endure German bombing raids on London.

Newspapers reported blitzkrieg successes of the Nazis in France and their jubilation at taking Paris. What would be their next move? Would this monster, Hitler, now set out to dominate the world? It was frustrating to be denied our radio at such a time.

Letters from New York arrived regularly. Our friends Paul Meinberg and family from Gütersloh had just arrived in America, indicating that the American quota system must still be operating. Could this apply to our marooned relatives? Clara wanted to move to Cologne to look after Louis but the Gestapo would not allow her to relocate, nor would they give permission to Louis to join her in Gütersloh.

Via the family in the States, we kept up correspondence with those still in Germany. Their replies were always short. They had to be careful. All mail was censored. We now heard rumours that Jewish families from Germany were being uprooted and sent to southern France. True or not, it was the first indication of the 'resettlement' of Jews.

* * *

Ella and I joined the National Council of Jewish Women, giving us opportunities to make new acquaintances, improve our English and do community work. I recall one particular meeting which resolved to send food and clothing to German refugees interned in a camp in Victoria.[91] Before the outbreak of war these men had taken refuge in England, where they later came to be regarded as security risks. Two thousand were crammed onto the ship, HMS *Dunera*, and deported to Australia, together with 250 antagonistic German prisoners of war and 200 Italians. All were ill treated by their British guards on the long sea journey. The Australian Jewish community lobbied to have these men released, eventually achieving this in 1942. We came to know many who, on release, came to Sydney. One, Dr Siegfried Cohn, became principal founder of the Kingsford-Maroubra Synagogue. His daughter, Miriam, became my niece when she married my nephew Walter.

Ella, Leopold, Karl and I were invited to the home of Mr and Mrs Mel Solomon of Bellevue Hill for a meeting of Youth Aliyah. Silva Steigrad spoke in moving terms about Youth Aliyah, which had agents in Europe rescuing young Jews, an initiative needing large sums of money. We were glad to contribute. Perhaps an organisation like this could rescue our nephew Lutz Schöneberg. Youth Aliyah brought young people out of Europe to Palestine before, during and after the war. Alas, Lutz was not one of the fortunate ones.

Sydney now felt like home to us, for we had a sizeable group of relatives and friends. On a social evening at Irma and George Krug's place in Clovelly, we met the Casparis, who brought the news that Germany had just invaded Russia. It was 22 June 1941, Clara's birthday.

* * *

Hitler was now fighting on many fronts. The First World War had demonstrated that to be victorious he must defeat Russia before the start of winter. If he could

---

[91] At the time of the Nazi conquest of France and the Dunkirk retreat, the British government became concerned their internees were a security risk, and requested assistance from Commonwealth countries. Canada and Australia both agreed to accept some of these internees. In mid-1940, 2542 men were sent to Australia on the *Dunera*, a hellish voyage in which all suffered privation. Many were brutalised, abused and robbed of their property by their British guards. Once in Australia they joined refugees at Hay and later at Tatura. (Source: Rutland, S. *Edge of the Diaspora*.)

not achieve this, 'General Winter' would defeat him with deep snow, muddy roads and extreme cold. The steady advance of the Germans concerned us. We hoped the Russian retreat was a tactical move to trap them deep into Russia during winter.

Soon afterwards, Finland joined the Axis, declared war on Russia and together with the Germans besieged Leningrad. That monumental siege would last 880 days, until 27 January 1944, when the railway to Moscow would be re-opened.

The first snow flurries in Russia fell on 12 September, signalling the inevitability of a winter campaign. By October the temperature had already dropped to eight degrees below zero. The Germans began to feel the lack of appropriate winter clothing. Despite the hardships, their infantry reached a suburb of Moscow, but was driven back by General Zhukov on 6 December 1941, the day before Japan entered the war. The north and south lifelines to Russia from the West remained open.

After an unbroken chain of victories, Hitler's forces began to retreat for the first time. The myth of an invincible German army was broken. It took another year and a second winter before the German army was repulsed at Stalingrad. The irrevocable retreat of the Wehrmacht to the West began.

* * *

On Sunday 7 December 1941, Japanese bombers attacked the American naval base at Pearl Harbour catching everyone by surprise. We were alarmed by the spread of the war to the Pacific. On 11 December Hitler declared war on the United States. The balance of power changed with the involvement of America and its vast resources. Surely this would shorten the war.

On 3 May 1942, a Japanese submarine released three midget submarines into Sydney Harbour. A torpedo aimed at the US cruiser *Chicago* struck HMAS *Kuttabul*, a naval dormitory ship, killing nineteen sailors and wounding ten. The mother submarine shelled coastal suburbs, including residential areas of Rose Bay.

As there was a possibility of Japanese air strikes, shop windows had to be shuttered and every home had to have blackout curtains. Streetlights were dimmed. Karl now worked till long after closing time to cater for increased demand. The streets were dark when I walked home alone from the tram stop, an experience I hated.

Sydney hosted American servicemen, who had a considerable social and economic effect on the city. Our Vienna almonds proved popular, even being sent home to the United States. As there were no imports we were dependent on local products, which were in short supply. Though Karl made trips to the Murrumbidgee irrigation area and sent agents to South Australia to buy almonds, our stocks were far from adequate. Consequently, we reduced shop hours, opening at eleven to a queue of customers. We used the earlier hours of the day to process the goods, which included our new popular line, Vienna almonds dipped in chocolate. I didn't pre-package. That way it would take longer to serve each of the queuing customers and keep the shop open for business till three o'clock. This was a very stressful way of working. After closing, preparations for the next day would begin. We had two employees, Lisa Meyer (later Lisa Eltham), who helped Karl with the manufacturing, and another girl behind the counter. Paul and Walter still helped out, as did Erica and Ursula in the pre-Xmas weeks.

Each customer was rationed to 115 grams of only one of our products, but anyone in uniform or a customer sending a parcel to someone in the forces could buy 230 grams. When larger quantities of raw materials were available, we increased the amount for those in uniform.

Ration cards for butter, meat, tea and sugar were introduced. Shared by our two families the rations were adequate, although some items were just not available. We were now a household of ten, as our nephew Ralph had finally agreed to come back to Sydney to a job in a knitting mill. In our limited 'semi' there was no bed space for him, so we found him a room close-by with cousins of Sylvia Mendels. There were now five young people in the house, all getting on well together and growing up as siblings. Attending Sydney Boys' High, Paul and Walter worked hard at school, Leopold helping them with homework when needed.

7

The New Yorkers passed on the sad news that Clara[92] had been sent to the East.[93] About the same time we received a note from Dagobert Schöneberg[94] through the Red Cross with the bald statement: 'We are about to travel to the East', a coded message that Dagobert, Paula and young Lutz were being deported. We were distraught.

Our nephews Werner Herzberg and John Lind were called up by the American army. Werner was sent to Italy and John elsewhere in Europe. It was Werner who mailed us the first airletter we had ever seen; it was in miniature. When wounded in one eye he was repatriated to New York.

Most of Europe was suffering under Hitler's grim regime. Towards the end of 1942, the West first learned that Jews deported to concentration camps in the East were being gassed. In November a protest meeting was held in the Sydney Town Hall. The Lord Mayor presided, and among the speakers were Anglican Archbishop Mowll and the rabbi of the Great Synagogue, Rabbi Israel Porush. The meeting followed one in London chaired by the Archbishop of Canterbury. There was no protest from the Pope in Rome.

In July 1943 Mussolini and his Fascist regime were ousted by a group of court officials and Italian monarchist generals. The Allies were inching their

---

[92]   Clara was forced to move to Bielefeld 10 December 1941, was deported to Riga on 13 December 1941, and *umgebracht* (annihilated) near Riga in 1942.

[93]   See Appendix 10

[94]   Dagobert, Paula and Lutz Schöneberg were forced out of their home on 19 July 1939 and had to move to a *Judenhaus* (Jewish house) in Dortmund. On 1 February 1942 they were deported to the ghetto of Riga. Dagobert and Paula disappeared after the *Selektion* on 27 July 1944.

way northwards against the German forces. With Mussolini gone, the Germans took over full control in the areas not yet liberated. Under Mussolini, no Jews had been deported from Italy. With the German occupation deportations began.

Then at last! The Second Front!

On 6 June 1944, a vast Allied armada slipped across the English Channel in weather the Germans thought too rough to permit an invasion. They had also been misled about the likely location of the landing. Thousands upon thousands of troops landed on the beaches of Normandy. The Germans, caught by surprise, offered furious resistance. By afternoon the Americans had toeholds on two beaches, the British on a third, penetrating inland two to six miles. Hitler, needing so many troops in the East, found that his widely publicised defensive Atlantic Wall was breached within a few hours. The much-touted Luftwaffe had been driven from the air and the German navy from the sea. The battle was far from over, but the outcome was not in doubt.

A small anti-Hitler group within the German army, including high-ranking officers, had been plotting to murder Hitler and overthrow his regime, convinced he was dragging Germany to complete disaster. The opportunity arose in July 1944.

On 20 July Count von Stauffenberg, a lieutenant colonel, succeeded in smuggling a briefcase containing a time-bomb into Hitler's headquarters, Wolfsschanze (Wolf's Lair), in East Prussia. Wanting better access to the documents, one of the generals had inadvertently shifted the briefcase under the table out of position, to the far side of the table frame. The explosion killed four officers but not Hitler, who survived the blast, protected by the massive table and its frame. He was badly shaken, his hair singed, his legs burnt, his right arm bruised and his back lacerated by a falling beam. After the immediate shock passed, he screamed and ranted, ordering the SS to shoot anyone about whom there might be the slightest suspicion.

Many officers were shot. Some were forced to shoot themselves. Others were tried in show trials, then hanged with piano wire. That attempt was the last overt opposition to Hitler from the Wehrmacht. The once-mighty army, its leaders now muzzled, would go down with him. They fully realised he was leading Germany into the greatest defeat in the history of their beloved Fatherland.

A week later, in blind retribution for the attempt on Hitler's life, thousands of Jews in ghettos and concentration camps were sacrificed, among them Paula and Dagobert Schöneberg. And, as this family tragedy played out in Europe, in Australia we were unknowing.

By the middle of August 1944 the Russian summer offensives had brought the Red Army to the border of East Prussia and had penetrated Finland. In six weeks they advanced 400 miles to the Vistula, opposite Warsaw. In the south a new attack resulted in the reconquest of Romania and its Ploesti oilfields, the only source of natural oil for the German armies. In August, Bulgaria withdrew from the war and in September, Finland. France was liberated quickly, as were Belgium and Holland. By the end of August the German armies had lost 500,000 men and almost all their trucks, artillery and tanks in the West. His military virtually defeated, Hitler gave up neither the fight nor the deportations![95]

We followed the news of the war keenly, especially as fighting was now taking place in towns and villages of Holland, the Rhineland and Westphalia, areas familiar to us. The Germans were retreating from one place after another. On 25 April 1945 the Russians encircled Berlin. On the same day they met the Americans on the river Elbe. In the last days of April the Russians battered their way into the city. With it came news the world had been waiting for.

Hitler was dead. He had taken his own life. The date was 30 April 1945.

The Thousand Year Reich was at an end.

On 7 May 1945 Germany surrendered.

Peace came to Europe.

The killing in Europe would cease. Would any of our family have survived? Where and how could we find them?

---

[95] Despite the fact that the war had been going badly for them, the Germans were still busy deporting Jews to concentration camps, using valuable resources, trains and manpower. Having lost the protection of the Italians, the Jews of Northern Italy were deported, together with masses of Italian soldiers. From 15 May till November 1944 the Jews of Hungary were deported, mainly to Auschwitz. On 6 June 1944, the day of the Normandy landing, Corfu's 1795 Jews were deported, as well as the 260 Jews of Crete, who were put on a boat which was scuttled and all deportees drowned. The Jews of Rhodes were deported on 17 July.

8

There were victory celebrations in all Allied countries. In central Sydney, people danced in the streets of the city and strangers embraced. In Martin Place there were speeches, jubilation and singing. Leopold and our teenagers went into the city to join the celebrations. It was well past midnight when they set out for home. There were no buses or trams so they walked much of the way before catching a lift from a truck driver.

The newspapers featured the liberation of the concentration camps and death camps. They told about gas chambers and shooting *Aktions*. Pictures showed human beings starved to skeletons, too weak to walk. In every cinema, newsreels of the camps demonstrated that men could follow an ideology to extreme sadism and to extermination of human beings.

Noble is Man?

Every decent soul who saw those pictures shuddered.

The manner in which the Nazis had dealt with their victims was now published for all the world to see, but many Germans claimed ignorance of the camps and what had taken place there.[96]

Germany was laid waste. The newspapers displayed pictures of the destruction. Hitler's mantra about Jews as Germany's misfortune found him in his last days still calling on his successors 'to resist international Jewry'.

---

[96] This proposition is disputed. After the *Kristallnacht*, Germans all over the country knew that Jews had been sent to these camps. There were many concentration camps in Germany with many citizens living nearby. Hundreds of thousands, both civilian and military, had jobs connected with those camps. Trains travelling to other death camps in all parts of Europe were not invisible. Staff manning those trains must have known what they were carrying and where they were going.

9

The postal services in Germany were at a standstill, as were the railways. We were frustrated at being unable to begin a search for surviving family.

George and Irma Krug came to the Nut Shop with great news. Our cousin Alfred Bock and his wife, Culle (Carola), Irma's sister, with their two children, had been liberated in Holland by Canadian troops. Alfred's father, his bachelor brother Ernst, sister Lina Simons with husband and daughter, had all survived the war years by living underground. They were malnourished and in great need, despite having received a distribution of food and clothing from humanitarian agencies. We immediately sent parcels of warm clothing, tins of food, and of course our Vienna almonds.

Jewish communities received lists of survivors and we were desolate when not a single relative or friend appeared on any list. Perhaps the lists were incomplete. Somebody might still write. A young Lutz might have survived the camps. We placed an advertisement in the German language newspaper *Aufbau* (Construction), an American journal. We gave the Linds' New York address for replies, as the *Aufbau* had a large German-Jewish readership in the States and internationally.

The advertisement in German read as follows:

Does anybody know the whereabouts of the following individuals?

Clara HERZBERG, from Gütersloh
Louis NEUGARTEN, from Rüdinghausen-Annen, last of Cologne
Dagobert David SCHÖNEBERG, from Schüren-Dortmund

Paula SCHÖNEBERG, from Schüren-Dortmund

Lutz SCHÖNEBERG, from Schüren-Dortmund

Paul NEUGARTEN, from Dortmund

Please write to:

Mr & Mrs Emil Lind

602 West 157 St, Apt 4c

New York 32, N Y

USA

Eventually the Linds forwarded us a copy of a letter, written on 6 January 1946, which they had received from Max Meyer[97] of Flüchtlingslageret[98], Ryd.

He wrote that Clara Herzberg had arrived in the Riga Ghetto in December 1941, and Paul Neugarten, brother of Rosa's Louis, a little later; that out of 25,000 German and Austrian Jews deported to the Riga Ghetto only 1,000 survived. Max had been unable to find the names of Clara Herzberg and Paul Neugarten listed among the survivors, but he did know about Lutz Schöneberg. Lutz had been sent to a work camp, Salaspils, near Riga. When its role changed to accommodate political prisoners, Lutz had been returned to Riga, very ill. He was nursed back to 'health' by his parents. They were together in the ghetto until July 1944, when Paula and Dagobert Schöneberg, with many others, were taken at a *Selektion* and not seen again.[99]

Max held out no hope for them. He knew Lutz had tuberculosis. A friend of Max had met Lutz recently in Neustadt, near Lübeck, and believed he was recovering and would most probably return to Schüren. He gave us to understand we would have no trouble finding Lutz, who would appreciate parcels of food and clothing. Max and his wife had affidavits for New York. He would tell the Linds further details, face to face.

Ilse and Rolf's father, Louis Neugarten, was sent to Theresienstadt on 27 June 1942. In fact, there had been a Red Cross note from him to his children in London, just before his deportation. After the war, all we could learn was: 'Ultimate destination and date of death unknown'.

---

[97] There were connections between the Meyers and Schönebergs. Dagobert's sister was married to Hermann Ahrenberg. In turn Hermann's sister was the wife of Julius, brother to Max Meyer.

[98] Displaced Persons Camp.

[99] See Appendix 11

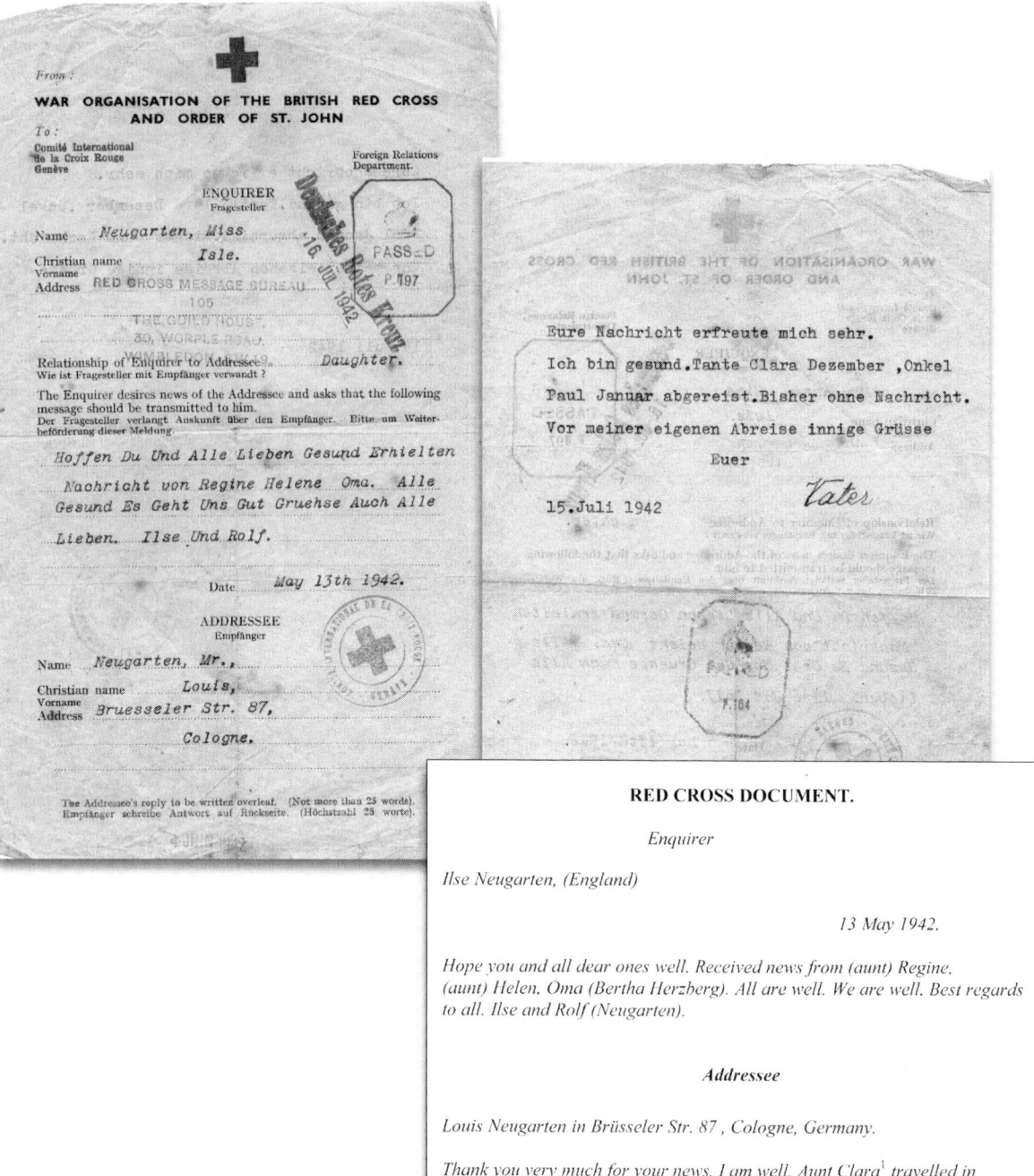

Eure Nachricht erfreute mich sehr.

Ich bin gesund.Tante Clara Dezember ,Onkel

Paul Januar abgereist.Bisher ohne Nachricht.

Vor meiner eigenen Abreise innige Grüsse

Euer

Vater

15.Juli 1942

RED CROSS DOCUMENT.

Enquirer

Ilse Neugarten, (England)

13 May 1942.

*Hope you and all dear ones well. Received news from (aunt) Regine,
(aunt) Helen, Oma (Bertha Herzberg). All are well. We are well. Best regards
to all. Ilse and Rolf (Neugarten).*

Addressee

Louis Neugarten in Brüsseler Str. 87 , Cologne, Germany.

*Thank you very much for your news. I am well. Aunt Clara[1] travelled in
December, Uncle Paul (Neugarten) in January. Until now no news. Before my
own departure,[2] all my love,*

Your
Father.

July 15 1942

---

[1] Deportation to Riga.
[2] Deportation to Theresienstadt.

Final exchange between Louis
Neugarten and his children, Ilse
and Rolf.

Stolpernstein (stumble-stone), a brass plaque set into the pavement outside a house from which a Jew had been deported. In 2009, ten thousand of these were already in place throughout Germany. This *Stolpernstein* commemorates Klara (Clara) Herzberg née Levy, born 1886, deported 1941, died in Riga.

The entrance to the Bielefeld Railway Station, where two permanent 'memorial tables' (encircled) are inscribed with the names of Jews from the surrounding districts deported through this station. The names of the Gütersloh deportees appear below. Among the names is the Hebrew quotation:
'That the generation to come will know of this, and the children who will be born, in their turn will stand up to proclaim it to their children.' (Psalm 78.6)

Lutz Schöneberg was the sole surviving family member of those we had left in Germany.

We set out to find him, contacting the Red Cross to search for him in Schüren. We wrote to his relatives in Madeira, Chile and South Africa, asking them to do likewise, accepting it would be some time before anyone would hear direct news, as communications in Germany were still poor.

After months of waiting we received a letter from Lutz's South African cousin, Ilse Bergmann (née Neugarten), confirming that Lutz had survived and giving his address, obtained through the Red Cross. We immediately wrote and sent food and clothing.

Weeks passed before his reply, saying that he could not contact us earlier, our address having been lost during the war years. He was now reasonably well, living in Schüren with the Eichwald family, who employed him in their butcher shop. Eichwald was Jewish and had survived the war in Germany because his wife was Catholic.

We were anxious to have Lutz come to Australia and set about getting him a permit, a difficult task, even though we and the Herzbergs guaranteed financial security. Lutz would not travel by boat, due to memories of his almost fatal experience on the *Cap Arcona* in the Bay of Lübeck in the last days of the war.

* * *

We moved to our own home in Eastlakes in February 1945. The Herzbergs and Oma stayed on in Randwick for a further year, till they bought a house in Kingsford.

At the end of 1945, Paul and Walter both passed their school leaving certificate, with excellent results. Walter went to Sydney University to do a science degree. Paul, though interested in science, came into our rapidly growing business and went for a time to night school studying accountancy. He travelled to the United States in February 1948 for a confectionery course with a spell of practical experience organised for him by Emil Lind.

In January 1946 Ralph Sommer became engaged to a Melbourne girl, Becky Berkon. They married in June and settled in Melbourne.

10

At last all formalities were completed and we sent Lutz his ticket. The aeroplane on which he was to travel was chartered by the American Jewish Joint Distribution Committee. Ahead of his departure for Australia from Paris, Lutz spent three enjoyable months in that exciting city.

There were no long-distance passenger jets so planes had to refuel frequently. On the way to Karachi, while over the Arabian Desert, the plane developed engine trouble and made an emergency landing in Basra. As Iraq was at war with Israel and the passengers were without visas, they were interned at the airport hotel, a stressful experience for Jews who had been incarcerated in concentration camps.

We first heard of this delay when we rang the Australian Jewish Welfare Society (AJWS) to find out the expected time of arrival. AJWS asked the Australian Government to use their influence to free the passengers. They were detained for two weeks before the plane was allowed to continue its flight.

On Friday 27 July 1948, Lutz landed at Mascot Airport. It was nearly midnight when Karl, Leopold and Lutz climbed our thirty-two steps in Eastlakes. Ella, Oma and I had been waiting for hours. The table was set. Hot, strong coffee, sandwiches and cake were waiting for them. I was shocked at the haggard appearance of the young man with a scarred left eye. The bones at the back of his neck were prominent under a big scar. I could find in this man no semblance of the plump fifteen-year-old I remembered so well. Was this really Lutz?

Next morning, after Karl had left for business and Erica for Sydney Girls'

High School, I knocked on Lutz's door to tell him a warm bath was waiting for him. While he was having breakfast I asked about his childhood and reminisced about holidays he had spent with us in Harsewinkel. He remembered everything. I gradually realised this really was our nephew. Any change in his appearance was evidence of harsh times endured.

He wouldn't talk to us about the fate of his parents, just said, 'Give me time. I'll tell you later. It was too terrible.' Then he would change the subject. 'My first tasks are to learn English as quickly as possible and find a good job.'

Lutz soon settled in. When Paul came home from America a few months later, the two boys shared a room. Lutz was like a brother to our children and like a son to us. We took every opportunity to speak English with him, Paul helping him with his English every night.

He had done his apprenticeship in Germany so was soon able to take a job as a butcher, but had to learn the different cuts of meat and the different techniques of making small-goods because of the warmer climate in Australia. He learned quickly and was happy at work.

In no time he had a social life. Paul and Erica brought home their friends, and Walter and Ursula came over often. The house was always full of young people.

* * *

It was an unwritten law to be together with the Herzbergs Friday nights after dinner, either at our place or theirs. One evening Lutz 'opened up' about the fate of his parents. We listened in silence:

> Days after the attempt on Hitler's life in July 1944, all men over fifty and women over forty-five in the Riga Ghetto were rounded up and taken away, my parents included. From previous *Selektions* in the camps, I knew I would never see them again.

He wouldn't talk about the terrible years in the camps, only about the last days in German hands:

> It was clear that the formerly powerful Nazis were defeated. About mid-April 1945 we were taken from Stutthof concentration camp, first by land and then by barge, to Lübeck Bay, there loaded onto the

once-luxury liner *Cap Arcona*, together with thousands of prisoners, both camp inmates and prisoners of war of all nationalities. The Nazis beat us with rubber truncheons. I was severely injured about my face and neck and my left eye was permanently blinded. They herded us into the holds and locked us in. Our ship and two others were attacked by British aircraft and set afire. Miraculously some of us managed to break out of the hold and jump into the icy Baltic. I was one of those.[100]

How I was rescued I don't know. I had lost consciousness. I woke up in a British naval hospital near Lübeck, where medical staff nursed me back to health. Slowly my stomach learned to accept the nourishing food offered. I intended to travel to Schüren once I was strong enough but was delayed till trains were running again. When I arrived in Schüren the people living in our home would not allow me in. As you know, I then went to the Eichwalds.

Many migrants who came to Sydney were survivors of concentration camps and even of the Riga Ghetto. Lutz knew some of them, kept up friendships, and occasionally brought one or other home.

* * *

Attempts to bring the young Neugartens to Australia before and during the war had been unsuccessful. Ilse was working as a live-in maid, earning very little, and wrote that she was quite lonely. Her brother, Rolf, married Gina Zlotnicki and now had an anchor in England. In September 1949 we finally managed to bring Ilse to Sydney and she lived with Leopold and Ella. I had a relapse of rheumatic fever a few days after her arrival and asked her to stay with us, for I needed help in the house while I was unwell. She was with us for nearly two years.

Before the war, my sister Helen's daughter, Inge Lind, was engaged to Moritz (Maurice) Schweizer, Executive Director of the Jewish community organisation of Essen. She migrated to New York, but Maurice felt obligated to stay behind to help departing emigrants and make arrangements for his aged father and other elderly relatives, before following Inge to the United States. War trapped him in Holland. He survived several concentration camps,

---

[100] Of the 4,500 prisoners on board, 350 survived the historic tragedy of *Cap Arcona*.

including Westerbork, Auschwitz and Bergen-Belsen. In April 1945 he was on a train heading for Theresienstadt, referred to as the 'Lost Transport', for it shuttled and zig-zagged along the collapsing rail system, unable to find an intact route. Many deportees died of typhus and malnutrition during the two-week journey and were buried in mass graves. The train was intercepted by the Red Army in Tröbitz and the prisoners were liberated, but still more deaths occurred. Though ill himself, Maurice performed sanctified Jewish burials for each individual victim and kept complete records. The names are memorialised on a wall at the Or Chadash School in Kfar Chassidim, near Haifa, Israel. Years later a *Siddur* in the Art Scroll series was dedicated to his memory.

Even though encouraged to accept one of several proposals of marriage, Inge, a beautiful young woman, refused, hoping and praying that Moritz would survive. Shortly after the war in Europe ended, her prayers were answered when a telegram arrived from Moritz. Visa difficulties delayed his migration to the United States. They married in New York, set up house in Chicago and later retired to Miami. Sadly, they had no children.

My mother, Bertha Herzberg, 'matriarch and crown of the family' passed away on 31 May 1950, loved, respected and missed by everyone who had known her. Once again our world had been diminished.

11

In March 1951, Karl and I went on our first overseas trip. In our absence Ilse kept house for Paul, Lutz and Erica. After our return Ilse went to work in The Nut Shop and moved in with the Herzbergs. In February 1953, she married Alfons Hynek.

Lutz settled in well. He worked long hours, had free board and lodging with us and was able to build up his savings. With loans from the Herzbergs and from us, he bought a butcher shop in Newtown in partnership with a former inmate from the Riga Ghetto. Additionally, they developed a small-goods factory. Leopold helped with the bookkeeping, until they were well established. After the sudden death of his business partner in 1955, Lutz became the sole owner.

He would introduce his girlfriends to us as though we were his parents. He had been with us for almost six years, when, on holiday in the Blue Mountains, he met Helen Hofmann. Helen and her mother had survived the horrors of several concentration camps, including Auschwitz and Bergen-Belsen. She had the telltale, tattooed number on her arm. In the camps Helen had lost father, brother, grandmother and many other relatives. Like Lutz, she also kept her sad story to herself. It was too painful to remember.

We liked Helen right away and agreed she would be a fine partner. They were married in January 1954 at the Temple Emanuel and, after a *Kiddusch* at the synagogue, we celebrated with a wedding breakfast for closest family in our home.

(l-r): Paul, Erica, and parents Kate and Karl Mendels.

(l-r): Walter, Ursula and parents
Ella and Leopold Herzberg.

Wedding of Lutz Shonberg and Helen Hoffman, January 1954.
Back row (l-r): Jeanne and Frank List (formerly Lieblich, Marta Reach's brother),
Walter, Leon, Sylvia (obscured) Karl, Paul, Ralph Sommer. Front row (l-r): Ella,
Leopold, Marta Reach (mother of the bride), Walter Reach, Kate, Erica, Ilse, Alfons,
Ursula. Seated: Helen and Lutz. Children (l-r): Raphael, Anna, David (children of
Leon and Sylvia Mendels).

12

Now, as I end my story, I say, *'J'ACCUSE!'*

I accuse not only the bestial Hitler and his sadistic henchmen, I also accuse the governments of countries that locked their gates to Jews in despair, not granting adequate numbers of permits, visas or affidavits while limiting quotas.

Australia, New Zealand, the United States and Canada, as well as the South American and African nations, could have absorbed more refugees, allowing European Jews to escape the grasp of the Nazis. Many Jews thus rescued would have been happy to cultivate barren land as they had done in Palestine during the time of the Mandate and since the establishment of the State of Israel.

Those migrants who came to Australia during the 1930s and after the war have contributed much to the economy, the industry and the culture of this country.

I am so grateful that our families were among those approved to found new homes in this G-d-blesséd country, Australia.

Kate Mendels, Sydney 1971

FAMILY ALBUM OF KATE AND LEOPOLD

Family of Kate's daughter Erica (Blum/Schwarz)

Erica with husband Oscar.

Standing (l-r): Erica, Jeremy, Timothy
Seated: David Blum.

(l-r): Mark Blum, Ilana, Daniella, Michelle (née Melman).

Family of Kate's son Paul

(l-r): Paul, Adam, Richard Hyman, Joshua, Rivka (née Azulay),
Vicki, Leora, Esther (née Benjamin).

(l-r): Jackie (née Stark), Daniel, Martin, Zachary. Front: Bradley.

Family of Leopold's daughter Ursula

Ursula with husband Ivan.

(l-r): Eitan, Liora, David (Lashansky), Michal, Lawrence, Sylvia (née Becher), Tamara.

(l-r): Leah, Yossi, Leonie, Talya, Zalman (Bassin), Isaac Balbin, Batsheva, Leah (née Moss), Tzvi Yehuda.

(l-r): Nathan, Jemma holding Lily, Gideon, Amelie, Camit (née Mimun).

Family of Leopold's son Walter

(l-r): Stephen, Jessica, Carol (née Wolf), Michael.

(l-r): Leah, Ian, Benjamin, Judith (née Nysenholc).

(l-r): Brian Mayer, Raphael, Suzanne, David, Miriam, Walter, Jonah. Front: Daniel.

Epilogue

In my mind's eye I can still see my Aunt Kate sitting at her typewriter in the front verandah of her home at 7 Cecil Rd Rose Bay, Sydney, recording our families' story. She felt sure that in years to come her descendants would appreciate the pictures she was painting of life in small Jewish communities in Germany, of the effects of the First World War, of the rise of Nazism and of the eventual migration. Her work shows that throughout all those dramatic times, the value of family and the family's values, together with their love of their Jewish heritage, were of utmost importance to them.

My father, Leopold, believed it was vital to document in detail the inhuman behavior he had seen and experienced during *Kristallnacht* and subsequently in Buchenwald concentration camp; and to do so as soon as he could after his arrival in Australia. He remained a noble citizen, a wonderful example to all, despite all he had endured both during the four years of the First World War and as a Jew under the Nazis. Sadly, he didn't live to meet any of his grandchildren, of whom he would have been justly proud.

Through these chronicles the offspring of my parents and of my Aunt Kate and Uncle Karl, will meet their forebears and come to know them.

Ursula Cher, Melbourne 2010

APPENDICES

Appendix 1
Economic History of the Jews of Gütersloh

In the year 1565 Gütersloh became a part of the County of Rheda. Shortly thereafter the Count allowed a number of *Schutzjuden* (Jews protected by the authorities, in this case by the Count) into his lands, specifying the town of Rheda and the village of Gütersloh as an area in which to sojourn. For this the Jews continuously had to pay a substantial *Schutzgebühr* (protection tax) into the Count's coffers. Due to imposed restrictions denying them entry to most occupations, Jews lived almost exclusively from trade. This placed them as challenging competitors for non-Jewish merchants in Gütersloh. In 1745 the Rheda authorities raised the level of tax on all merchants, thus stirring up the indignation of the entire business community in the county. In a petition the merchants of Gütersloh turned to the government and urgently requested exemption from the tax.

One of their arguments was that uncultivated county moorland could not support any merchants who might be forced to seek a living outside the towns. All the non-Jewish businessmen of the area signed the petition! This discriminatory petition was inherently a 'strike' by disgruntled non-Jewish merchants against Jewish competition.

The Jews were at an additional disadvantage. As most lenders of money were Jewish, this being one of the limited occupations open to them, when non-Jewish merchants became bankrupt, Jews as creditors lost substantial capital.

Source: Barlev, Jehuda. *The Jews and Jewish Community in Gütersloh 1671–1943*, page 91.

Appendix 2
German Jewish Soldiers 1914–1918

Of the 550,000 Jews in Germany, 100,000 men became soldiers: 80% of these served at the frontline; 30,000 were decorated for bravery; 19,000 were promoted; 2,000 earned officer status; tens of thousands were wounded; 12,000 were killed. Given their constitutional status of citizenship, Jews had seen enlistment as the opportunity to prove their commitment to the Fatherland. The Kaiser is quoted as saying, 'I look at my army and see only Germans.'

German expectations in 1914 of a swift and certain victory were stymied by trench warfare and the British blockade. Shortages of raw materials and food supplies stimulated a search for a scapegoat. Anti-Semitic groups and political parties brought pressure on the Minister for War, Adolf Wild von Hohenborn, who, despite protests from the Reichstag and the press, ordered the *Judenzählung* (Jew census) in the military in October 1916. This was the self-same minister who signed the memorial testament commemorating Paul Herzberg's ultimate sacrifice. Some commanders at the front gave short home leave for many of the Jewish soldiers so they would not be there for the count. The results were not made public, ostensibly to spare Jewish feelings. The truth was that the census disproved the allegation that German Jewry was shirking its duty.

That their fellow countrymen so quickly and openly turned on them was a major source of dismay and the beginning of rapid decline in what historians have called 'the Jewish–German symbiosis'. Anti-Semitism was once again encouraged courtesy of the German army, foreshadowing official discrimination and persecution to come.

Sources:
The Jewish Roll of Honour: A Memorial Book compiled by Leo Lowenstein; Angress Werner T, 'The German Army's 'Judenzählung' of 1916: Genesis – Consequences – Significance';
Elon, Alon, *The Pity of It All.*

Appendix 3

Letter from Leopold Herzberg, written three and a half weeks before *Kristallnacht*, to brother-in-law Leon (Ludwig) in Sydney

Gütersloh, 15.10.38

Dear Ludwig,

Even though we wrote only three days ago, you shall have another letter today, the purpose being to send you the attached report that appeared in today's *Family Magazine*. Apparently the report was written over your way; I would be very pleased to hear your opinion regarding the various points made. If according to this report 22,000 immigration applications by Jews have been submitted, then considering the quota number allocated to me (it is somewhat over 21,000) from Canberra, I must be pretty near the end of the list. By the way, how come Karl has not received any acknowledgement at all from Canberra? Do you believe that we (my use of 'we' always means both our families in Harsewinkel and Gütersloh, as we really would like to stay together) have any chance of a permit, if only 10% of those applying are being considered? I beg you to answer these questions and give us your views of the article as quickly as possible. If we had some idea what to expect, that would be very helpful not only for the purchases we have to make, but particularly for the disposition of our business affairs.

You have actually not told us anything of your own situation for a long time. Are you now more satisfied with your status at work and are there prospects of becoming a partner? That would be quite something and you could be proud that after only two years in a foreign land you had achieved so much. You also don't write about the Weissbrems anymore. Is your friend still in the same job and has his father found work? You write least of all about your 'intended' and her family. This subject is of great interest to us all, but particularly to the ladies. Dear Oma in Harsewinkel has made a wonderful recovery, but she has difficulty walking. A few weeks ago we wrote to Ralph and sent the letter, in which we included a few photographs, by ordinary mail. I presume that in the meantime, it has arrived. How is he actually coping with English at school? This is of particular interest to me, in regard to our children.

For today, best regards from your brother-in-law,

Leopold Herzberg

Please reply immediately and give regards to Ralph, Gronsfelds, Lehmanns and Weissbrems.

Appendix 4
Night of 9–10 November 1938:
Heydrich's Instructions

Secret

Most Urgent telegram from Munich, November 10, 1938, 1:20 a.m. **#**

To:

All Headquarters and Stations of the State Police

All districts and Sub-districts of the SD (*)

Urgent! For immediate attention of Chief or his deputy!

Re: Measures against Jews tonight

Following the attempt on the life of Secretary of the Legation vom Rath in Paris, demonstrations against the Jews are to be expected in all parts of the Reich in the course of the coming night, November 9–10, 1938. The instructions below are to be applied in dealing with these events:

1. The Chiefs of the State Police, or their deputies, must immediately upon receipt of this telegram contact, by telephone, the political leaders in their areas – *Gauleiter* or *Kreisleiter* – who have jurisdiction in their districts and arrange a joint meeting with the inspector or commander of the Order Police to discuss the arrangements for the demonstrations. At these discussions the political leaders will be informed that the German Police has received instructions, detailed below, from the *Reichsführer* SS and the Chief of the German Police, with which the political leadership is requested to coordinate its own measures:

   a) Only such measures are to be taken as do not endanger German lives or property (i.e., synagogues are to be burned down only where there is no danger of fire in neighboring buildings).

   b) Places of business and apartments belonging to Jews may be destroyed but not looted. The police (force) is instructed to supervise the observance of this order and to arrest looters.

   c) In commercial streets particular care is to be taken that non-Jewish businesses are completely protected against damage.

   d) Foreign citizens – even if they are Jews – are not to be molested.

2. On the assumption that the guidelines detailed under para. 1 are observed, the demonstrations are not to be prevented by the Police (force), which is only to supervise the observance of the guidelines.

3. On receipt of this telegram Police will seize all archives to be found in all synagogues and offices of the Jewish communities so as to prevent their destruction during the demonstrations. This refers only to material of historical value, not to contemporary tax records, etc. The archives are to be handed over to the locally responsible officers of the SD.

4. The control of the measures of the Security Police concerning the demonstrations against the Jews is vested in the organs of the State Police, unless inspectors of the Security Police have given their own instructions. Officials of the Criminal Police, members of the SD, of the Reserves and the SS in general may be used to carry out the measures taken by the Security Police.

5. As soon as the course of events during the night permits the release of the officials required, as many Jews in all districts – especially the rich – as can be accommodated in existing prisons are to be arrested. For the time being only healthy male Jews, who are not too old, are to be detained. After the detentions have been carried out the appropriate concentration camps are to be contacted immediately for the prompt accommodation of the Jews in the camps. Special care is to be taken that the Jews arrested in accordance with these instructions are not ill treated.[101]

Signed: Heydrich,
SS *Gruppenführer*

(*SD Sicherheitsdienst = Security Service)

Source: Nürnberg Documents PS-3051. http://www.jewishvirtuallibrary. org/jsource/Holocaust/Heydrichkristal.html

---

[101] Heydrich's instructions that Jews arrested were not to be ill treated was certainly not adhered to, evidenced by what happened within 2 hours after dispatch of this telegram. The Herzberg house was attacked together with thousands of others and Jews physically and emotionally traumatized throughout Germany.

Appendix 5
At the Gütersloh Synagogue on the Night of 9–10 November 1938

In 1938 Mrs Auguste Gottsleben, aged sixty-two and disabled, was living in the synagogue premises with her son Rudi, aged twenty-seven. They were Protestants employed by the Jewish community for the maintenance of the synagogue, the neighbouring small school and garden, in exchange for the right to live in a small residence in the synagogue building. During the night of 9–10 November the building was set alight. Fast asleep, they were unaware that the property was actually being burnt down around them. Mrs Gottsleben's daughter and son-in-law (Paula Rocklage, age thirty-seven, and Wilhelm Rocklage, age forty-one), living in the Königstrasse opposite Türmer Guesthouse, were rudely wakened by the townsfolk of Gütersloh at about two in the morning with cries that the synagogue had been set on fire, with her mother and brother in the burning house! The couple went as quickly as they could to the site of the fire. Attempts were made to deny them access through the barrier. Only through frantic indications that family members were still in the burning building were they allowed into the synagogue residence. They brought out their totally distraught family, having to carry their mother, Auguste. They also took out whatever they could snatch (bedding, some linen, a few clothes). Everything else, all furniture, most clothes and linen, were [sic] burned. Mother and son received no restitution or compensation.

The activists of the pogrom night in Gütersloh took staves of wood from Schröder's Bakery (Feldstrasse 19), used as fuel for the ovens, and with these, smashed hardware and china at the Herzberg's, for example, and then set the various fires. As Mrs Kiel (née Schröder) reported: during the day a great 'procession of the population' went down the Feldstrasse to the sites of the fires.

Based on reports by Mr Wilhelm Rocklage, Mrs Erica Siekmann, née Gottsleben, (Johann-Sewerin-Strasse 19) and Mr Fritz Krümpelmann (Putzhagen 20). Gütersloh, 12.8.1984. In Barlev, Jehuda, *The Jews and Jewish Community in Gütersloh 1671–1943*, page 98.

Appendix 6
Buchenwald Concentration Camp

Buchenwald was the German concentration camp on the Ettersberg Mountain, in the Thüringer Forest near Weimar. Opened on 19 July 1937 to house prisoners from several smaller camps being disbanded, its first inmates were 'professional' criminals. They were, however, soon followed by political prisoners. The political prisoners, among whom were several Jews, appropriated for themselves such administrative posts as were available to prisoners. Prior to World War II, Buchenwald was considered one of the worst of the concentration camps.

The first Jews arriving as a group were political prisoners from a round-up of 'asocial' Jews in June 1938. Shortly thereafter 2,200 Austrian Jews were transferred from Dachau concentration camp. Later that year, the mass arrests after *Kristallnacht* more than doubled the number of Jewish prisoners. The 10,000 new Jewish prisoners, quartered in recently built huts, suffered far more than the non-Jews, 244 dying during the first month of their imprisonment. Most of the prisoners were released by the spring of 1939.

(Source: *Encyclopaedia Judaica*)

Appendix 7
Letter from the Buchenwald Foundation, 2009
(Translation opposite page)

Stiftung Gedenkstätten
Buchenwald und Mittelbau-Dora

Gedenkstätte Buchenwald

Gedenkstätte Buchenwald, Direktion Haus 2, 99427 Weimar

Frau
Ursula Cher
54 Arrona Rd
Caulfield North
Melbourne
VICTORIA 3161
AUSTRALIEN

Ihre Zeichen/Ihre Nachricht vom	Unsere Zeichen/Unsere Nachricht vom	Durchwahl-Nr.	Datum 21.04.09

Sehr geehrte Frau Cher,

aus den bei uns vorhandenen Unterlagen, die sich aus unvollständigem Sammlungsmaterial zusammensetzen, geht hervor, dass Ihr Schwiegervater **Leopold Herzberg** unter die Häftlingsnummern 28978 als jüdischer Häftlinge im KZ Buchenwald registriert war. Diese Häftlingsnummern wurden nur für diese besondere Verhaftungsaktion vom November 1938, der sog. Kristallnacht, vergeben. Am 12. November 1938 kamen ca. 4000 jüdische Männer nach Buchenwald, unter Ihnen Leopold Herzberg. Das Nummernbuch belegt, dass am 27. November 1938 Ihr Schwiegervater als sog. Aktions-Jude aus dem Konzentrationslager Buchenwald entlassen wurde. Im Thüringischen Hauptstaatsarchiv Weimar existiert die Geldkartei des Lagers im Original. Dort sind die Häftlinge der Verhaftungsaktion vom November 1938 enthalten, da sie sich das Geld für die Heimfahrt von ihren Angehörigen schicken lassen mussten. Weitere Informationen stehen uns leider nicht zur Verfügung.

In der Anlage erhalten Sie:
- Auszug aus dem Liste vom 27.11.1938
- Kopie der Bericht von Leopold Herzberg (Kopie aus Yad Vashem Archives)

Um weitere Informationen zu erhalten, gibt es für Sie die Möglichkeit im **Thüringischen Hauptstaatsarchiv Weimar, Marstallstraße 2** in **99423 Weimar** sowie beim **Internationalen Suchdienst des Roten Kreuzes, Große Allee 5 - 9** in **34444 Bad Arolsen** anzufragen.

Mit freundlichen Grüßen

Sabine Stein
Archiv

Gedenkstätte Buchenwald
Direktion - Haus 2
99427 Weimar-Buchenwald
Internet: http://www.buchenwald.de

Tel.: +49 (0) 3643 430 0
Fax.: +49 (0) 3643 430 100
Besucheranmeldung: 430 200
E-Mail: buchenwald@buchenwald.de

Bankverbindung:
Sparkasse Mittelthüringen
BLZ 820 510 00
Konto-Nr. 0301 009 171

Translation of Appendix 7

Memorial Foundations Buchenwald
Buchenwald and Mittlebau-Dora

Buchenwald Foundation, Administration Building 2, 99427 Weimar

Mrs Ursula Cher
54 Aroona Rd
Caulfield North
Melbourne
Victoria 3161
Australia

21.4.09

Dear Mrs Cher,

Our existing documents gathered from records (incomplete) indicate that your father-in-law [sic], Leopold Herzberg, Prisoner Number 28978, is on the register as a Jewish prisoner in Buchenwald Concentration Camp. This set of prisoner numbers was allocated to those particular prisoners of the November 1938 *Aktion* (round-up), known as *Kristallnacht*. On the one day, 12 November 1938, about 4000 Jewish men arrived at Buchenwald, amongst them Leopold Herzberg. The enclosed extract from the roll book confirms that your father-in-law [sic] referred to as an *Aktions-Jude* (a Jew rounded up during *Kristallnacht*) was released from Buchenwald Concentration Camp on 27 November 1938. The original financial files of the camp, held in the Türingisches State Archives in the city of Weimar, record the money a family had to send for the fare home on release of a prisoner. Unfortunately we don't have further information at our disposal.

The attachments include:
Extract of the List of 27.11.38
Copy of Leopold Herzberg's own story (Copy from Yad Vashem Archives)

For possible further information you could contact the Thüringischen Hauptstaatsarchiv Weimar, Marstallstrasse 2, 99423 Weimar as well as International Tracing Services of the Red Cross, Grosse Allee 5 – 9 in 34444 Bad-Arolsen.

With kind regards,

Signed for
Sabine Stein (Archives)

Appendix 8
Immigration to Australia

In the early 1930s, the Australian Federal Cabinet wished to maintain the ratio of British stock in Australia at 97% of the population. Thus, for a non-British family to be allowed to enter Australia as migrants, they were required to possess £500 'landing money'. (The average wage in Australia was about £3 at the time.)

In 1936 a German Jewish Relief Fund (GJRF) was established in Australia to raise money to guarantee and assist migrants. It asked the government to waive the £500 and accept guarantees from the local Jewish community. Later that year the minimum amount of landing money required was reduced to £50 per family for those migrants guaranteed by relatives or friends. At the same time the government conceded that responsible organisations such as the GJRF could henceforth act as sponsor/guarantor. In 1937 the Australian Jewish Welfare Society was formed to co-ordinate all activities concerning application for admission, reception and integration of refugees.

On 6 July 1938 the American President Franklin D Roosevelt convened an intergovernmental conference in the city of Evian on Lake Geneva to address the growing problems of the refugees from Nazism. The conference decided that governments were not obligated to find the finance for this, nor were they obligated to alter existing legislation regarding the quota levels. The finance should come from existing private organisations. Australia was a participant at the conference.

On 1 December 1938, following *Kristallnacht*, the Australian Government decided to admit 15,000 Jewish refugees over the next three years: 3,500 per annum for those who fulfilled landing money requirements and 1,500 refugees. On the whole this proposition was well received by all sections of government. Even conservative elements accepted this decision, seeing the quota as a restriction adequate to protect Australia from being 'flooded' with Jews, who might achieve too much influence in the country! The number of refugees admitted before war broke out in September 1939 did not reach even half that number.

(Sources: Rutland, Suzanne D. *Edge of the Diaspora* and Andgel, Anne. *Fifty Years of Caring*.)

Appendix 9
Letter from Louis Neugarten to family in New York and Sydney

Dear ones all,   11th November 1941

I feel I must write to you once again to enquire after you all. Hope you, Mother (Bertha Herzberg), and all the family (in Australia) are well. I hear news of you from Clara who exchanges letters with you regularly. I am so glad that I was able to go once more to Gütersloh and Dortmund last summer. Just happened to be at the time of Clara's (Herzberg) birthday. Now we are restricted to contact by mail (as travel is no longer allowed).

Since 30 September I have been working in a lumberyard, together with thirty acquaintances of similar age. The work is tolerable but the hours are long. I get up at five thirty in the morning and leave the house at six fifteen, returning home only at seven at night. I had a very severe cold and tooth infection, and was on sick leave for three weeks. Now I am much better and must go back the day after tomorrow. Every day after work I pick up my food from a place close by. It is very good and I just have to warm it up. I take some for my lunch next day, and have the opportunity to heat it up at work. It is thanks to your cousin Emil that my room is nice and warm. We get on very well.

Two transports, each of 1000 persons, were recently evacuated from here to Litzmanstadt. On 8 December, the third transport, again of 1000, will go to Minsk. Amongst them are many of my good friends and acquaintances. It is almost one and a half years since dear Rosa passed away, and as painful as the loss was and still is, yet I repeatedly tell myself that it is a blessing that she was spared so much unpleasantness.

I can't understand that Leopold (Herzberg) and Karl (Mendels) are not able to do anything for me, not even with the help of an organisation. That leaves me no possibilities and so I have accepted that I will spend the rest of my days here.

My dear ones I wish you all the very best, with kind regards,

Your brother-in-law and uncle,

Louis (Neugarten, aged 65)

(As the United States was not yet in the war, all letters to Australia were sent via America.)

Appendix 10
Deportation of the Jews of Gütersloh

Transportation of German Jews into extermination camps began in November 1941. Clara Herzberg and the couple Bernard and Hannchen Levi from Gütersloh were 'moved' on 10 December to Bielefeld and then 'resettled' on 13 December 1941 to Riga, Latvia. Deportees had been notified (Editor's note: by Registration Order) approximately two weeks before, that they were to be 'resettled'.

The Registration Order declared that:

'Each individual must bring the following:
1. Money, to a limit of 100 Marks
2. One suitcase containing all necessities, maximum weight 50 kilos, that is,
    Full range of clothing
    Bedding and eiderdown
    Food for eight days (bread, flour, legumes)
    Rations for two days' march (sandwiches)
Articles not permitted:
    Bank bills, shares, savings and account books; pets; valuables of any kind; gold, silver, platinum (with the exception of wedding rings).
Ration cards are to be kept separate and handed in to the administration office. The Jews must not take more than they can carry on a short march.'

From 10 December the deportees were gathered in the hall of the Kyffhäuser Guesthouse on the Kesselbrink, the town centre of Bielefeld that was turned into a reception centre by the local Gestapo. Here the Jews were encamped on the scantily straw-covered floor of the hall till their transportation on 13 December. According to an eyewitness the sanitary facilities were catastrophic.

The Gestapo used the two- to three-day stopover for thorough searches and luggage inspections. With the exception of wedding rings, all other valuables, personal papers and even family photos were confiscated.

All luggage happened to get lost on arrival in Riga.

(Source: Barlev, Jehuda. *The Jews and Jewish Community in Gütersloh 1671–1943*.)

Appendix 11
Selektion in Riga, ostensibly to Dünamünde

There were continual *Selektion*s made from Riga. The Jews were told they were to go as a workforce to the city of Dünamünde to work in fish-canning factories. The plan sounded credible. The Baltic Sea was rich in fish, and everyone knew that workers were badly needed everywhere. To the old and hungry, working with fish implied access to food as well as a degree of security and reprieve from the cold. While most selected for this work were elderly or ailing or parents with small children, some of the ghetto functionaries were chosen as well. A number of physicians were also put on the lists, ostensibly to take care of workers who might get sick.

On 26 March 1942 at a further *Selektion* of German Jews, the SS asked for 1500 'workers'. There were many who refused to be separated from parents, others who were tempted by the promise of easy indoor work and the likelihood of better food at such a location. Four hundred more Jews than the SS had asked for left the city that Sunday morning. They were taken, not to the distant labour camp, but to the nearby Bikernieker Forest. On the following day several trucks returned to the Riga Ghetto, and were unloaded. Their cargo was an assortment of personal effects of the people who had been 'resettled'. Clothes had been taken off in haste (still turned inside out), stockings attached to girdles and shoes encrusted with mud. The trucks also yielded nursing bottles, children's toys, spectacles, bags filled with food, and satchels containing photographs and documents.

The women from the ghetto were ordered to sort the clothes. The best items were to be sent to Germany, the rest to be distributed among people of the ghetto. The women recognised many of the clothes: some by the names that had been sewn into them, some by the identity cards still in the pockets; and there were, of course, dresses, coats and suits which they had seen on their friends and neighbours when they had left the ghetto only a few days before.

Soon everyone in the ghetto knew about the cargo that the trucks had brought and the conditions of the clothes. It did not take any great imagination to understand what had happened to their owners. No longer did anyone scoff at the tales told to them earlier by the Latvian Jews, nor think that this could happen only to *Ostjuden* (Jews from Eastern Europe), never to Jews from Germany. In many houses in the ghetto, *Kaddisch* was recited. The German ghetto was plunged into despair.

Among those murdered at the Bikernieker Forest that day was Chief Rabbi Joseph Carlebach.

(Source: Gilbert, Martin. *The Holocaust*.)

Clara Herzberg arrived in Riga in the second half of December 1941. She was killed sometime in 1942. We do not know if she was taken at that particular *Selektion*. We do not know where she met her death.

GLOSSARY

The Hebrew and Jiddisch words listed in this Glossary without markers (#,*) are rendered in phonetics as used by the Jews in Germany.
# denotes German language,
* denotes transliterated Hebrew (Ivrit).

Aktion#	a planned raid or round-up (of Jews)
Barches (Challah)*	a plaited bread for Shabbat
Barmizwo (Bar Mitzvah)*	a thirteen-year-old boy's rite of passage to religious obligations
Basmizvo (Bat Mitzvah)*	a twelve-year-old girl's rite of passage to religious obligations
Bensch	to bless, to pray Grace after Meals
Brissmille (Brit Milah)*	ritual circumcision
Broches (Brachot)*	blessings
Bürgermeister#	mayor
Butterbrot#	sandwich
*Chanukah**	Jewish Festival of Lights
Chasen (Chazan)*	cantor
Chasser (Chazir)*	pig; meat of a pig
Chaul hamaueid (Chol hamoed)*	the intermediate, semi-holydays between the beginning and end of both Pesach and Sukkoth
Chein	charm, style, good taste
Chevro Kadischo (Chevra Kaddishah)*	Jewish burial society
Chuppe (Chuppah)*	wedding canopy
*Daven**	to pray, to lead communal prayers
Ersatz#	synthetic, substitute
Fleischig	any food that is meat, has meat content, or has had contact with meat; applicable to crockery and cutlery
Frau#	Mrs

Fräulein#	Miss
Hallel*	a liturgical unit of psalms of praise recited on festivals/occasions
Herr#	Mr
Ja-aleh (Ya-aleh*)	prayer added to liturgy on certain festivals and New Moon
Jaum Kippur (Yom Kippur*)	Day of Atonement
Jiddisch	German-Jewish spelling of Yiddish, the daily language of Eastern European Jews
Jigdal (Yigdal*)	hymn, as part of weekly services
Jontef (Yom Tov*)	Jewish religious holy day
Jude#	Jew
Kaddisch (Kaddish*)	prayer of praise recited in the presence of a *minyan* during services, but particularly associated with mourning
Kapo#	concentration camp prisoner given authority over fellow inmates
Kaschrus (Kashrut*)	Jewish dietary laws
Kavoneh (Kavanah*)	devotion during religious observances
Kiddusch (Kiddush*)	blessing over wine
Kinnim*	lice
Kittel	white cotton garment worn by Jewish men on various occasions; also shroud for Jewish male; see Sargenes (below)
Kol Nidre*(All vows)	opening declamation at the Eve of Yom Kippur service, annulling religious vows
Kommandant#	commanding officer
Kommandantenhaus#	headquarters
Kristallnacht#	Night of Broken Glass, 9–10 November 1938
Lechem*	bread
Lieder#	classical German art songs
Luftwaffe#	German air force
Matzo (Matzah*)	unleavened bread

Mauhel (Mohel*)	ritual circumciser
Mauze (Motzi*)	blessing over bread
Menubbel	small, deformed or ugly person
Milchig	milk product or food containing milk derivative or food that has had contact with milk; applicable to crockery and cutlery
Minche (Minchah*)	afternoon service; afternoon prayer
Minjen (Minyan*)	a group of ten adult males required for liturgical purposes (prayers, etc.)
Misrach (Mizrach*) (east)	a religious decorative work hung on an eastern wall showing the direction from Europe, of the Temple Mount in Jerusalem
Mizwo (Mitzvah*)	a good deed, as in the 613 biblical obligations (Mitzvot*)
Mogen Dovid (Magen David*)	Star of David, Shield of David
Moischelchen	fables, stories
Nebbich	pitiful person
Ne-ile (Neilah*)	concluding service on Yom Kippur
Nigun*	melody, particularly a liturgical melody
Nigunim*	plural of Nigun
Oma#	Grandma
Pesach*	Festival of Passover
Pfennig#	German coin, a hundredth of a Mark
Ponem (Panim*)	face; facial expression
Purim*	Festival of Drawing Lots, celebrating the survival of the Jews in Persia (485–465 B.C.E.)
Rausch Haschono (Rosh Hashanah*)	Jewish New Year
Risches	anti-Semitism.
Sargenes/Zargenes	See Kittel
Schabbes (Shabbat*)	Jewish Sabbath
Schacharis (Shacharit*)	morning service; morning prayer

Schauchet (Shochet*)	kosher slaughterer
Schechite (Shechitah*)	kosher slaughter of animals
Schiwe (Shivah*)	seven-day period of mourning, after a burial
Schlemihl (m)	unskilful, awkward dullard
Schlemilte (f)	unskilful, awkward dullard
Schnorrer	Jewish beggar
Schmecheln	to grin
Schir Ha-maalaus	a psalm sung or recited before Grace after
(Shir Ha-maalot*)	Meals on Shabbat, festivals, festive occasions.
Schlaumo (Shlomoh*)	Solomon
Schul (Bet Haknesset*)	synagogue
Seelenfeier# (Yizkor*)	memorial service for the departed
Selektion#	selecting prisoners in concentration camps and ghettos; e.g., according to health, age, fitness for a particular purpose; almost always adverse
Semiraus (Zemirot*)	songs sung at the table on Shabbat
Siddur*	prayer book
Simcho (Simchah*)	celebration
Strasse#	street
Stussen#	pranks, playing nonsensical tricks
Suckes (Succot*)	Festival of Tabernacles
Tal*	(dew) a prayer for rain and dew
Tefille (Tefillah*)	prayer
Wurst#	sausage, salami

BIBLIOGRAPHY

Andgel, Anne. *Fifty Years of Caring: the history of the Australian Jewish Welfare Society 1936–1986*. Sydney: The Australian Jewish Welfare Society and the Australian Jewish Historical Society, 1988.

Angress, Werner T. 'The German Army's 'Judenzählung' of 1916: Genesis – Consequences – Significance.' In *The Leo Baeck Institute Yearbook* 23(1). London, 1978.

Aliav, Ruth; Mann, Peggy. *The Last Escape: the launching of the largest secret rescue movement of all times*. London: Victor Gollancz, 1974.

Barlev, Jehuda. *Juden und Jüdische Gemeinde in Gütersloh 1671–1943* (*The Jews and Jewish Community in Gütersloh 1671–1943*). Gütersloh: Town of Gütersloh, 1988. (Information sourced is translated by Ursula Cher.)

Elon, Amos. *The Pity of It All*: *a portrait of Jews in Germany 1743–1933*. New York, Metropolitan Books. Henry Holt and Company, 2002

Encyclopaedia Britannica, 15th edition. Chicago: Encyclopaedia Britannica, 1972.

Encyclopaedia Judaica, Edited by Cecil Roth and Geoffrey Wigoder. Jerusalem: Keter, 1972.

Gilbert, Martin. *The Holocaust*. London: Guild Publishing, 1978.

Gilbert, Martin. *The Second World War*. New York: Henry Holt, 1991.

The Jewish Roll of Honour: A Memorial Book. Compiled by Leo Lowenstein. Berlin: The Reich Association of Jewish Combat Veterans, 1932.

Rutland, Suzanne D. *Edge of the Diaspora: two centuries of Jewish settlement in Australia*. Sydney: Collins Australia, 1988.

Shirer, William L. *The Rise and Fall of the Third Reich*. New York: Fawcett, 1960.

Snowman, Daniel. *The Hitler Emigrés*. London: Chatto and Windus, 2005

Weinberg, Werner. *Lexicon of the Religious Vocabulary and Usage of German Jews*. Stuttgart: Froman-Holzboog, 1994.

www.ushmm.org (Accessed 6 October 2009). Fair use of Roll Call Photograph.

For Further Reading

Friedlaender, Saul. *Nazi Germany and the Jews, 1933-1939*. New York: Harper Collins 1997

Kaplan, Marion M. (ed.) *Jewish Daily Life in Germany, 1618-1945*. Oxford & New York: Oxford University Press 2005

Kaplan, Marion M. *Between Dignity and Despair. Jewish Life in Nazi Germany*. Oxford & New York: Oxford University Press 1998

Matthaeus, Juergen, Roseman, Mark. (eds.) *Jewish Responses to Persecution*. Vol. 1 *1933-1938*, Lanham: Alta Mira Press, 2010 (*Documenting Life and Destruction. Holocaust Sources in Context*. US Holocaust Memorial Museum, Washington DC)

Meyer, Michael. (ed.) *German-Jewish History in Modern Times*. Vol. 1: *Tradition and Enlightenment, 1600-1780*. Vol. 2: *Emancipation and Acculturation, 1780-1871*. Vol. 3: *Integration in Dispute, 1871-1918*. Vol. 4: *Renewal and Destruction, 1918-1945*. New York: Columbia University Press 1996-1998

Richarz, Monika. (ed.) *Jewish Life in Germany. Memoirs from Three Centuries*. Trans: Rosenfeld SP, Rosenfeld S. Bloomington & Indianapolis: Indiana University Press 1991